FOUNDATIONS TODAY SERIES
2002 EDITION

FOUNDATION YEARBOOK

Facts and Figures on Private and Community Foundations

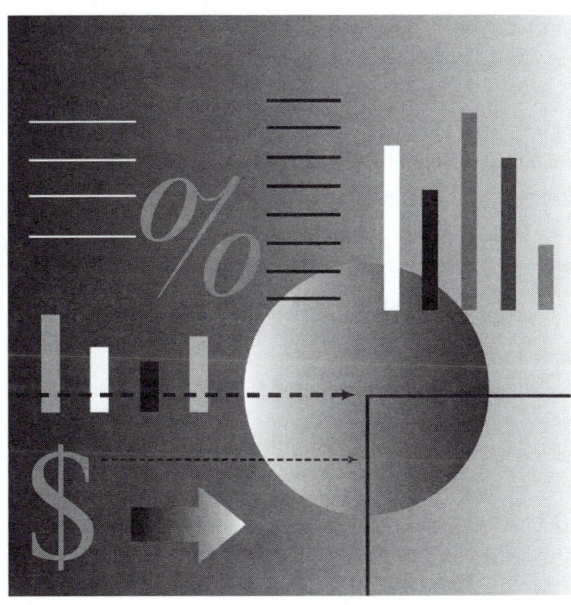

Steven Lawrence
Director of Research

Dia Ganguly
Research Assistant

THE FOUNDATION CENTER

CONTRIBUTING STAFF

Loren Renz	Vice President for Research
Kathye Giesler	Publishing Database Administrator
Emmy So	Database Operations Assistant
Crystal Mandler	Senior Programmer/Analyst
Lucy Wang	Programmer
Cheryl L. Loe	Director of Design and Production
Christine Innamorato	Production Associate

ABOUT THE REPORT

The original research upon which this report is based was conducted by the Foundation Center. Data from the report may not be cited or reproduced without attribution to *Foundation Yearbook* and the Foundation Center. Other reports in the *Foundations Today Series* of annual research studies include *Foundation Giving Trends, Foundation Growth and Giving Estimates, Foundation Staffing,* and *Foundation Reporting*. In addition, the Center produces numerous studies on special topics including:

- *Arts Funding Update,* 2002.
- *Giving in the Aftermath of 9/11: Foundations and Corporations Respond,* 2002.
- *California Foundations: A Profile of the State's Grantmaking Community,* 2001.
- *Health Funding Update,* 2001.
- *The PRI Directory: Charitable Loans and Other Program-Related Investments of Foundations,* 2001.
- *International Grantmaking II: An Update on U.S. Foundation Trends,* 2000.
- *Family Foundations: A Profile of Funders and Trends,* 2000.
- *Arts Funding 2000: Funder Perspectives on Current and Future Trends,* 1999.
- *Southeastern Foundations II: A Profile of the Region's Grantmaking Community,* 1999.
- *Health Policy Grantmaking: A Report on Foundation Trends,* 1998.

ABOUT THE FOUNDATION CENTER

The Foundation Center's mission is to support and improve institutional philanthropy by promoting public understanding of the field and helping grantseekers succeed. To achieve our mission, we:

- Collect, organize, and communicate information on U.S. philanthropy
- Conduct and facilitate research on trends in the field
- Provide education and training on the grantseeking process
- Ensure public access to information and services through our World Wide Web site, print and electronic publications, five library/learning centers, and a national network of cooperating collections.

Founded in 1956, the Center is the nation's leading authority on institutional philanthropy and is dedicated to serving grantseekers, grantmakers, researchers, policymakers, the media, and the general public.

ACKNOWLEDGMENTS

The authors gratefully acknowledge the many Foundation Center staff whose work provides the information base necessary for this analysis. We also thank the many foundations that participate in the Center's annual survey, providing more detailed information not otherwise available.

Copyright © 2002 by the Foundation Center. All rights reserved.
Printed and bound in the United States of America.
Book design and production by Cheryl L. Loe and Christine Innamorato.
Cover design by Apicella Design.

ISBN 0-931923-03-5   ISSN 1528-1663

This report is available exclusively through subscription to the annual *Foundations Today Series* of research reports. Subscriptions are $95.00 each and include five reports.
Discounts are available on bulk subscriptions. To order by phone or for more information, call toll-free (800) 424-9836.

Contents

Tables and Figures .... *v*
Foreword .... *ix*
Key Findings .... *x*

CHAPTER 1: The State of Foundation Giving, 2002 1

CHAPTER 2: Foundation Giving and Growth 7
  Overview of Growth Through 2000 7
  2000 Giving 7
  2000 Assets 12
  2000 Gifts Received 14
  Growth of the Top 25 Foundations 17
  Large and Small Foundations 21

CHAPTER 3: Foundations by Region and State 31
  Regional Trends, 1975 to 2000 31
  State-Level Trends, 1975 to 2000 37
  Regional and State-Level Distribution by Foundation Type, 2000 42
  New Foundation Creation 45

CHAPTER 4: Giving and Growth of Independent, Corporate, and Community Foundations 47
  Growth in Giving, 2001 and 2000 47
  Growth and Distribution by Foundation Type, 2000 49
  Independent Foundations 49
  Corporate Foundations 57
  Community Foundations 67
  Grantmaking Operating Foundations 73

CHAPTER 5: Foundation Development 75
  Overview through 2000 75
  Foundation Creation Before 1970 75
  Foundation Creation in the 1970s 77
  Foundation Creation in the 1980s and 1990s 78
  Larger Foundation Creation 79
  Future Prospects for Foundation Creation 82

SPECIAL REPORTS
  Measures of Foundation Support, 2000 10
  Howard Hughes Medical Institute 19
  Foundations' Share of Private Philanthropy, 2000 27
  Family Foundations 58
  "New Health" Foundations 60
  Corporate Profits, Giving, and Foundations 63
  New Foundation Philanthropists 81

APPENDIX A: Methodology 85

APPENDIX B: Regulation of Private Foundations 89

APPENDIX C: Foundation Center Cooperating Collections 91

APPENDIX D: Bibliography 97

Tables and Figures

CHAPTER 1: The State of Foundation Giving, 2002
Figure 1. Growth of Foundation Giving, 1991 to 2001 2
Figure 2. Foundation Giving Per Capita, 1991 to 2000 2
Figure 3. Foundation Giving as a Share of GDP, 1991 to 2000 3
Figure 4. Private (Non-Operating) and Independent Foundation Giving as a Share of Prior Years'
    Assets, 1988 to 2001 3
Figure 5. Total Giving by Foundations, 1975 to 2001 4

CHAPTER 2: Foundation Giving and Growth

2000 Giving
Table 1. 2000 Aggregate Fiscal Data by Foundation Type 7
Table 2. Comparison of 2000 to 1999 Aggregate Fiscal Data 8
Figure 6. Effect of Inflation on Foundation Giving, 1975 to 2000 9
Table 3. Growth of Foundation Giving Adjusted for Inflation 9
Table 4. Number of Grantmaking Foundations, Assets, Total Giving, and Gifts Received 10

2000 Assets
Figure 7. Effect of Inflation on Foundation Assets, 1975 to 2000 13
Table 5. Growth of Foundation Assets Adjusted for Inflation 14

2000 Gifts Received
Table 6. Growth of Gifts Received Adjusted for Inflation 15
Table 7. Number of Foundations Receiving Total Gifts of $5 Million or Over and Aggregate Dollar
    Value, 2000 15

Growth of the Top 25 Foundations
Table 8. Comparison of the 25 Largest Foundations by Total Giving, 1999 to 2000 17
Table 9. Comparison of the 25 Largest Foundations by Assets, 1999 to 2000 17
Table 10. Ten Largest Foundations of 1990: Growth of Assets and Total Giving, 1990 to 2000 21

Large and Small Foundations
Table 11. Analysis of Foundations by Asset Size, 2000 22
Figure 8. Distribution of Foundations and Foundation Assets by Asset Range, 2000 22
Table 12. Analysis of Foundations by Total Giving Range, 2000 23
Figure 9. Largest Foundations by Total Giving and Percentage of 2000 Giving 23
Figure 10. Largest Foundations by Asset Size and Percentage of 2000 Assets 23
Table 13. 50 Largest Foundations by Total Giving, 2000 24
Table 14. 50 Largest Foundations by Assets, 2000 25
Table 15. 50 Largest Foundations by Gifts Received, 2000 26
Figure P1. Distribution of Private Philanthropic Giving, 2000 27
Table P1. 2000 Private Philanthropic Giving 27
Figure P2. Growth of Private Philanthropic Giving by Source, 1975 to 2000 28
Figure P3. Giving by Independent and Community Foundations and Corporations/Corporate
    Foundations as a Share of All Private Giving 29

CHAPTER 3: Foundations by Region and State

Regional Trends, 1975 to 2000
Table 16. 2000 Fiscal Data of Grantmaking Foundations by Region and State, 2000 32
Figure 11. Growth of Foundation Number, Giving, and Assets by Region, 1999 to 2000 33
Figure 12. Growth of Foundation Number by Region, 1975 to 2000 34

Figure 13. Increase in Number of Grantmaking Foundations Created by Region, 1975 to 2000 34
Figure 14. Growth of Foundation Giving by Region, 1975 to 2000 35
Figure 15. Foundation Giving by Region, 1975 and 2000 35
Figure 16. Growth of Foundation Assets by Region, 1975 to 2000 36
Figure 17. Foundation Assets by Region, 1975 and 2000 37

State-Level Trends, 1975 to 2000
Figure 18. Top Ten States by Growth of Foundation Giving, 1990 to 2000 38
Table 17. Foundation Giving Per Capita and as a Share of Gross State Product, 2000 39
Figure 19. Distribution of Foundation Giving by State, 1975 and 2000 40
Table 18. Top Ten States by Total Giving Reported, 2000 40
Figure 20. Top Ten States by Growth of Foundation Assets, 1999 to 2000 41
Figure 21. Distribution of Foundation Assets by State, 1975 and 2000 41

Regional and State-Level Distribution by Foundation Type, 2000
Table 19. 2000 Fiscal Data by Region and Foundation Type 42
Figure 22. Distribution of Foundation Giving by Type and Region, 2000 43
Table 20. 2000 Fiscal Data of Corporate and Community Grantmaking Foundations by Region
    and State 44
Figure 23. Decade of Establishment for Larger U.S. Foundations by Region 45

CHAPTER 4: Giving and Growth of Independent, Corporate, and Community Foundations
Figure 24. General Characteristics of Four Types of Foundations 48

Growth in Giving, 2001 and 2000
Figure 25. Growth of Foundation Giving by Type, 1999 to 2001 49
Figure 26. Growth of Foundation Giving by Type, 1991 to 2001 49
Figure 27. 2000 Number of Foundations by Foundation Type 50
Table 21. Comparison of 2000 to 1999 Total Number of Foundations 50
Figure 28. 2000 Giving by Foundation Type 50
Table 22. Comparison of 2000 to 1999 Total Giving 50
Figure 29. 2000 Assets by Foundation Type 51
Table 23. Comparison of 2000 to 1999 Assets 51
Figure 30. 2000 Gifts Received by Foundation Type 51
Table 24. Comparison of 2000 to 1999 Gifts Received 51

Independent Foundations
Table 25. Analysis of Independent Foundations by Total Giving Range, 2000 51
Table 26. 50 Largest Independent Foundations by Total Giving, 2000 52
Table 27. Analysis of Independent Foundations by Asset Range, 2000 53
Table 28. 50 Largest Independent Foundations by Asset Size, 2000 54
Table 29. Largest Independent Foundations by Gifts Received, 2000 56
Table 30. Growth of Independent Foundation Giving and Assets, 1987 to 2000 57
Table F1. 25 Largest Family Foundations by Total Giving, 2000 59
Table H1. 25 Largest Private "New Health" Foundations by Total Giving, 2000 60

Corporate Foundations
Table 31. Analysis of Corporate Foundations by Total Giving Range, 2000 61
Table 32. Corporate Foundation Giving by Industry, 2000 61
Table 33. 50 Largest Corporate Foundations by Total Giving, 2000 62
Table 34. Analysis of Corporate Foundations by Asset Range, 2000 64
Table 35. 50 Largest Corporate Foundations by Asset Size, 2000 65
Table 36. Largest Corporate Foundations by Gifts Received, 2000 66
Table 37. Growth of Corporate Foundation Giving and Assets, 1987 to 2000 67

Community Foundations

Table 38. Analysis of Community Foundations by Total Giving Range, 2000 68
Table 39. 25 Largest Community Foundations by Total Giving, 2000 69
Table 40. Analysis of Community Foundations by Asset Range, 2000. 69
Table 41. 25 Largest Community Foundations by Asset Size, 2000 70
Table 42. Largest Community Foundations by Gifts Received, 2000 71
Table 43. Growth of Community Foundation Giving and Assets, 1981 to 2000 72

Grantmaking Operating Foundations

Table 44. Ten Largest Grantmaking Operating Foundations by Total Giving, 2000 73
Table 45. Analysis of Grantmaking Operating Foundations by Asset Range, 2000. 74
Table 46. Ten Largest Grantmaking Operating Foundations by Asset Size, 2000. 74

CHAPTER 5: Foundation Development

Overview through 2000

Figure 31. Number of Grantmaking Foundations, 1975 to 2000 76
Table 47. Number of Grantmaking Foundations by Type, 1975 to 2000 76

Foundation Creation Before 1970

Table 48. Period of Establishment for Larger Foundations by Asset Categories 77
Table 49. Growth of Number of Larger Foundations by Decade 77
Table 50. Growth of Number of Larger Foundations by Decade and Foundation Type. 78

Larger Foundation Creation

Figure 32. Decade of Establishment of Active Grantmaking Foundations with Assets of at Least
$1 Million or Making Grants of $100,000 or More 79
Figure 33. Establishment of Larger Foundations by Year, 1970 to 1998 80
Table 51. Number and Assets of Larger Foundations Created per Year After 1969. 80
Table 52. Period of Establishment for Larger Foundations by Foundation Type with Aggregate Assets .. 82
Table 53. Foundations Created Since 1990 with Assets of $125 Million or More 83
Table 54. Foundations Created Since 1990 with Total Giving of $10 Million or More. 84

Foreword

Through numerous research reports published over the past two decades, the Foundation Center has created for the field an increasingly refined and detailed portrait of foundation philanthropy. This rich collection of facts and figures on private and community foundations and their grantmaking interests begins with 1975 and continues through over 25 years of foundation development. In the 1990s, the principal vehicle for presenting and interpreting this growing body of data on foundation growth and giving trends was *Foundation Giving,* an annual statistical yearbook. From 1991 to 1999, *Foundation Giving* doubled in size, paralleling the meteoric growth of the foundation field, and demonstrating the Center's continuous efforts to enhance and expand its examination of foundations.

In 2000, we introduced the *Foundations Today Series,* the successor to *Foundation Giving.* The *Foundations Today Series* organizes foundation trends into five annual reports on the current state of foundations and their giving. The series approach allows us to present information in a more timely and tailored way. The first report of the series, *Foundation Giving Trends,* presents a picture of how just over 1,000 of the top U.S. foundations distributed their grant dollars in 2000. *Foundation Growth and Giving Estimates* provides highly informed predictions of giving trends in 2001. Foundation Yearbook tracks foundation growth and development for the nearly 56,600 foundations active in 2000. Finally, *Foundation Staffing* and *Foundation Reporting* present key trends related to the internal practices of foundations.

While concentrating on trends of the most recent year, reports in the *Foundations Today Series* also compare growth and giving patterns retrospectively. The series is the only source providing a comprehensive historical record on foundation fiscal data; new foundation development; changes in levels of support by grant subject or purpose, recipient type, type of support, and population group; and changes in levels of foundation staffing and reporting.

Recognizing that foundations are an increasingly diverse community, the *Foundations Today Series* has been designed to satisfy information needs concerning, first, the universe of nearly 56,600 grantmaking foundations, and, second, specific segments of that universe. A wealth of summary data can be found for independent, family, corporate, community, and grantmaking operating foundations. Foundation statistics are further segmented regionally and by state. Finally, the behavior of large and small foundations and the patterns of large and small grants are independently evaluated.

We look forward to your comments on the *Foundations Today Series* and welcome suggestions to enhance or improve the series.

Loren Renz
Vice President for Research

Key Findings

Despite the onset of a recession, continuing stock market declines, and national paralysis immediately following the September 11th terrorist attacks, U.S. foundations managed to follow five straight years of double-digit giving increases with a 5 percent gain in giving in 2001. By foundation type, independent and family foundations provided the strongest boost to giving overall, followed by community foundations. For corporate foundations, the change in giving fell slightly below the rate of inflation.

Across the country, the number of grantmaking foundations grew by a record amount in the latest year. Foundations in the West continued to experience the fastest rate of growth in number, giving, and assets through 2000, and the West is poised to surpass the South in share of foundation giving. Nonetheless, the South reported the biggest gain in actual number of foundations in the latest year, while the Northeast showed the largest increase in actual grant dollars.

Foundation Yearbook, 2002 Edition, documents the growth in actual number, giving, and assets of all active U.S. foundations from 1975 through 2000 and provides estimates of foundation giving through 2001. The report provides an overview of the state of foundation giving in the current year and beyond; comparisons of foundation activities by foundation size; breakdowns of foundation resources by geographic location and grantmaker type; and a brief history of foundation development since the early 1900s. *Foundation Yearbook* is part of the *Foundations Today Series* of annual research reports on foundation growth and trends in foundation giving.

Findings presented in *Foundation Yearbook* are based on aggregate fiscal data collected by the Foundation Center on all active U.S. foundations. Estimates for 2001 are based on survey figures reported by more than 1,800 large and mid-size foundations combined with year-end fiscal indicators.

State of Foundation Giving, 2002

- Giving reached an estimated $29.0 billion in 2001, up $1.4 billion

- Giving in 2002 expected to remain flat

- Over the long term, modest growth in giving appears likely

Foundation Giving and Growth

- Giving by the nation's nearly 56,600 grantmaking foundations rose 18.2 percent in 2000 to $27.6 billion

- Funding by the top 25 foundations increased nearly 22 percent in 2000, surpassing foundations overall

- Assets of all active U.S. foundations rose to $486.1 billion in 2000, up 8.4 percent from the prior year

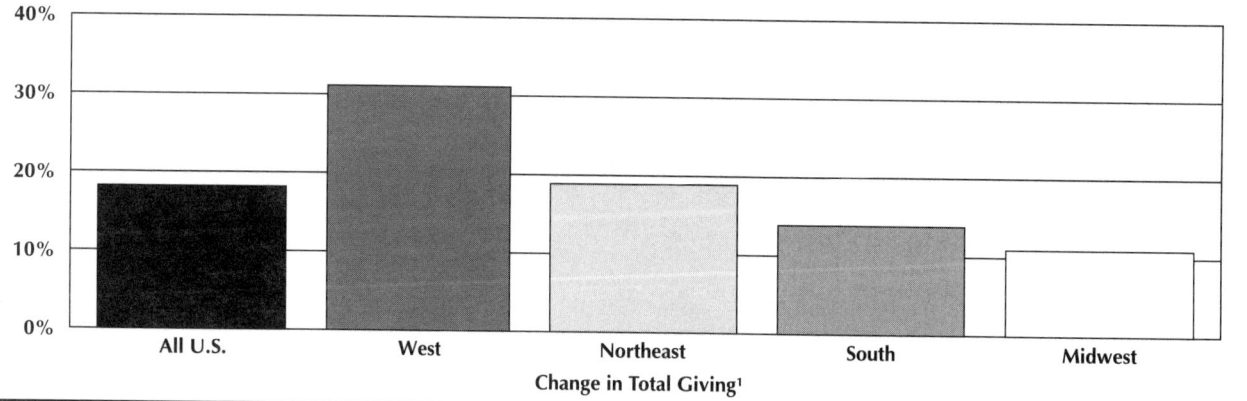

The West continued to show the fastest growth in foundation giving between 1999 and 2000

Change in Total Giving[1]

Source *Foundation Yearbook,* 2002.
[1] Percent change based on unadjusted dollars.

Key Findings

- Endowments of the top 25 foundations grew 12.2 percent in the latest year, exceeding overall asset gains but falling well behind growth in giving among top funders

- Gifts and bequests from donors to their foundations decreased nearly 14 percent in 2000, following record gifts in 1999

- Despite decline, 2000 gifts totaled $27.6 billion—second highest level on record

- 719 foundations received at least $5 million in gifts and bequests from their donors in the latest year, up 3 percent from 1999

Foundations by Region and State

Regions:

- West experienced fastest rate of growth in number of foundations in 2000

- Nearly half of larger Western foundations were established in the 1990s

- South reported largest gain in actual number of foundations since 1975

- West experienced fastest rate of growth in giving in latest year and since 1975

- West poised to surpass South by share of foundation giving in next few years

- Northeast showed largest increase in actual grant dollars in 2000

- Led by the Bill & Melinda Gates Foundation, West ranked first in rate of growth of assets and actual dollar gains for third consecutive year

- West increased its share of all U.S. foundation assets

- Corporate foundations in Midwest accounted for largest share of corporate foundation giving by region; community foundations in Midwest and West provided largest shares of community foundation giving by region

States:

- Washington State experienced most rapid rate of growth in giving in 2000

- New York and California led in actual grant dollar gains in latest year

- New York foundations ranked first by overall giving and giving as a share of Gross State Product; funders in the state ranked second based on giving per capita

- The District of Columbia ranked first based on giving per capita—due to its small population and the presence of a few large national and international funders

- Alaska ranked first by rate of growth in assets in 2000

- New York topped all states in actual 2000 asset dollar gains

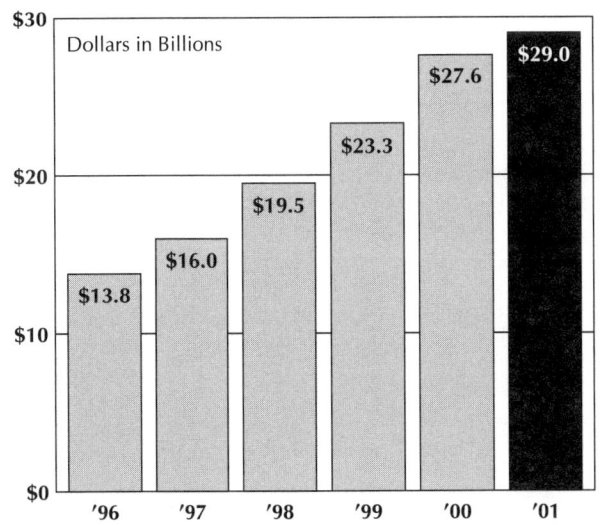

Foundation giving has more than doubled since 1996*

Source: *Foundation Yearbook*, 2002.
*Figures estimated for 2001. All figures based on unadjusted dollars.

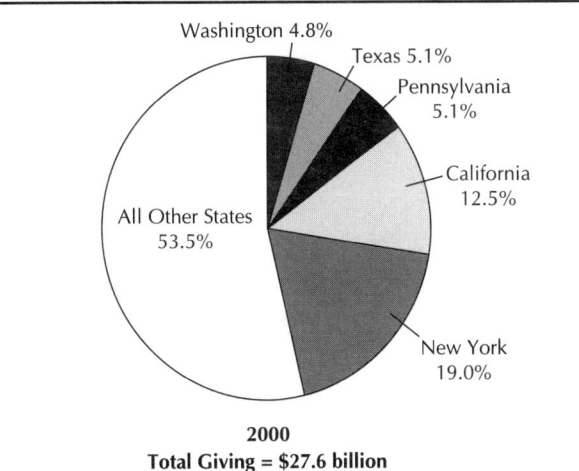

Foundations in five states accounted for close to half of 2000 giving

2000 Total Giving = $27.6 billion

Source: *Foundation Yearbook*, 2002.

Led by Gates Foundation, Washington State surpassed all others in the rate of growth in foundation giving between 1999 and 2000*

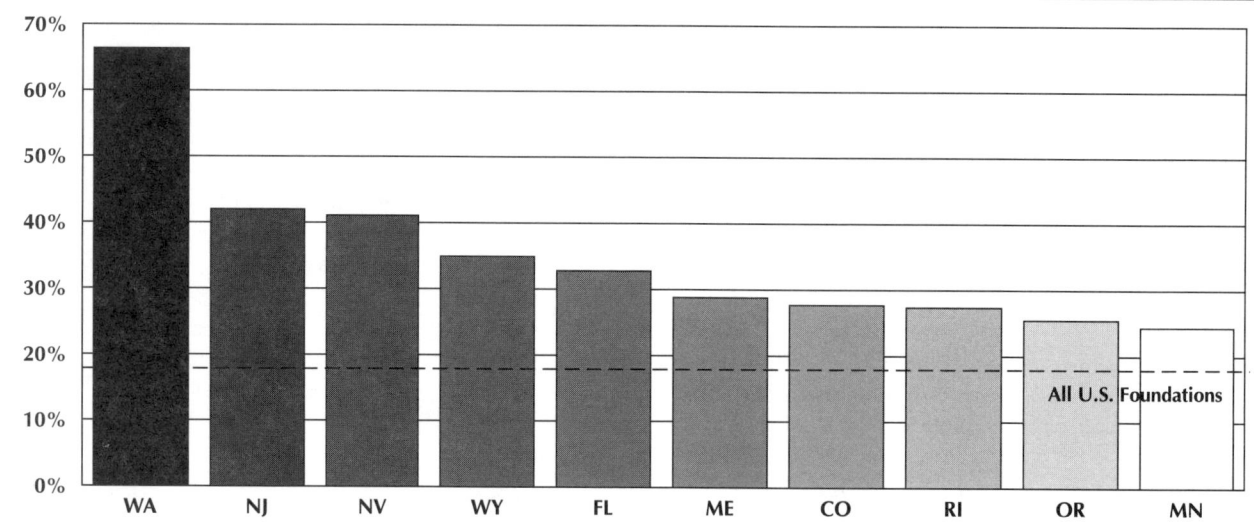

Source: *Foundation Yearbook*, 2002.
*Percent change based on unadjusted dollars.

Giving and Growth of Independent, Corporate, and Community Foundations

- Giving by independent foundations grew an estimated 5.4 percent in 2001, following an 18.7 percent actual gain in 2000

- Independent foundation assets increased 7.2 percent in 2000, falling behind overall growth

- Independent foundation giving in 2001 as a share of the prior year's assets totaled 5.5 percent, down slightly from 5.6 percent in 2000, but matching 1999's share

The West continued to increase its share of foundation assets in 2000*

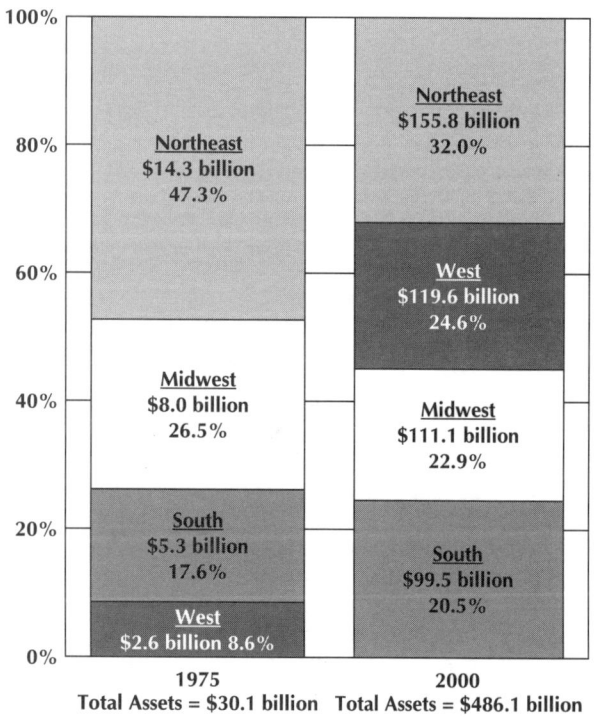

Source: *Foundation Yearbook*, 2002.
*Figures based on unadjusted dollars. Excludes assets of foundations based in the Caribbean and South Pacific, which accounted for 0.0 percent of total foundation assets in 1975 and 2000.

Foundation Profile, 1999 to 2000*

	1999	2000	% Change
All Foundations			
No. of Foundations:	50,201	56,582	12.7
Total Giving:	$ 23,321	$ 27,563	18.2
Total Assets:	$448,612	$486,085	8.4
Gifts Received:	$ 32,076	$ 27,614	-13.9
Independent			
No. of Foundations:	44,824	50,532	12.7
Total Giving:	$ 17,989	$ 21,346	18.7
Total Assets:	$381,365	$408,749	7.2
Gifts Received:	$ 24,097	$ 19,156	-20.5
Corporate			
No. of Foundations:	2,019	2,018	0.0
Total Giving:	$ 2,814	$ 2,985	6.1
Total Assets:	$ 15,258	$ 15,899	4.2
Gifts Received:	$ 3,313	$ 2,902	-12.4
Community			
No. of Foundations:	519	560	7.9
Total Giving:	$ 1,849	$ 2,166	17.1
Total Assets:	$ 27,649	$ 30,464	10.2
Gifts Received:	$ 3,295	$ 3,829	16.2
Operating			
No. of Foundations:	2,839	3,472	22.3
Total Giving:	$ 669	$ 1,065	59.2
Total Assets:	$ 24,340	$ 30,973	27.3
Gifts Received:	$ 1,371	$ 1,727	26.0

Source: *Foundation Yearbook*, 2002.
*Dollars in millions. Percent change represents current dollars. Includes only foundations that awarded grants in the latest fiscal year.

Key Findings

- 53 active private new health foundations, a subset of independent foundations, held assets of $8.1 billion in 2000 and gave $362.4 million

- Corporate foundation giving grew an estimated 2.6 percent in 2001, down from a 6.1 percent actual gain in 2000

- Assets of corporate foundations increased only 4.2 percent in 2000

- Gifts from companies to their foundations (pay-in) decreased 12.4 percent

- Pay-in fell behind giving (payout) in the latest year by close to 3 percent, placing a modest drain on corporate foundation assets

- Giving by community foundations grew an estimated 4.6 percent in 2001, following a 17.1 percent rise in 2000

- Community foundations' assets grew 10.2 percent in the latest year, roughly half of the prior year's increase

Foundation Development

- Foundation community grew by a record 12.7 percent in 2000

- Actual number of grantmaking foundations climbed by a record 6,381

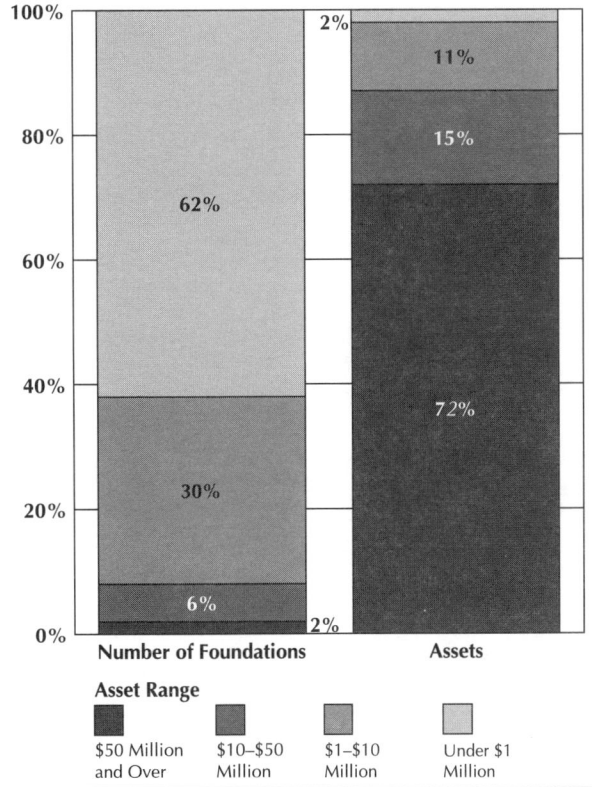

Only two percent of foundations or just over 1,100 held more than seven out of ten asset dollars in 2000

Source: *Foundation Yearbook*, 2002.

- Over two-fifths of larger foundations were formed in 1990s

- More than three-fifths of larger foundations were created since 1980

Foundation giving grew ahead of inflation during recessions over the last quarter-century*

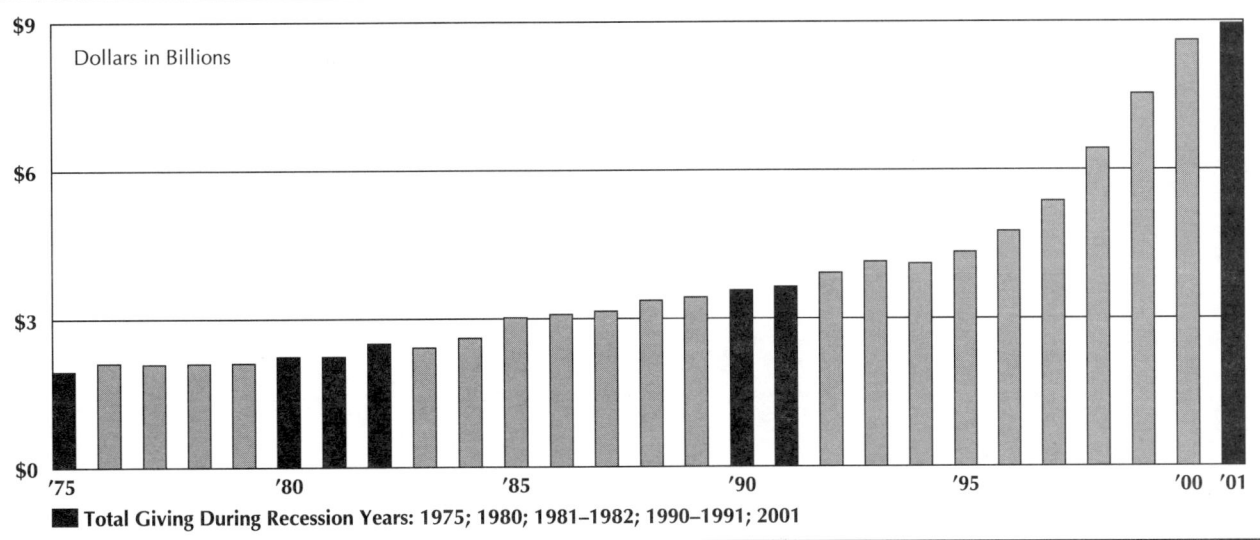

■ Total Giving During Recession Years: 1975; 1980; 1981–1982; 1990–1991; 2001

Source: *Foundation Yearbook*, 2002.
*Figures estimated for 2001. Constant 1975 dollars based on annual average Consumer Price Index, all urban consumers, U.S. Department of Labor, Bureau of Labor Statistics, as of March 2002.

CHAPTER 1

The State of Foundation Giving, 2002

- Giving reaches an estimated $29.0 billion in 2001, up $1.4 billion
- Giving in 2002 expected to remain flat
- Over the long term, modest growth in giving appears likely

In the minds of many Americans, the mid-1990s through the start of the new millennium seemed a halcyon time. The hallmarks of that period—unprecedented economic prosperity, a surge in Internet use and rapid growth in the technology sector, falling crime rates, and an unchallenged climate of political stability and domestic well-being—were seen as the prerogatives of a hard-working nation and the world's only superpower. Now, that reality could not seem more distant or naïve. Beginning with the decline of stock prices in the technology sector in late 2000 and accelerated by the September 11, 2001, attacks on New York and Washington, DC, this country's citizens came to feel that many of the gains of the last half-decade could vanish.

In the country's nonprofit sector, this new environment initially generated fear that charitable support—from individuals, corporations, and foundations—would diminish sharply for all but those organizations directly responding to the aftermath of 9/11. Even before this tragic event occurred, however, some third sector watchers posited reductions in charitable giving, including giving by foundations. They maintained that changes in giving were directly tied to the nation's economic performance. Thus, any reduction in wealth, such as that precipitated by 2001's falling stock market and economic recession, would lead to immediate decreases in charitable support.

For nonprofit organizations that had benefited from the unprecedented rise in foundation giving over the last half-decade, these predictions were especially troubling. Between 1995 and 2000, U.S. foundations reported five consecutive years of double-digit growth in their giving, and their overall support more than doubled during this period. As a result, foundations' share of all private giving climbed from roughly 10 percent at mid-decade to 13.5 percent at the start of the new century.[1] Beyond providing more support to a greater number of nonprofits, these vastly increased foundation resources encouraged many nonprofits to enhance their work by expanding programs and launching capital campaigns. A sudden cutback in foundation giving would consequently harm a greater number of organizations and put in doubt many of their more ambitious plans.

Despite this fear and the gloomy prognostications of some experts in the sector, giving by foundations did not fall in 2001. In fact, the nation's nearly 56,600 grantmaking foundations contributed an estimated $29.0 billion in grants in 2001 (Figure 1), up $1.4 billion. This 5.1 percent increase fell behind the prior year's 18.2 percent rise and represented the smallest annual gain in giving since 1994. Still, in the second consecutive year of declining stock values and amidst a recession, the increase in foundation giving outstripped inflation. Continued higher spending by many leading foundations (often fulfilling commitments made in the boom years of the late 1990s), along with exceptional giving in the aftermath of the 9/11 attacks,[2] helped to maintain positive growth. Newly established independent foundations also contributed to the overall increase in foundation giving.

---

1. See Brown, M., *Giving USA 2001: The Annual Report on Philanthropy*, New York: AAFRC Trust for Philanthropy, 2001. Figures on foundations' share of private giving include independent, corporate, community, and grantmaking operating foundations.
2. In response to the 9/11 attacks, independent and community foundations pledged nearly $195 million, of which roughly three-fifths was paid out in 2001. Corporations and corporate foundations pledged $621.5 million, of which approximately two-thirds was paid out in 2001. (Due to combined reporting of pledges, the precise amount paid out by corporate foundations cannot be determined.) For information on institutional giving in response to 9/11, see Renz, L., *Giving in the Aftermath of 9/11: Foundations and Corporations Respond*, New York: Foundation Center, 2002.

Independent foundations showed the greatest growth in giving in 2001, relative to other types of foundations. Giving by independent foundations, including family and new health foundations, rose an estimated 5.4 percent, following an actual 18.7 percent gain in 2000. Community foundations followed, with giving up an estimated 4.6 percent in 2001, following a 17.1 percent increase in 2000. This gain represented the slowest growth in community foundation giving since 1994 and reflected the sensitivity of their individual donors to changes in the economy. (For more detailed comparisons of estimated giving by foundation type, see Chapter 4.)

Corporate foundation giving grew an estimated 2.6 percent in 2001. After inflation, support by corporate foundations slipped 0.2 percent. This year of flat giving came on the heels of a 6.1 percent increase in 2000 and a 15.0 percent rise in 1999. Slower growth in giving compared to other types of foundations reflected the vulnerability of corporate funders to reduced profits. Partially offsetting expected corporate belt-tightening was the tremendous outpouring of support by corporations and their foundations in response to the 9/11 attacks.

The continuing growth in foundation giving through 2001 meant that their overall support more than doubled since 1996. Even adjusted for inflation, giving by foundations almost doubled during this period. By most standard economic measures, foundations realized remarkable growth in a very short period. For example, Figure 2 shows that inflation-adjusted foundation giving per capita grew by four-fifths (80.0 percent) from $45.47 in 1996 to $81.83 in 2000. As a share of Gross Domestic Product (GDP), inflation-adjusted foundation giving climbed by 46.4 percent over the same period (Figure 3).[3] Driving this growth in foundation giving was the rapid increase in both the number and the assets of foundations.

The dizzying climb of the stock market and the robust health of the economy were the key factors responsible for the increased value of existing foundation assets in the latter half of the 1990s and the record amount of new gifts and bequests from donors to their foundations. The rapid rise in personal wealth

---

3. Between 1995 and 2000, private charitable giving from all sources—including individuals, corporations, and foundations—as a share of Gross Domestic Product rose 17.6 percent, from 1.7 percent to 2.0 percent. For additional information, see *Giving USA 2001*.

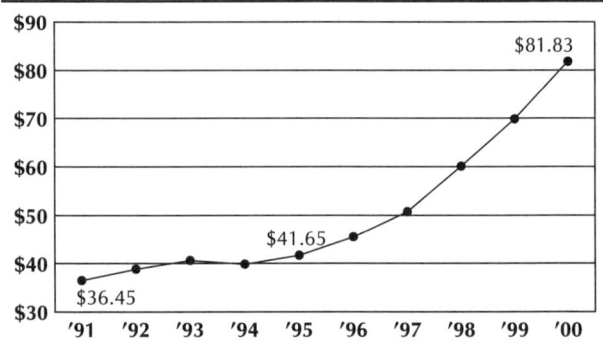

FIGURE 2. Foundation Giving Per Capita, 1991 to 2000 (Constant Dollars)*

Source: *Foundation Yearbook*, 2002.
*Constant 1991 dollars based on annual average Consumer Price Index, all urban consumers, U.S. Department of Labor, Bureau of Labor Statistics, as of March 2002. Figures on U.S. population for 2000 from *Statistical Abstracts of the United States: 2001*.

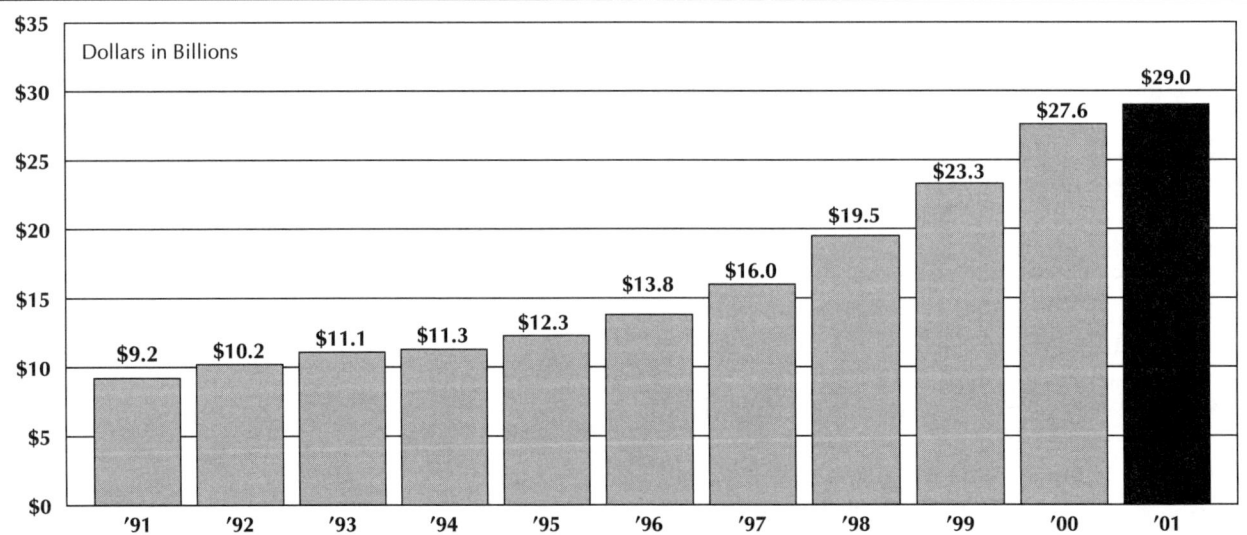

FIGURE 1. Growth of Foundation Giving 1991 to 2001*

Source: *Foundation Yearbook*, 2002.
*Figures estimated for 2000. All figures based on unadjusted dollars.

during this period also created an environment in which a record number of individuals chose to create foundations.

In the new reality of 2002, a weak recovery from the nation's first recession in ten years and two years of roiling instability in the stock market make a rapid return to robust economic health unlikely. Moreover, the country faces ongoing threats of terrorist activity and a loss of confidence in the business community following the Enron collapse, which could undermine economic recovery. These factors suggest a pessimistic outlook for the growth of existing U.S. foundations and the establishment of new ones.

Yet, despite uncertainty in the current economic and political climate, several factors indicate that foundation giving will remain relatively stable in 2002. Most importantly, many foundations—including most of the nation's largest ones—hold permanent investment assets and follow long-term payout strategies. While these foundations may not increase their grant budgets during periods of depressed markets, they generally try to avoid steep reductions in giving during recessions. In contrast, individuals' personal giving usually mirrors fairly directly real or anticipated changes in their net worth.

Also helping to stabilize foundation giving in periods of economic decline is the federal payout requirement for private, non-operating foundations. By law, independent and corporate foundations must pay out each year in charitable distributions at least 5 percent of the value of their investments in the preceding year. (They may carry forward over several years payout in excess of 5 percent.) Figure 4 shows that independent foundation giving as a share of prior year's assets totaled 5.5 percent in 2001, down slightly from 5.6 percent in 2000. For corporate foundations, the share slipped from 19.6 percent to 19.3 percent. (Unlike larger independent foundations, corporate foun-

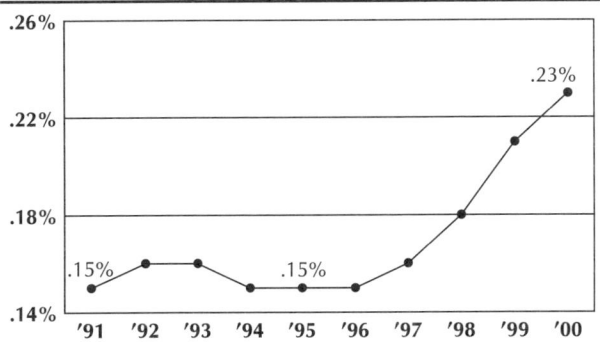

FIGURE 3. Foundation Giving as a Share of GDP, 1991 to 2000 (Constant Dollars)*

Source: *Foundation Yearbook*, 2002.
*Constant 1991 dollars based on annual average Consumer Price Index, all urban consumers, U.S. Department of Labor, Bureau of Labor Statistics, as of March 2002. Figures on 2000 U.S. Gross Domestic Product (GDP) from *Statistical Abstracts of the United States: 2001.*

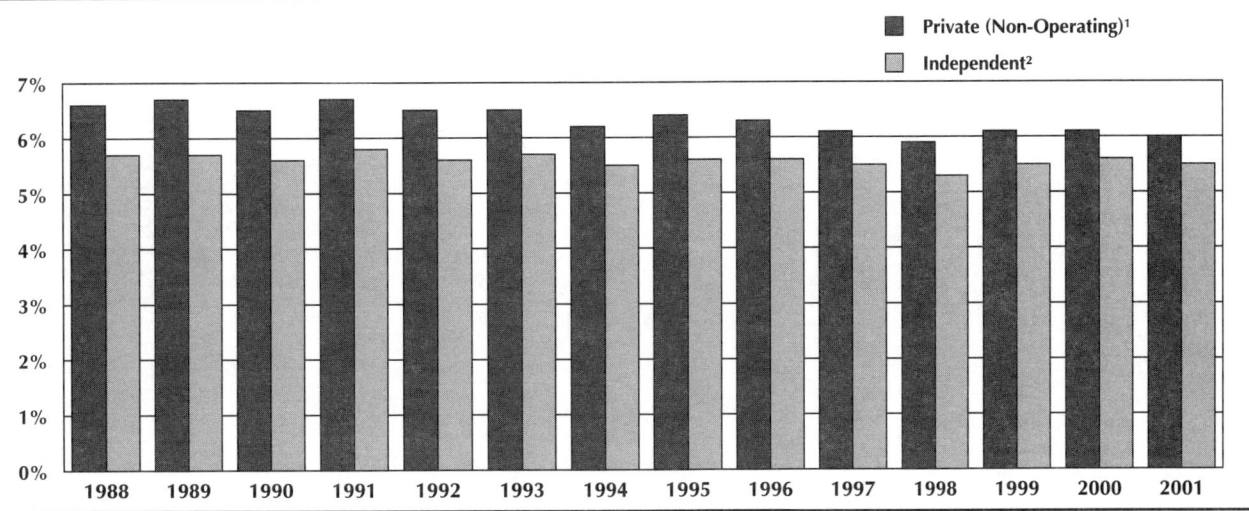

FIGURE 4. Private (Non-Operating) and Independent Foundation Giving as a Share of Prior Year's Assets, 1988 to 2001*

Source: *Foundation Yearbook*, 2002.
*Giving figures for 2001 based on estimates.
[1]Figures exclude private foundations that have been defined by the IRS as "Operating" foundations. These foundations are not subject to the same payout requirement as other private foundations. Community foundations are excluded as they are grantmaking public charities, not private foundations.
[2]Figures exclude private foundations identified by the Foundation Center as serving as vehicles for corporate philanthropy, many of which operate as "pass-through" foundations.
Note: Private (non-operating) foundations are required to pay out each year at least 5 percent of the value of their investments in the preceding year. (They may carry forward payout in excess of 5 percent over several years.) "Qualifying Distributions" is the amount used in calculating the required 5 percent payout and includes total giving, as well as reasonable administrative expenses, set-asides, PRIs, operating program expenses, and the amount paid to acquire assets used directory for charitable purposes. Actual payout can only be calculated for individual foundations. The ratio of total giving to prior year asset values therefore serves as only a rough proxy for payout.

dations generally do not maintain substantial endowments and instead fund grant budgets through annual gifts from their corporate donors—hence, the higher ratio of giving to prior year's assets. Nonetheless, some corporations will make additional gifts into their foundations' endowments in periods of higher earnings, which can be used to stabilize giving during periods of lower earning.) By comparison, community foundations are under no obligation to maintain mandated levels of giving during rocky economic times. Still, their giving typically amounts to between 7 percent and 8 percent of the value of their prior year's assets, with new gifts from individual donors combining with earnings on investments to fund grants budgets.

Figure 5 illustrates the changes in foundation giving in inflation-adjusted dollars since 1975 (the first year for which comprehensive information is available). During the recessions of 1980, 1981-82, and 1990-91, foundation giving in real dollars did not decline and, in fact, *increased slightly*. Still, the latest recession (unlike those in the 1980s and 1990s) has been accompanied by two straight years of stock market declines. Looking at 2002, this suggests that, although foundation giving cannot be expected to grow, it most likely will not show a pronounced reduction. In fact, among the nation's nearly 56,600 funders, giving patterns will vary. Many foundations will maintain a steady level of giving, and decreases in giving by some funders may be offset by increases among others, particularly new foundations whose grantmaking programs started up in the last few years or foundations whose investments have fared well in the current environment.

The relative stability of foundation giving compared to giving by individuals or corporations means that foundations will represent an even greater share of private charitable support. Moreover, with cutbacks in government support for nonprofits, due to the recession and the reallocation of federal resources, nonprofit organizations will face even greater competition for foundation support.

Beyond 2002, the establishment of new and often very large foundations and the exceptionally large gifts and bequests still being given by donors to their existing foundations will help to ensure the short-term stability of and longer-term return to growth in foundation giving. While information on foundation creation at the end of the 1990s and into 2000 remains incomplete, the number of larger foundations established during the past decade has already exceeded the record-high birth rates witnessed in the 1980s. In 2000 alone, the number of active foundations overall increased by a record 6,400, far surpassing the prior year's record gain of 3,400. As many of these new foundations receive additional assets over the next ten to 20 years, they will contribute new resources to the nation's nonprofit community.

Among up-and-coming grantmakers is a $5 billion family foundation established by Intel Corporation founder Gordon Moore. In 2001, the Gordon I. and Betty E. Moore Foundation made future commitments totaling over $750 million. Ultimately, Mr. Moore expects to give most of his fortune to the foundation. On

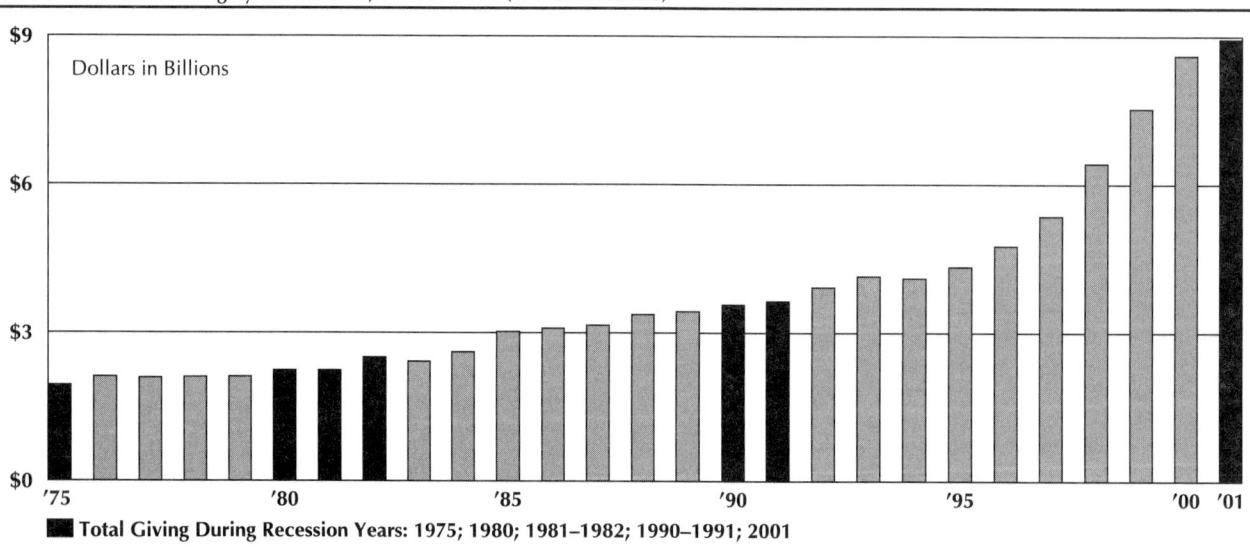

FIGURE 5. Total Giving by Foundations, 1975 to 2001 (Constant Dollars)*

Source: *Foundation Yearbook*, 2002.
*Figures estimated for 2001. Constant 1975 dollars based on annual average Consumer Price Index, all urban consumers, U.S. Department of Labor, Bureau of Labor Statistics, as of March 2002.

a similar scale, the William and Flora Hewlett Foundation will benefit from a multi-billion-dollar bequest from the estate of William Hewlett over the next several years that could raise its assets to approximately $7 billion, placing it among the top ten foundations by assets.

In addition, a 1998 change in federal tax policy will continue to aid the growth of new and existing foundations. A temporary provision in the tax law permitting living donors to deduct the current market value of gifts of appreciated property to private foundations expired in 1994. It was reinstated twice after 1995 for brief periods, encouraging gifts from donors and new foundation creation, but it expired again in mid-1998. After strong lobbying by foundation associations and nonprofit groups, the provision was finally made a permanent part of the tax code in 1998.[4]

4. Alternatively, reductions in personal income and estate tax rates could slow the establishment of new foundations and reduce the growth of existing foundations through gifts or bequests. As evidenced by the decline in the rate of foundation formation immediately following the 1986 personal income tax reductions, decreases in taxes on wealthy individuals lower the incentive for charitable giving.

The U.S. nonprofit community continues to benefit from foundation giving that in 2001 was more than double the amount it received in the mid-1990s. In fact, despite the country's first recession in ten years, a continuing stock market decline, and national uncertainty in the wake of the 9/11 terrorist attacks, foundation giving rose ahead of inflation last year. Looking ahead to 2002 and beyond, the prospects for maintaining current levels of giving appear reasonable. Yet the sluggish performance of the stock market over the past two years and the continued weak state of the economic recovery have taken a toll on foundation endowments. Barring a dramatic and sustained upturn in the nation's economic fortunes, it appears unlikely that foundations can offer more than modest increases in support in the near future.

June 2002

CHAPTER 2

Foundation Giving and Growth

Overview of Growth Through 2000

- Number of foundations reaches nearly 56,600, more than doubling since 1987

- Annual giving reaches $27.6 billion, doubling since 1996

- Endowment values climb to $486.1 billion, more than doubling since 1995

- Gifts to foundations from their donors total $27.6 billion, doubling since 1997

The beginning of the technology sector's decline and the first signs of a general economic slowdown could not dampen the exceptional growth in new foundation creation and double-digit increases in foundation support. By number and giving, foundations experienced very strong one-year growth in 2000. The number of grantmaking foundations grew a record 12.7 percent, surpassing the more than 7 percent increase reported in 1999 and representing more than triple the growth rate seen in the years 1994 through 1996. Giving rose 18.2 percent, falling below the 19.9 percent increase reported in 1999 and the record 21.7 percent gain recorded in 1998. Still, actual grant dollars increased by an unprecedented $4.2 billion. In contrast, assets rose 8.4 percent, about half of the increase realized in the two prior years. Finally, gifts into foundations slipped by roughly one-seventh (13.9 percent), although they accounted for the second highest actual amount of gifts on record.

2000 Giving

- Giving rises 18.2 percent, continuing double-digit gains

- Giving totals $27.6 billion, up a record $4.2 billion

Foundations gave nearly $27.6 billion in 2000, up 18.2 percent over 1999 (Table 1 and Table 2). Measured against inflation, growth was 14.3 percent. While the percentage increase in giving fell below the two prior years' gains, this marked the fifth consecutive year of very robust growth—giving has jumped $13.7 billion (99.1 percent) since 1996—and the ninth year since 1988 in which grants grew by more than 5 percent in real terms. This striking performance over the last

TABLE 1. 2000 Aggregate Fiscal Data by Foundation Type (Dollars in thousands)*

Foundation Type	Number of Foundations	%	Assets	%	Gifts Received	%	Qualifying Distributions[1]	%	Total Giving[2]	%	PRIs/ Loans	%
Independent	50,532	89.3	$408,749,391	84.1	$19,155,555	69.4	$22,853,261	74.9	$21,346,232	77.4	$183,289	81.2
Corporate	2,018	3.6	15,899,090	3.3	2,902,208	10.5	3,130,172	10.3	2,984,645	10.8	11,641	5.2
Community	560	1.0	30,463,674	6.3	3,828,552	13.9	2,205,594	7.2	2,166,343	7.9	7,098	3.1
Operating	3,472	6.1	30,973,156	6.4	1,727,480	6.3	2,308,533	7.6	1,065,947	3.9	23,595	10.5
Total	56,582	100.0	$486,085,311	100.0	$27,613,795	100.0	$30,497,560	100.0	$27,563,166	100.0	$408,912	100.0

Source: *Foundation Yearbook*, 2002.
*Due to rounding, figures may not add up.
[1]Qualifying distributions is the amount used in calculating the required 5 percent payout for private foundations; includes total giving, as well as reasonable administrative expenses, set-asides, PRIs, operating program expenses, and the amount paid to acquire assets used directly for charitable purposes.
[2]Includes grants, scholarships, and employee matching gifts; excludes set-asides, loans, PRIs, and program expenses.

decade has increased foundations' share of all private giving by more than half.[1] Moreover, actual grant dollars grew by a record $4.2 billion in the latest year.

Growth was spurred by several factors, chief among them the bullish performance of the stock market from 1995 through 1999. The resulting boom in endowment values led to sharp increases in giving levels starting in 1996. In 2000, giving increased 18.2 percent—the fourth largest increase reported since the Foundation Center began keeping records on all grantmaking foundations in 1975—despite the beginning of an economic downturn, especially in the technology sector. This increase in giving followed a 16.5 percent rise in 1999 assets. A one-year delay is consistent with payout requirements and with the spending policies of the large endowed foundations, which seek to maintain a steady level of growth.

Grants budgets are generally determined by the previous year's average asset value. Thus, sharp gains or losses in asset values in the current year—especially those falling in the last quarter—generally do not affect payout levels until the following year. Still, in periods of exceptional growth, foundations may choose to make extraordinary one-time awards for special purposes.

Beyond the economic and stock market boom of the late 1990s, three other factors helped raise grantmaking in 2000. First was the continued high level of new gifts and bequests from many donors to their foundations, including an additional $5.1 billion gift into the Washington State-based Bill & Melinda Gates Foundation. In the latest year, the Gates Foundation's giving climbed by more than four-fifths to almost $1 billion. Second was the continued development of new foundations. Giving by foundations reporting for the first time—especially independent and family foundations—added almost $710 million to overall giving in 2000, accounting for one-sixth (16.7 percent) of the total $4.2 billion increase noted above. The third factor was the rapid growth in giving reported by several newly large foundations, such as the William and Flora Hewlett Foundation (CA).

2000 Giving by Foundation Type. Giving by independent and community foundations continued to grow at a strong pace in 2000, while corporate foundations began to show the impact of the economic slowdown. Independent foundations reported the fastest growth in giving in the latest year, with their grant dollars rising 18.7 percent. This followed a 20.5 percent increase in 1999 and a similar 20.7 percent gain in 1998. Community foundations reported a 17.1 percent increase in giving in 2000, following a record 26.9 percent rise in 1999. By comparison, corporate foundation giving increased just 6.1 percent in the latest year, less than half of the 15.0 percent gain recorded in 1999 and approximately one-third of the 18.4 percent rise reported in 1998. This dip occurred despite an increase in corporate pretax income in 2000.

Regardless of foundation type, giving by the larger endowed foundations grew more quickly than grants from the smaller foundations. (See a review of trends of the 25 largest foundations on page 17.) Still, even the categories of smaller funders reported relatively strong increases in 2000. (For more detailed comparisons of giving by foundation type, see Chapter 4.)

2000 Giving by Region. Led by the Bill & Melinda Gates Foundation and the David & Lucile Packard Foundation (CA), grantmakers in the West continued to report the fastest growth in giving in the latest year. Overall, Western foundations raised giving by 31.1 percent in 2000, surpassing grantmakers in the Northeast (18.9 percent), South (13.9 percent), and Midwest (11.0 percent). Still, a comparison of growth in actual grant dollars showed the Northeast leading, with an increase in giving of $1.5 billion, followed by the West ($1.4 billion), South ($724.3 million), and Midwest ($640.8 million). (For more detailed comparisons of giving by region, see Chapter 3.)

Growth of Giving, 1975 to 2000

Figure 6 and Table 3 illustrate growth in foundation giving and the impact of inflation since 1975, the first year for which the Foundation Center produced summary data on all grantmaking foundations. Table 4 compares the growth of number of foundations, giving, assets, and gifts received. At the start of the 1980s, the prospects for foundations were dim. Giving barely kept pace with inflation. Not only was the number of grantmaking foundations shrinking, but so too was the real value of foundation endowments. High inflation and difficult market conditions were partly

---

1. See page 27 for a special report on "Foundations' Share of Private Philanthropy, 2000."

TABLE 2. Comparison of 2000 to 1999 Aggregate Fiscal Data*

Foundation Type	1999	2000	% change
No. of Foundations	50,201	56,582	12.7
Total Giving[1]	$ 23,321,482	$ 27,563,166	18.2
Total Assets	$448,610,710	$486,085,311	8.4
Gifts Received	$ 32,076,674	$ 27,613,795	-13.9

Source: *Foundation Yearbook,* 2002.
*Dollars in thousands. Percent change represents current dollars. Includes only foundations that awarded grants in the latest fiscal year.
[1]Includes grants, scholarships, and employee matching gifts; excludes set-asides, loans, PRIs, and program expenses.

Foundation Giving and Growth

FIGURE 6.   Effect of Inflation on Foundation Giving, 1975 to 2000

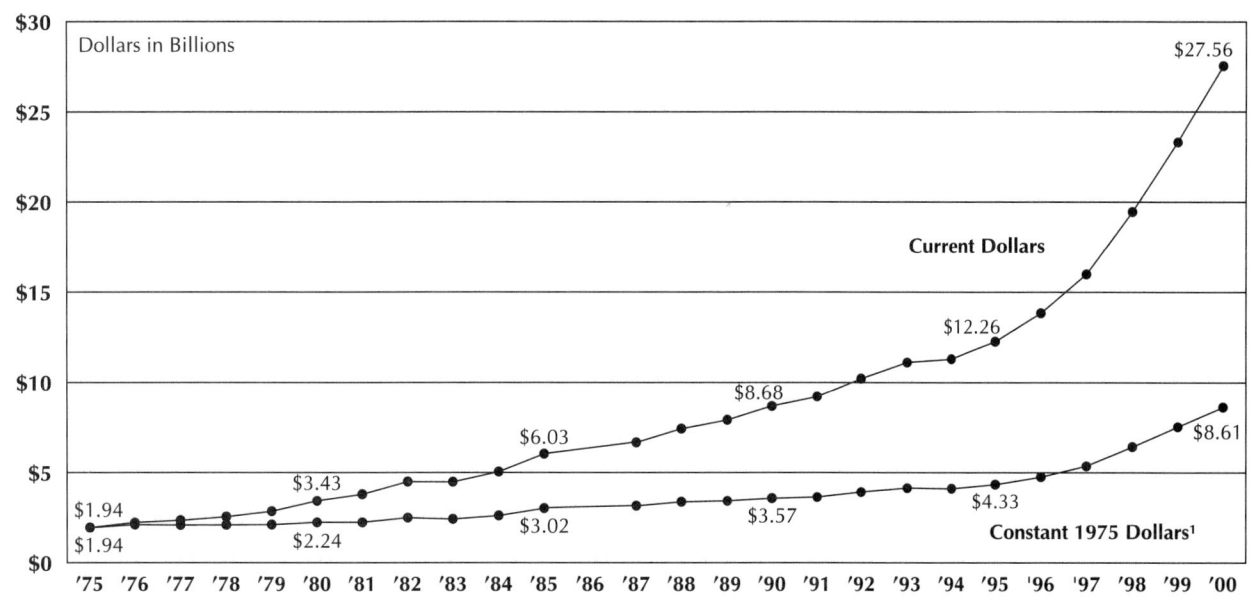

Source: *Foundation Yearbook,* 2002.
[1] Percent change in 1975 dollars based on annual average Consumer Price Index, all urban consumers, U.S. Department of Labor, Bureau of Labor Statistitics, as of March 2002.

TABLE 3.   Growth of Foundation Giving Adjusted for Inflation*

Year	Current Total Giving Amount	% Change	1975=100	Constant Total Giving Amount	% Change	1975=100
1975	$ 1.94		100.0	$1.94		100.0
1976	2.23	14.9	114.9	2.11	8.7	108.7
1977	2.35	5.4	121.1	2.09	(1.1)	107.5
1978	2.55	8.5	131.4	2.10	0.9	108.5
1979	2.85	11.8	146.9	2.11	0.4	108.9
1980	3.43	20.4	176.8	2.24	6.0	115.4
1981	3.79	10.5	195.4	2.24	0.2	115.6
1982	4.49	18.5	231.4	2.50	11.6	129.0
1983	4.48	-0.2	230.9	2.42	(3.3)	124.7
1984	5.04	12.5	259.8	2.61	7.8	134.5
1985	6.03	19.6	310.8	3.02	15.5	155.4
1986	—	—	—	—	—	—
1987	6.66	—	343.3	3.15	—	162.6
1988	7.42	11.4	382.5	3.37	7.0	173.9
1989	7.91	6.6	407.7	3.43	1.7	176.9
1990	8.68	9.7	447.4	3.57	4.1	184.2
1991	9.21	6.1	474.7	3.64	1.8	187.5
1992	10.21	10.9	526.3	3.92	7.6	201.8
1993	11.11	8.8	572.7	4.14	5.7	213.2
1994	11.29	1.6	582.0	4.10	(0.9)	211.3
1995	12.26	8.6	632.0	4.33	5.6	223.1
1996	13.84	12.9	713.4	4.75	9.6	244.6
1997	15.99	15.5	824.2	5.36	12.8	276.3
1998	19.46	21.7	1,003.1	6.42	19.8	331.0
1999	23.32	19.9	1,202.1	7.53	17.3	388.1
2000	27.56	18.2	1,420.6	8.61	14.3	443.8

Source: *Foundation Yearbook,* 2002. Dates approximate; reporting years varied.
*Dollars in billions. Constant 1975 dollars based on annual average Consumer Price Index, all urban consumers, U.S. Department of Labor, Bureau of Labor Statistics, as of March 2002.
— = not available

TABLE 4. Number of Grantmaking Foundations, Assets, Total Giving, and Gifts Received*

Year	Number	1975=100	Assets	1975=100	Total Giving[1]	1975=100	Gifts Received	1978=100
1975	21,877	100.0	$ 30.13	100.0	$ 1.94	100.0	—	—
1976	21,447	98.0	34.78	115.4	2.23	114.9	—	—
1977	22,152	101.2	35.37	117.4	2.35	121.1	—	—
1978	22,484	102.7	37.27	123.7	2.55	131.4	$ 1.61	100.0
1979	22,535	103.0	41.59	138.0	2.85	146.9	2.21	137.3
1980	22,088	100.9	48.17	159.9	3.43	176.8	1.98	123.0
1981	21,967	100.4	47.57	157.9	3.79	195.4	2.39	148.4
1982	23,770	108.6	58.67	194.7	4.49	231.4	4.00	248.4
1983	24,261	110.8	67.87	225.3	4.48	230.9	2.71	168.3
1984	24,859	113.6	74.05	245.8	5.04	259.8	3.36	208.7
1985	25,639	117.2	102.06	338.7	6.03	310.8	4.73	293.8
1986	—	—	—	—	—	—	—	—
1987	27,661	126.4	115.44	383.1	6.66	343.3	4.96	308.1
1988	30,338	138.7	122.08	405.2	7.42	382.5	5.16	320.5
1989	31,990	146.2	137.54	456.5	7.91	407.7	5.52	342.9
1990	32,401	148.1	142.48	472.9	8.68	447.4	4.97	308.7
1991	33,356	152.5	162.91	540.7	9.21	474.7	5.47	339.8
1992	35,765	163.5	176.82	586.9	10.21	526.3	6.18	383.9
1993	37,571	171.7	189.21	628.0	11.11	572.7	7.76	482.0
1994	38,807	177.4	195.79	649.8	11.29	582.0	8.08	501.9
1995	40,140	183.5	226.74	752.5	12.26	632.0	10.26	637.3
1996	41,588	190.0	267.58	888.1	13.84	713.4	16.02	995.0
1997	44,146	201.8	329.91	1,095.0	15.99	824.2	15.83	983.2
1998	46,832	214.1	385.05	1,278.0	19.46	1,003.1	22.57	1,401.9
1999	50,201	229.5	448.61	1,488.9	23.32	1,202.1	32.08	1,992.5
2000	56,582	258.6	486.09	1,613.3	27.56	1,420.6	27.61	1,714.9

Source: *Foundation Yearbook,* 2002. Dates approximate; reporting years varied.
*Dollars in billions.
— = not available
[1]Includes grants, scholarships, and employee matching gifts; excludes set-asides, loans, PRIs, and program expenses.

Measures of Foundation Support, 2000

- 2000 qualifying distributions total $30.5 billion
- **Foundation payout exceeds Federal requirement**
- Grants to individuals total almost $545 million
- **Loans and other charitable investments total $226 million**
- Top 21,000 foundations award more than 965,000 grants

If asked how to measure the extent of foundations' charitable support, most people would suggest counting up all of the money that funders give to organizations in the form of grants. While this measure would accurately reflect the vast majority of foundations' charitable activities, it would by no means capture all of their philanthropic support.

Foundations employ a number of tools to promote their charitable mission. For example, beyond making grants to organizations, funders can make charitable loans and other forms of below-market-rate investments—also know as program-related investments (PRIs)—as well as grants and loans to individuals. These types of charitable support offer several opportunities for measurement. Moreover, minimum levels of private foundation support have been set by the Federal government, providing another opportunity for measuring foundations' charitable activities.

The following sections detail several ways, beyond grantmaking to organizations, by which to measure foundation support:

Qualifying Distributions. Qualifying distributions represent the total amount that foundations disbursed for charitable activities in a given fiscal year that can be counted toward their Federal payout requirement (see below). Grants to organizations constitute the vast majority of qualifying distributions, an amount that also includes grants to individuals, charitable investments, set asides, most operating expenses, and other charitable expenditures, e.g., the costs for convening a conference on the U.S. health care system, offering office space to nonprofits, and providing technical assistance (see Table 1). Between 1999 and 2000, qualifying distributions grew from $25.7 billion to $30.5 billion, up 18.6 percent (just exceeding the increase in grants).

Payout. U.S. law requires that all private, non-operating foundations pay out a minimum of 5 percent of the value of their assets in the preceding year as charitable distributions.[1] While we cannot precisely measure aggregate payout, 2000 giving represented 5.6 percent of independent foundation assets at the close of 1999, up from 5.5 percent (see Figure 4 in Chapter 1). For all private (non-operating) foundations, which includes independent and corporate foundations, the ratio decreased slightly from 6.1 percent in 1999 to 6.0 percent in the latest year. The ratio of independent and corporate foundations' qualifying distributions to assets was 6.6 percent.[2]

The ratio varies by foundation type and size. In general, corporate foundations and smaller foundations that do not maintain endowments pay out at a higher rate than the large endowed foundations. In contrast, most large independent foundations, with income derived solely from their endowments, adhere to a 5 percent payout strategy, in compliance with IRS regulations.[3]

Grants to Individuals. Of the total $27.6 billion in foundation giving awarded in 2000, the Foundation Center identified almost $544.8 million in scholarships and other grants to individuals, up 7.3 percent from $507.5 million in 1999. While the total amount has increased substantially since the early 1990s, grants paid directly to individuals represented a tiny share of overall giving (2.0 percent). Still, in 2000 close to 184,000 individuals benefited from grants and scholarships made directly by foundations.[4]

Program-Related Investments (PRIs). Foundations provided $225.6 million in low- or no-interest loans and charitable investments—known as PRIs—for projects closely related to their grantmaking interests (Table 1). (They provided an additional $35.5 million in loans to individuals, primarily for tuition assistance.) The use of this type of alternative financing decreased 7.5 percent in 2000 from $243.9 million in 1999. Some of the leading independent foundation PRI providers in 2000 included the Ford and John D. and Catherine T. MacArthur foundations. Notable corporate foundations included the Prudential and Fannie Mae foundations. A number of community foundations, such as the Cleveland Foundation, operate small loan programs for local nonprofits.[5] Despite a decrease in the amount of PRI financing, the number of active PRI providers has remained fairly stable. Approximately 200 foundations were identified in 2000.

Number of Grants. Foundation Center staff identified 965,198 grants made by the nearly 21,000 foundations with assets of at least $1 million or grants of at least $100,000.[6] These grants are accounted for in *The Foundation Directory, The Foundation Directory, Part 2*, and the *Guide to U.S. Foundations*. Over two out of three grants were made by independent foundations, one out of five by corporate foundations, and one out of nine by community foundations. Only 1 percent of grants were made by operating foundations.

---

1. The principal purpose of operating foundations is to conduct their own programs or provide a direct service. Therefore, they are not required to meet the same payout requirement as other private foundations.
2. These ratios are merely representative and do not equal actual payout, which is calculated individually for each foundation based on a five-year formula that allows for carrying forward distributions in excess of the 5 percent requirement.
3. A 2000 study, "Spending Policies and Investment Planning for Foundations," assessed the impact of foundation spending policies on the value of their portfolios. The report, prepared by DeMarche Associates for the Council on Foundations, concludes that foundations cannot maintain payout rates of 6 percent or higher without undermining the purchasing power of their portfolios. A 2000 study prepared by Cambridge Associates for the Council of Michigan Foundations, "Sustainable Payout for Foundations," reached a similar conclusion.
4. Grants to individuals were reported by 1,151 of the 10,000 foundations listed in *The Foundation Directory*, 2002 Edition. Although the Foundation Center does not maintain comprehensive data on individual giving of all foundations, descriptive entries on more than 4,300 large and small grantmakers that award grants to individuals are provided in the 2001 edition of *Foundation Grants to Individuals*.
5. The latest information on charitable investing was released in the Foundation Center's 2001 publication, *The PRI Directory: Charitable Loans and Other Program-Related Investments by Foundations*.
6. Unlike information on grant dollars awarded, data on the number of grants awarded may be incomplete for a few funders. Therefore, the total figure for number of grants awarded by these foundations is probably somewhat higher.

to blame. From 1975 to 1981, giving grew faster than assets in nearly every year. However, as assets eroded in real terms, the prospects for increased giving diminished.

Beyond the stagnant economy, much of the decline has been attributed to payout requirements imposed under the 1969 Tax Reform Act, a comprehensive body of regulations governing private foundations, which has been amended several times (see Appendix B, "Regulation of Private Foundations"). Under modifications introduced in 1976, foundations were required to distribute for charitable purposes all of their adjusted net income or 5 percent of the market value of that year's investment assets, whichever was greater.

In the late 1970s, a period of low investment income and high inflation, foundations were forced to dig deep into capital to satisfy payout requirements, and the real value of assets dropped. In 1981, following intensive lobbying, Congress lowered the payout rate to a minimum of 5 percent of the market value of the foundation's investment assets in the preceding year. The distribution requirement has remained at this level ever since.

By the mid-1980s, a combination of lower inflation, higher corporate profits, and soaring stock values helped to reverse the trend toward asset decline. Foundations experienced their first real growth spurt in more than a decade (see "2000 Assets" below). The fast-rising asset base in turn assured a steady increase in the level of annual grants.

From 1980 to 2000, giving multiplied more than eight times, from $3.4 billion to $27.6 billion. In constant dollars, giving grew close to four times (284.4 percent). Giving increased rapidly between 1981 and 1988. In real terms, grants jumped 50 percent over seven years, growing on average 6.0 percent a year. Between 1988 and 2000, giving grew an additional 155.5 percent after inflation, or an average 8.1 percent a year, but the pace was uneven. The growth rate slowed from 1988 to 1991 and remained unsteady through 1994. In the past few years, however, the growth rate picked up steam. From 1996 through 2000, for example, it averaged 16.0 percent a year after inflation.

2000 Assets

- **Foundation assets rise to $486.1 billion, up 8.4 percent**
- **Stock market loses and a lower level of new gifts slow growth**

The beginning of the technology bust in mid-2000, an overall cooling in the economy after five years of rapid growth, and lower levels of new gifts into foundations resulted in slower growth in foundation resources. Overall, foundation assets grew 8.4 percent in the latest year to $486.1 billion (Table 2). This relatively modest rise followed five straight years of double-digit growth, including more than 16 percent gains in foundation assets in 1998 and 1999. Still, foundation assets have grown by over four-fifths (81.7 percent) since 1996.

Although they cannot be directly compared, changes in the value of foundation endowments typically follow the direction of U.S. investment markets. For example, the Standard and Poor's 500 stock index fell 10.1 percent between 1999 and 2000, while the Wilshire 5000 stock index declined 10.9 percent and the technology heavy NASDAQ plummeted 39.3 percent. By comparison, the Dow Jones Industrial average posted a modest 1.9 percent gain and the New York Stock Exchange composite index increased 1.0 percent. Compared with these top-performing indexes, foundation endowments showed relatively stronger growth of 8.4 percent.

Among factors accounting for this difference in returns is that only a portion of foundation assets are invested in the U.S. stock market.[2] In addition, not all asset growth is derived from investments. In 2000, gifts and bequests to foundations from their donors—while falling below 1999's record level—added substantially to asset values.

In years of strong market growth, the largest endowed foundations have invariably outperformed mid-size and smaller foundations in terms of asset value gains. By comparison, in the weak 2000 market year, assets of the very largest foundations ($250 million or more) grew 8.5 percent, while those with smaller assets ($5 million or less) experienced growth of roughly 11 percent or more. Regardless, it should be noted that, in all asset size ranges, the endowments of new funders and the value of large new gifts and bequests contributed to growth.

2000 Assets by Foundation Type. All types of foundations experienced much more modest asset increases in 2000, compared to the prior five-year period. Community foundations reported the fastest growth—a one-tenth (10.2 percent) rise from $27.6 billion to $30.5 billion. New gifts into community foundations

---

2. To avoid risk or for lack of professional management, smaller endowed foundations tend to invest less heavily in the stock market and more in fixed income assets, including bonds and money market funds. Larger foundations invest more in stocks, but their investments are also more diversified and may not match yields reported by the fastest growing stock indexes. In the *Foundation Management Report*, 10th edition, Council on Foundations, 2001, Table 2.1, the report's authors note that based on the latest member survey, close to two-thirds (65%) of the average foundation portfolio is composed of stocks and nearly one-fourth (24%) is made up of fixed income assets.

accounted for close to one-fifth (18.9 percent) of this gain. The assets of independent foundations, a group that comprises the vast majority of grantmakers, climbed $27.4 billion or 7.2 percent. This modest growth fell well below 1999's 16.6 percent rise. Established foundations were responsible for the lion's share of growth. Nevertheless, $8.2 billion in assets (three-tenths) was provided by newly reporting independents. Finally, assets of corporate foundations rose 4.2 percent to $15.9 billion, roughly one-quarter of the 16.4 percent increase reported in 1999.

Contributing to the slower growth in corporate foundation assets was a decrease in company gifts into their foundations. Overall, new gifts (pay-in) declined 12.4 percent in 2000, following a 24.8 percent gain in 1999 and a record 41.7 percent jump in 1998. Moreover, giving (payout) exceeded pay-in by about $82 million or 2.8 percent, placing a modest drain on the value of corporate foundation assets. Helping to boost corporate foundation assets, however, were the 60 corporate foundations new to the pool of active grantmakers in 2000, which provided $251.6 million or 39.2 percent of asset growth. (For more detailed comparisons of assets by foundation type, see Chapter 4.)

2000 Assets by Region. Foundations in the West led in asset growth in terms of both percentage increase and gain in actual dollars, although gains were much more modest than in recent years. Overall, Western foundation assets rose 11.7 percent, surpassing the Midwest (9.5 percent), Northeast (6.7 percent), and South (5.9 percent). Actual Western foundation asset dollars grew $12.6 billion, with an additional $5.1 billion gift into the Bill & Melinda Gates Foundation accounting for about two-fifths of this gain. By comparison, the assets of foundations in the Northeast and Midwest rose $9.7 billion and $9.6 billion, respectively, while those of grantmakers in the South increased $5.6 billion. (For more detailed comparisons of assets by region, see Chapter 3.)

Growth of Assets, 1975 to 2000

Even more than giving, assets grew at a record pace through the mid-1980s, but slowed in the years following. Between 1981 and 1987, inflation-adjusted endowment values soared 94 percent (Figure 7 and Table 5). In contrast, they rose just 28 percent from 1988 to 1994. On average, annual growth plummeted from double-digit percentages in the mid-1980s to less than 5 percent after 1986. Between 1995 and 1999, however, assets climbed an average of 16.0 percent per year in real terms, higher than in the mid-1980s.

Whereas assets grew much faster than giving in the mid-1980s, the pace equaled out after 1986. In the first half of the 1990s, giving grew faster than assets in three out of six years, despite the addition of new foundations and a rise in gifts to foundations. Between 1995 and 1997, however, as the stock market boomed and

FIGURE 7. Effect of Inflation on Foundation Assets, 1975 to 2000

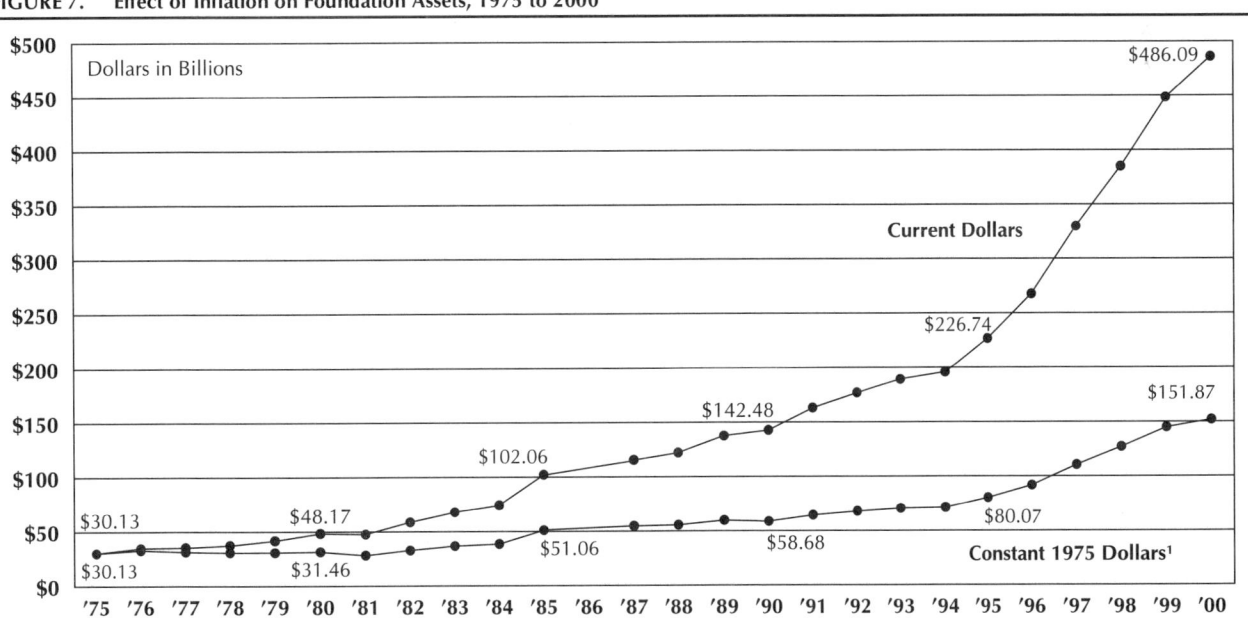

Source: *Foundation Yearbook*, 2002.
[1] Percent change in 1975 dollars based on annual average Consumer Price Index, all urban consumers, U.S. Department of Labor, Bureau of Labor Statistitics, as of March 2002.

new gifts reached record levels, growth in assets outpaced giving by a substantial margin for the first time in a decade. Beginning in 1998, growth in giving once again surpassed asset gains, as foundations' grantmaking began to catch up with the rapid run-up in endowment values. The double-digit growth in foundation assets that ran from 1995 through 1999 launched a new era of rapid growth in foundation giving and raised expectations about future performance. In real terms, giving increased 17.3 percent in 1999 and 14.3 percent in 2000. Prospects dampened as stock market declines led to far more modest asset growth in 2000, and giving outpaced inflation by only a slim margin—2.2 percent—in 2001. Yet while a remarkable period of double-digit annual growth in foundation assets and giving has come to a close, the giving capacity of foundations is immeasurably greater than five years ago. Moreover, foundations now account for a far larger share of private contributions than they did in the mid-1990s and can be expected to play an even larger role in helping to address societal needs over the coming years.

2000 Gifts Received

- Gifts and bequests from donors to foundations decrease by one-seventh
- New gifts total $27.6 billion—second highest level on record
- Gifts to community foundations grow, while independent and corporate foundations experience declines
- Number of very large gifts from donors slips

Variations in the growth patterns of grantmakers often result from new gifts to endowments or from differences in the funding policies of endowed and non-endowed (sometimes called "pass-through") foundations. Grants of endowed foundations are generally paid from investment income, while principal is left to grow. In contrast, many corporate foundations and family foundations with living donors maintain only a small asset base, instead funding grants from annual gifts.

TABLE 5. Growth of Foundation Assets Adjusted for Inflation*

| | Current Asset Dollars | | | Constant Asset Dollars | | |
Year	Amount	% Change	1975=100	Amount	% Change	1975=100
1975	$ 30.13		100.0	$ 30.13		100.0
1976	34.78	15.4	115.4	32.88	9.1	109.1
1977	35.37	1.7	117.4	31.41	(4.5)	104.2
1978	37.27	5.4	123.7	30.75	(2.1)	102.1
1979	41.59	11.6	138.0	30.84	0.2	102.3
1980	48.17	15.8	159.9	31.46	2.0	104.4
1981	47.57	(1.2)	157.9	28.15	(10.5)	93.4
1982	58.67	23.3	194.7	32.71	16.2	108.6
1983	67.87	15.7	225.3	36.66	12.1	121.7
1984	74.05	9.1	245.8	38.37	4.6	127.3
1985	102.06	37.8	338.7	51.06	33.1	169.4
1986	—	—	—	—	—	—
1987	115.44	—	383.1	54.67	—	181.3
1988	122.08	5.8	405.2	55.54	1.6	184.1
1989	137.54	12.7	456.5	59.71	7.5	197.9
1990	142.48	3.6	472.9	58.68	(1.7)	194.5
1991	162.91	14.3	540.7	64.37	9.7	213.4
1992	176.82	8.5	586.9	67.82	5.4	224.9
1993	189.21	7.0	628.0	70.49	3.9	233.6
1994	195.79	3.5	649.8	71.08	0.9	235.7
1995	226.74	15.8	752.5	80.07	12.6	265.5
1996	267.58	18.0	888.1	92.22	14.6	304.3
1997	329.91	23.3	1,095.0	110.61	19.9	365.0
1998	385.05	16.7	1,278.0	127.11	14.9	419.5
1999	448.61	16.5	1,488.9	144.87	14.0	478.0
2000	486.10	8.4	1,613.3	151.87	4.8	501.1

Source: *Foundation Yearbook*, 2002. Dates approximate; reporting years varied.
*Dollars in billions. Constant 1975 dollars based on annual average Consumer Price Index, all urban consumers, U.S. Department of Labor, Bureau of Labor Statistics, as of March 2002.
— = not available

Gifts and bequests from donors to their foundations decreased by 13.9 percent in 2000, from $32.1 billion to $27.6 billion. New gifts were boosted in the prior year by a record $11.5 billion gift from Bill and Melinda Gates to the Bill & Melinda Gates Foundation. By comparison, the largest gift reported in 2000—an additional $5.1 billion gift to the Gates Foundation—amounted to less than half of the prior year's amount. As a result, new gifts in the latest year provided less of a boost to the growth of foundation assets (Table 2). Nonetheless, these new gifts from donors totaled more than two and one-half times the $10.3 billion in gifts reported in 1995 and represented the second highest level of new gifts on record (Table 6). In addition, the $27.6 billion total included $3.1 billion in gifts from donors to new foundations.

Unlike for giving and assets, growth of new gifts is unpredictable. Typically, the largest gifts are triggered by one-time events, such as a donor's death. Consequently, while living donors provided the single largest gift in 2000, many of the largest gifts to foundations resulted from bequests, and the frequency of such large gifts has increased over the past several years. This suggests that foundations may be experiencing the much publicized transfer of wealth that is expected as the World War II generation passes on. Evidence supporting this development includes a five and one-half-fold increase in the annual amount of gifts and bequests since 1990.

Number of Large Gifts. Of the nation's 56,582 grantmaking foundations, 24,743 (43.7 percent) received gifts from their donors in 2000, but only a relatively few received substantial gifts. In the latest year, 719 foundations received at least $5 million in bequests and gifts (Table 7), an increase of 3.0 percent from 1999. In contrast, the number of funders receiving gifts of $10 million or more decreased by more than one-sixth, from 348 to 288. Nonetheless, community foundations reported growth of 10.9 percent in the number of very large gifts in 2000, while both independent and corporate foundations experienced declines (26.7 percent and 1.9 percent, respectively).

TABLE 7. Number of Foundations Receiving Total Gifts of $5 Million or Over and Aggregate Dollar Value, 2000*

Foundation Type	$5 million or more No. of Foundations	Amount	$10 million or more No. of Foundations	Amount
Independent	442	$13,696,036	154	$11,179,561
Corporate	104	2,262,811	51	1,908,083
Community	130	3,330,186	71	2,901,338
Operating	43	1,260,542	12	723,316
Total	719	$20,549,575	288	$16,712,298

Source: *Foundation Yearbook*, 2002.
*Dollars in thousands.

TABLE 6. Growth of Gifts Received Adjusted for Inflation*

	Current Dollars			Constant Dollars		
Year	Amount	% Change	1978=100	Amount	% Change	1978=100
1978	$ 1.61		100.0	$ 1.61		100.0
1979	2.21	37.3	137.3	1.99	23.4	123.4
1980	1.98	(10.4)	123.0	1.57	(21.1)	97.4
1981	2.39	20.7	148.4	1.71	9.4	106.5
1982	4.00	67.4	248.4	2.70	57.7	167.9
1983	2.71	(32.3)	168.3	1.77	(34.4)	110.2
1984	3.36	24.0	208.7	2.11	18.9	131.1
1985	4.73	40.8	293.8	2.87	35.9	178.2
1986	—	—	—	—	—	—
1987	4.96	—	308.1	2.85	—	176.8
1988	5.16	4.0	320.5	2.85	(0.0)	176.8
1989	5.52	7.0	342.9	2.90	2.1	180.4
1990	4.97	(10.0)	308.7	2.48	(14.6)	154.1
1991	5.47	9.9	339.8	2.62	5.6	162.7
1992	6.18	13.1	383.9	2.87	9.7	178.5
1993	7.76	25.6	482.0	3.50	22.0	217.7
1994	8.08	4.2	501.9	3.56	1.5	220.9
1995	10.26	27.0	637.3	4.39	23.5	272.8
1996	16.02	56.1	995.0	6.66	51.7	413.8
1997	15.83	(1.2)	983.2	6.43	(3.4)	399.6
1998	22.57	42.6	1,401.9	9.03	40.4	561.0
1999	32.08	42.1	1,992.3	12.55	39.0	779.5
2000	27.60	(13.9)	1,714.3	10.45	(16.7)	649.3

Source: *Foundation Yearbook*, 2002. Dates approximate; reporting years varied.
*Dollars in billions. Constant 1978 dollars based on annual average Consumer Price Index, all urban consumers, U.S. Department of Labor Bureau of Labor Statistics, as of March 2002.
— = not available

Not only did the overall number of very large gifts decrease, but the total value of gifts of $5 million or more slipped from $26.2 billion to $20.5 billion. Still, these large gifts accounted for almost three-quarters (74.4 percent) of the value of all gifts received (down from more than four-fifths in 1999).

Descriptions of the major gifts and their donors, and complete listings by foundation type of the top 50 independent, corporate, and community foundations by gifts received are provided in Chapter 4.

2000 Gifts Received by Foundation Type. In the latest year, changes in the level of gifts received varied according to foundation type. Gifts to independent foundations dropped by more than one-fifth from last year's record $24.1 billion to $19.2 billion. Excluding the $11.5 billion Gates gift in 1999 and the $5.1 billion gift in 2000 (noted above), however, independent foundations' gifts received would have grown by almost 12 percent to $14.1 billion in the latest year. (Moreover, all foundations, regardless of type, reported total gifts received of only $10.3 billion as recently as 1995.) Gifts from companies into their foundations decreased to $2.9 billion, a one-eighth (12.4 percent) dip from 1999. In all, nine companies made gifts of at least $50 million into their foundations in 2000, down from 12 in the prior year. Finally, in contrast to independent and corporate foundations, gifts into community foundations grew in 2000, rising by one-sixth (16.2 percent) to $3.8 billion. (For more detailed comparisons of gifts received by foundation type, see Chapter 4.)

2000 Gifts Received by Region. Most of the growth in gifts received in the latest year was concentrated among foundations in the Northeast. Overall, gifts into foundations in the Northeast increased $1.4 billion in 2000 to $7.2 billion. Southern foundations also reported 8.9 percent growth in gifts received to $5.0 billion. In contrast, new gifts to Midwestern foundations slipped 7.3 percent, while grantmakers in the West experienced a more than one-third (36.1 percent) drop in gifts received. Still, the decrease in 2000 gifts into Western foundations followed the receipt of a record $16.4 billion in new gifts in 1999. Moreover, foundations in the West received a total of $10.5 billion in new gifts in the latest year, surpassing all other regions. (For more detailed comparisons of gifts received by region, see Chapter 3.)

Growth of Gifts Received, 1978 to 2000

Long-term growth in gifts to foundations, principally in the form of bequests, has been far less predictable than increases in assets and giving. Nonetheless, in the 1980s, a rise in the number of gifts from living donors led to a more stable pattern of growth from this source. More recently, an increase in large bequests and a few exceptional gifts from living donors have greatly increased the level of contributions. Annual gifts to foundations have multiplied nearly fourteen-fold, from almost $2 billion in 1980 to $27.6 billion in 2000 (Table 6). After inflation, gifts have increased close to seven-fold. The second largest single gift to a foundation—the $5.1 billion gift from Bill and Melinda Gates to the Bill & Melinda Gates Foundation—was reported in 2000. This gift was preceded by a record $11.5 billion gift to the Gates Foundation in 1999 and another $4.8 billion gift in 1998, along with contributions to the David and Lucile Packard Foundation in 1996 and 1997 totaling $5.8 billion from the estate of David Packard.

Through the mid-1980s, gifts or bequests to foundations grew rapidly, reaching a level of $4.7 billion. With the exception of gifts to community foundations, the growth rate fell in the late-1980s, with total annual gifts fluctuating around the $5 billion level. Among family foundations with living donors, the drop in the rate of growth of new gifts after 1986 appeared linked to sharp reductions in personal income tax levels enacted by the Tax Reform Act of 1986. In general, higher tax rates increase incentives for all charitable giving. Finally, the decline in contributions from companies to their foundations in the late 1980s and into the 1990s due to business losses, leveraged buyouts, and recession, contributed to slow overall growth.

Starting in the early 1990s, gifts to foundations began to climb. Between 1991 and 1995, the amount of new gifts nearly doubled, surpassing $10.2 billion. In constant dollars, gifts increased by 68 percent. In 1996, the extraordinary bequest to the Packard Foundation caused new gifts to jump in a single year by more than half, reaching $16.0 billion. Contrary to expectations, the level of gifts from donors dipped only slightly in 1997, reflecting the ongoing strong growth of gifts in nearly all sectors, especially among community and independent foundations. Between 1997 and 1999, exceptional stock market growth, a strong economy, and record gifts into the Bill & Melinda Gates Foundation more than doubled gifts (up 102.6 percent). While another couple of multi-billion-dollar gifts have been pledged,[3] the slowing economy and softening stock market in late 2000 resulted in a lower level of new gifts paid into foundations overall. Still, new gifts into

---

3 These gifts include $5 billion from Intel Corporation founder Gordon Moore to establish the Gordon E. and Betty I. Moore Foundation, and a bequest from the estate of William Hewlett to the William and Flora Hewlett Foundation valued at approximately $3 billion. (These pledged gifts have not yet been transferred into the corpus of the foundations.)

Growth of the Top 25 Foundations

A comparison of 1999 and 2000 financial data for the 25 largest foundations by giving (Table 8) shows double-digit overall increases in giving. Yet while eight of the top foundations reported above-average growth in giving, seven funders reduced their giving in the latest year. Comparing changes in asset values of the 25 largest foundations (Table 9), only two-fifths (10) realized above-average growth in their endowments, while nine experienced declines. Of the six remaining foundations, four realized single-digit asset increases, while two reported less than 1 percent gains.

Giving

- Giving by the top 25 funders rises nearly 22 percent
- Growth in giving by top funders surpasses increase in overall giving
- Median giving increase for top 25 is 9.4 percent
- Gates Foundation reports largest growth in actual grant dollars

From 1999 to 2000, giving by the nation's 25 leading grantmakers grew 21.7 percent, compared with an 18.2 percent increase for all 56,582 grantmaking foundations. Giving by the largest funders increased from $4.8 billion to $5.9 billion, a $1.0 billion gain. In

TABLE 8. Comparison of the 25 Largest Foundations by Total Giving, 1999 to 2000*

	Foundation	Total Giving '99[1]	Total Giving '00[1]	% Change	Rank '99
1.	Bill & Melinda Gates Foundation	$ 549,433	$994,900	81.1	2
2.	Ford Foundation	514,401	652,091	26.8	3
3.	Lilly Endowment	558,287	583,891	4.6	1
4.	David and Lucile Packard Foundation	391,568	533,590	36.3	4
5.	Robert Wood Johnson Foundation	290,249	351,684	21.2	5
6.	Andrew W. Mellon Foundation	161,501	205,870	27.5	10
7.	California Endowment	178,411	189,663	6.3	9
8.	Pew Charitable Trusts	211,053	187,854	-11.0	6
9.	W. K. Kellogg Foundation	186,606	178,740	-4.2	8
10.	Ford Motor Company Fund	97,789	169,100	72.9	23
11.	John D. and Catherine T. MacArthur Foundation	158,582	164,023	3.4	11
12.	Rockefeller Foundation	149,343	163,392	9.4	13
13.	Starr Foundation	143,823	161,966	12.6	14
14.	Robert W. Woodruff Foundation	191,355	149,979	-21.6	7
15.	New York Community Trust	130,681	143,951	10.2	16
16.	Charles Stewart Mott Foundation	116,137	139,481	20.1	17
17.	William and Flora Hewlett Foundation	87,504	135,748	55.1	26
18.	Annenberg Foundation	133,488	132,384	-0.8	15
19.	Open Society Institute	152,974	116,343	-23.9	12
20.	Kresge Foundation	112,710	107,956	-4.2	19
21.	Robert R. McCormick Tribune Foundation	104,001	106,830	2.7	21
22.	Duke Endowment	80,230	106,030	32.2	28
23.	Annie E. Casey Foundation	103,945	101,013	-2.8	22
24.	Searle Patients in Need Foundation	22,404	95,976	328.4	127
25.	Bristol-Myers Squibb Patient Assistance Foundation	N/A	94,806	N/A	N/A
	Total	$4,826,475	$5,872,454	21.7	

Source: *Foundation Yearbook*, 2002.
*Dollars in thousands. Aggregate foundation fiscal information in other tables and figures is based on data provided to the Center as of February 2, 2002. Fiscal data on individual foundations included in this table may be more current.
[1] Includes grants, scholarships, and employee matching gifts; excludes set-asides, loans, PRIs and program expenses. For some operating foundations, program expenses are included.

TABLE 9. Comparison of the 25 Largest Foundations by Assets, 1999 to 2000*

	Foundation	Assets '99	Assets '00	% Change	Rank '99
1.	Bill & Melinda Gates Foundation	$15,515,455	$21,149,100	36.3	1
2.	Lilly Endowment	10,418,127	15,591,738	49.7	4
3.	Ford Foundation	11,960,280	14,659,683	22.6	3
4.	J. Paul Getty Trust	8,729,629	10,929,810	25.2	5
5.	David and Lucile Packard Foundation	13,144,242	9,793,213	-25.5	2
6.	Robert Wood Johnson Foundation	8,640,408	8,793,792	1.8	6
7.	Starr Foundation	4,486,499	6,255,917	39.4	11
8.	W. K. Kellogg Foundation	4,853,384	5,719,736	17.9	8
9.	Andrew W. Mellon Foundation	4,615,683	4,888,237	5.9	10
10.	Pew Charitable Trusts	4,894,418	4,800,776	-1.9	7
11.	John D. and Catherine T. MacArthur Foundation	4,629,519	4,479,154	-3.2	9
12.	William and Flora Hewlett Foundation	2,738,945	3,930,367	43.5	19
13.	Rockefeller Foundation	3,837,542	3,619,028	-5.7	13
14.	California Endowment	3,884,524	3,490,256	-10.1	12
15.	Robert W. Woodruff Foundation	3,114,438	3,139,654	0.8	16
16.	Annie E. Casey Foundation	3,626,230	3,001,942	-17.2	14
17.	Annenberg Foundation	2,755,835	2,932,206	6.4	18
18.	Charles Stewart Mott Foundation	3,229,256	2,881,803	-10.8	15
19.	Duke Endowment	2,335,496	2,874,017	23.1	23
20.	Casey Family Programs	2,810,532	2,811,001	0.0	17
21.	Kresge Foundation	2,575,425	2,770,531	7.6	20
22.	John S. and James L. Knight Foundation	1,888,543	2,198,985	16.4	28
23.	Freeman Foundation	1,602,821	2,113,689	31.9	34
24.	Harry and Jeanette Weinberg Foundation	2,174,892	2,063,325	-5.1	24
25.	Ewing Marion Kauffman Foundation	2,443,456	2,034,722	-16.7	22
	Total	$130,905,579	$146,922,681	12.2	

Source: *Foundation Yearbook*, 2002.
*Dollars in thousands. Aggregate foundation fiscal information in other tables and figures is based on data provided to the Center as of February 2, 2002. Fiscal data on individual foundations included in this table may be more current.

addition, these 25 funders accounted for roughly one-quarter (24.7 percent) of the $4.2 billion rise in giving by all foundations.

Although overall growth in giving remained strong among the top foundations in 2000, grantmakers included among the top 25 showed very mixed giving patterns. For example, the Searle Patients in Need Foundation (NJ) reported a more than fourfold (328.4 percent) rise in its giving, while the Bill & Melinda Gates Foundation increased giving by over four-fifths (81.1 percent) or $445.5 million—the largest actual increase in grant dollars recorded in 2000. Other foundations that raised their giving by at least $100 million in 2000 included the David and Lucile Packard Foundation and the Ford Foundation (NY). In contrast, two top 25 foundations reported cuts in giving of more than 20 percent—the Open Society Institute (NY) and the Robert W. Woodruff Foundation (GA)—while an additional five foundations reduced their giving between 0.8 and 11.0 percent.

A more equitable measure of change focuses on the median increase in giving. For the top funders, the median increase in 2000 was 9.4 percent, compared to an unparalleled 31.3 percent rise in the prior year. The median growth also represented less than half of the average increase. Among the top funders, four foundations raised their giving by more than half; six increased giving between 20 and 50 percent; seven raised giving between 0 and 20 percent; and seven reduced payments between 0.8 and 24 percent.

Variations in giving patterns among the leading funders can be attributed to differences in their investment performance over the most recent fiscal periods; dramatic influxes in assets through gifts and bequests from donors; or variations in fiscal reporting periods. They may also reflect differences in long-term grant distribution strategies or one-time distributions that skew funding levels for a single year.

In addition to the Gates, Packard, and Searle Patients in Need foundations, those reporting the largest percentage increases in giving included:

- Ford Motor Company Fund (MI), which raised giving by more than seven-tenths in 2000, from $97.8 million to $169.1 million. Overall, the foundation has increased its funding nearly fivefold since 1998. Supporting this growth in giving was a $200 million gift into the foundation from its parent company in 1999 and an additional $70 million gift in 2000.

- William and Flora Hewlett Foundation (CA), which increased giving by more than half, from $87.5 million to $135.7 million. The foundation focuses giving in the areas of conflict resolution, the environment, performing arts, education, population, and family and community development. It expects to increase giving more in the next several years, following receipt over three years of a multi-billion-dollar bequest from the estate of William Hewlett.

- Among the other leading foundations reporting above-average grant increases in 2000 were the Duke Endowment (NC), Andrew W. Mellon Foundation (NY), Ford Foundation, Robert Wood Johnson Foundation (NJ), and Charles Stewart Mott Foundation (MI). Most of these foundations reported double-digit asset gains in 1999 or 2000.

- Of the seven foundations reporting decreases in giving, this was the third consecutive decline for the W.K. Kellogg Foundation (MI). Since 1997, the foundation's grant payments have dropped from $260.8 million to $178.7 million. Still, the foundation's endowment grew by more than one-sixth in 2000, following several years of decline in the value of its principal holding, Kellogg Company stock. This suggests a possible increase in Kellogg Foundation giving in the coming year.

Rankings of most of the top ten foundations changed in the latest year. Only the Packard and Robert Wood Johnson foundations retained their ranks from 1999. Among those rising in rank were the first-ranked Gates Foundation and second-ranked Ford Foundation. One foundation was new to the top ten in the latest year: the Ford Motor Company Fund, which rose from twenty-third to tenth. Displaced from the top ten was the Robert W. Woodruff Foundation. Funders new to the top 25 included the William and Flora Hewlett Foundation, Duke Endowment, and Bristol-Myers Squibb Patient Assistance Foundation (NJ).

Compared with the top 25 foundations, the next 25 by size of giving reported more modest aggregate growth in 2000. Among these grantmakers, twenty raised the level of their grantmaking, including two by more than 100 percent. The median increase was 19.0 percent, while the aggregate change showed a much lower 10.3 percent rise (compared to 21.7 percent for the top 25 givers). The Doris Duke Charitable Foundation (NY) reported by far the largest percentage growth in giving, a more than tripling of grant dollars (up 228.8 percent) to $86.3 million. Established in 1996 through a bequest from tobacco heiress Doris Duke, the foundation has been ramping up its giving steadily over the past four years. It focuses giving in the areas of the performing arts, environment, and medical research.

Among other funders showing exceptional growth in giving was the Houston Endowment (TX), which more than doubled its grants paid to $66.1 million; and the Peninsula Community Foundation (CA), which raised its grant payments by over seven-tenths to $64.2 million.

A total of ten grantmakers were new to the list of foundations ranked 26 to 50 by giving in 2000. In addition to the Doris Duke Charitable Foundation, Houston Endowment, and Peninsula Community Foundation, these funders included the Lilly Cares Foundation (IN), which provided support totaling $86.7 million in the latest year.

Assets

- **Assets of the 25 largest foundations grow 12 percent**
- **Median asset increase for top 25 is less than 6 percent**
- **Gates and Lilly account for over two-thirds of asset growth among top 25**

From 1999 to 2000, the combined assets of the 25 largest endowed foundations grew 12.2 percent, surpassing the 8.4 percent growth rate for all foundations in the latest year but falling well below the 21.2 percent gain reported for the top 25 last year.[4] By dollar value, their endowments grew $16.0 billion, down from the $23.0 billion increase recorded in 1999. Yet if the Bill & Melinda Gates Foundation and the Lilly Endowment were excluded from the top 25 for both years, the average asset increase for the remaining foundations would slip to 5.0 percent—well below the average increase reported for all U.S. foundations. Overall, these two grantmakers accounted for more than two-thirds of asset growth among the top 25 foundations in the latest year.

Despite realizing more modest asset growth in the latest year, the top 25 foundations exceeded the growth rate reported by all of the major stock indexes. For example, both the 12.2 percent overall gain and median 5.9 percent increase in top foundation assets in 2000 compared favorably with the 1.9 percent rise in the Dow Jones Industrial Average, the 10.1 percent drop in the Standard and Poor's 500 index, and the 39.3 percent fall in the NASDAQ. Because many of the largest foundations maintain diversified investment portfolios, they often benefit from long-term stability at the expense of dramatic short-term gains. (Still, among grantmakers, the largest foundations typically experience the strongest performance in terms of asset growth.)

Two-fifths (10) of the 25 largest foundations by assets reported above-average asset growth in 2000, compared to 12 in 1999. The Lilly Endowment reported by the largest percentage increase—49.7 percent—after its assets grew $5.2 billion in the latest year to $15.6 billion. This rapid growth reflected gains in the value of Eli Lilly & Co. stock, the Endowment's principal holding. The William and Flora Hewlett Foundation reported the second fastest growth in its endowment, after its assets climbed $1.2 billion (43.5

---

4. For 2001, the onset of an economic recession and continuing stock market declines most likely resulted in no growth or a decrease in the overall value of assets among the top 25 foundations.

Howard Hughes Medical Institute

Exceptional new resources were added to organized philanthropy when the Howard Hughes Medical Institute (HHMI), a nonprofit organization whose principal purpose is the direct conduct of medical research, began a grants program in 1987, including support for colleges and universities to enhance life sciences education and research opportunities for students.

Formed by an endowment and holding assets of over $15.8 billion in fiscal 2001, HHMI is classified as a medical research organization under federal tax code. It is therefore not subject to the same regulations, payout requirements, limits on deductibility, and excise taxes that apply to private foundations (see Appendix B). Nonetheless, HHMI makes substantial charitable contributions, in addition to the spending required as a medical research organization. In 2001, HHMI made grants totaling $103.3 million in support of education and training in biomedical and related sciences, including $32.1 million in grants to individuals. If HHMI's grants were ranked with those of the largest private foundations, the Institute would place among the top twenty-three funders; in science education, it would be the largest grantmaker.

In recognition of its prominent role in philanthropy, information concerning HHMI's grant program has been added to Foundation Center publications. Yet because it is not a private or community foundation, data on HHMI are not included in the statistical analyses in this report.

percent) to $3.9 billion. The foundation has been diversifying its portfolio in recent years in anticipation of an influx of Hewlett-Packard Company stock from the estate of William Hewlett.

Other top 25 foundations to realize at least one-third gains in the value of their assets in the latest year included the Starr Foundation (NY), which reported a 39.4 percent increase in its assets to $6.3 billion; and the top-ranked Bill & Melinda Gates Foundation, which followed with a 36.3 percent rise in the value of its assets to $21.1 million. Nearly all of this growth resulted from an additional $5.1 billion from Bill and Melinda Gates in 2000, the third consecutive multi-billion-dollar gift from the foundation's founders.[5]

Among the top 25 funders, those reporting the largest increases in actual asset dollars after Gates and Lilly included:

- The Ford Foundation, with assets up by more than one-fifth in 2000 to $14.7 billion. This represented the second consecutive year of strong growth in the foundation's endowment. Based on positive investment returns, its assets climbed by $5 billion or just over half (50.6 percent) between 1998 and 2000.

- The J. Paul Getty Trust (CA), with its $10.9 billion in assets up by $2.2 billion or one-quarter (25.2 percent) from 1999. Although the foundation principally operates its own programs, through the Getty Grant Program it made grants in 2000 totaling $17.3 million to support research on the history of art, the advancement of the understanding of art, and the conservation of cultural heritage.

Other foundations among the top 25 posting asset gains of at least 10 percent included the Freeman Foundation, Duke Endowment, W.K. Kellogg Foundation, and John S. and James L. Knight Foundation (FL). All of these foundations benefited from strong stock performance. Six foundations reported asset growth of between 0 and 8 percent. In contrast, nine foundations experienced declines in their asset values in the latest yea—compared to four in 1999 and only one in 1998—and their losses ranged from 2 to 26 percent. These foundations included the David and Lucile Packard Foundation, Annie E. Casey Foundation (MD), Ewing Marion Kauffman Foundation (MO), Charles Stewart Mott Foundation, California Endowment, Rockefeller Foundation, Harry and Jeanette Weinberg Foundation, John D. and Catherine T. MacArthur Foundation, and Pew Charitable Trusts. The Packard Foundation experienced by far the largest drop in its assets, a 25.5 percent decline from $13.1 billion in 1999 to $9.8 billion in 2000. Nearly all of this decrease reflected the falling value of stock in Hewlett Packard and Company and its spin-off, Agilent Technologies, the foundation's principal holdings.

Six of the top ten foundations by assets changed rank in 2000. Based on its strong asset growth, the Lilly Endowment rose from fourth to second place rank. Of the other foundations to advance in rank, the J. Paul Getty Trust moved from fifth to fourth place, the Starr Foundation rose from eleventh to seventh place, and the Andrew W. Mellon Foundation stepped up from tenth to ninth place. The only foundation to leave the top ten in the latest year was the John D. and Catherine T. MacArthur Foundation, which slipped from ninth to eleventh place by assets.

In contrast to the positive overall asset growth seen among the top 25 foundations by assets, endowments of the foundations ranked between 26 and 50 by assets showed a modest overall decline in value. In 2000, assets decreased 3.5 percent for these grantmakers, compared to the 12.2 percent increase reported for the top group. Moreover, their median change in assets was a loss of 2.4 percent, compared to 5.9 percent growth for the top 25 by assets.

Four foundations ranked among the top 26 to 50 by assets realized at least 10 percent growth in their assets in 2000, compared to 15 in 1999. The foundations included: the Chicago Community Trust (IL), with assets up 22.9 percent to $1.3 billion; the Carnegie Corporation of New York (NY), with assets up 13.1 percent to $1.9 billion; the Samuel Roberts Noble Foundation (OK), with assets up 11.6 percent to $971.7 million; and the Wallace-Reader's Digest Funds, with an asset increase of 10.5 percent to $1.6 billion. All four of these foundations benefited from strong gains in their investments, while the Chicago Community Trust's assets were also boosted by gifts totaling $45.3 million. Finally, five foundations were new to the top 50 by assets in the latest year: the Ahmanson Foundation (CA), McKnight Foundation (MN), Packard Humanities Institute (CA), Robert R. McCormick Tribune Foundation (IL), and Samuel Roberts Noble Foundation.

---

5. Gifts into the Bill & Melinda Gates Foundation through the end of 2001 have since raised its value to over $24 billion.

Growth of the Top Ten Foundations, 1990 to 2000

Most of the nation's largest philanthropies were created and received their principal endowments long ago (see Chapter 5, "Foundation Development"). Nevertheless, new formation, new bequests, and a boom in investment markets in the late 1990s have brought about changes in the group of top foundations.

A comparison of the ten largest funders of 1990 by asset size (Table 10) with the largest foundations of 2000 (Table 9) showed that three foundations have been added and three displaced in recent years. The additions include the Bill & Melinda Gates Foundation (ranked first in 2000), the David and Lucile Packard Foundation (ranked fifth), and the Starr Foundation (ranked seventh). The Gates Foundation received the largest gifts into a foundation in 1998, 1999, and 2000; Packard experienced spectacular growth in the 1990s based on both bequests and investment performance; and the Starr Foundation benefited from strong growth in the value of its assets in recent years. Foundations displaced from the top ten included the MacArthur Foundation (ranked eleventh by assets in 2000), the Rockefeller Foundation (ranked thirteenth), and the Kresge Foundation, ranked twenty-first. Among the seven remaining foundations, Ford consistently ranked first until 1997, when the Lilly Endowment displaced it. In 1999, Lilly was displaced by Gates. Rankings of the other funders have fluctuated due to differences in asset growth patterns.

Top foundations in 2000 with the largest percentage increase in assets over the decade included:

- Lilly Endowment (IN)—assets grew more than four and two-fifths times, from $3.5 billion to $15.6 billion; asset rank remained consistent at third; giving increased more than five times, from $107.9 million to $583.9 million.

- Robert Wood Johnson Foundation (NJ)—assets tripled, from $2.9 billion to $8.8 billion; asset rank remained consistent at seventh; giving more than tripled, from $112.0 million to $351.7 million.

For most of the others, asset values in 2000 were about 55 to 130 percent greater than 1990 values, while growth of giving ranged from roughly one-fifth to a nearly tripling for the Ford and A.W. Mellon foundations. (Percentages reflect current value.) Giving increases for five of the top ten foundations either matched or outpaced asset growth, including Ford, Lilly, RWJ, Rockefeller, and A.W. Mellon.

Large and Small Foundations

- **Less than two-fifths of foundations control 98 percent of assets**

- **Only 361 foundations award grants totaling at least $10 million**

- **Larger foundations more likely to fund nationally and internationally, have defined programs, publish annual reports, and employ paid staff**

Of the 56,582 active grantmaking foundations, roughly 21,300 (37.7 percent) held assets of $1 million or more in 2000 (Table 11). This relatively small share of foundations accounted for 98 percent of total

TABLE 10. Ten Largest Foundations of 1990: Growth of Assets and Total Giving, 1990 to 2000*

Foundation Name	Assets 1990	Assets 2000	% Change	'00 Rank	Total Giving[1] 1990	Total Giving[1] 2000	% Change
1. Ford Foundation	$5,460,896	$14,659,683	168.4	3	$227,828	$652,091	186.2
2. J. Paul Getty Trust[2]	4,816,153	10,929,810	126.9	4	9,086	17,345	90.9
3. Lilly Endowment	3,543,648	15,591,738	340.0	2	107,931	583,891	441.0
4. W. K. Kellogg Foundation	3,509,461	5,719,736	63.0	8	121,974	178,740	46.5
5. John D. and Catherine T. MacArthur Foundation	3,077,581	4,479,154	45.5	11	115,676	164,023	41.8
6. Pew Charitable Trusts	3,076,892	4,800,776	56.0	10	155,114	187,854	21.1
7. Robert Wood Johnson Foundation	2,914,183	8,793,792	201.8	6	112,023	351,684	213.9
8. Rockefeller Foundation	1,962,761	3,619,028	84.4	13	74,414	163,392	119.6
9. Andrew W. Mellon Foundation	1,831,235	4,888,237	166.9	9	74,467	205,870	176.5
10. Kresge Foundation	1,214,209	2,770,531	128.2	21	48,792	107,956	121.3

Source: *Foundation Yearbook*, 2002.
*Dollars in thousands.
[1] Includes grants, scholarships, and employee matching gifts; excludes set-asides, loans, PRIs, and program expenses. For some operating foundations, program expenses are included.
[2] J. Paul Getty Trust, an operating foundation, started its grants program in 1984.

foundation assets and approximately 92 percent of giving. The number of large or very large foundations—those with assets of $50 million or over—rose from 1,045 in 1999 to 1,125 in 2000, up 7.7 percent. This group held 72.1 percent of assets (Figure 8) and was responsible for 58.2 percent of all giving. The smallest foundations—those more than 35,000 with assets of less than $1 million—held 2.0 percent of assets but accounted for 8.1 percent of giving.

A more equitable measure of foundation size, especially for non-endowed foundations, is total contributions. As revealed in Table 12, only 361 foundations (just under half of 1 percent) reported grants of $10 million or over, yet together they accounted for more than half (51.6 percent) of giving. Roughly 17,600 foundations (31.1 percent) awarded $100,000 or more in grants; their combined support represented 96.1 percent of giving.

Figures 9 and 10 demonstrate the share of assets and giving held in 2000 by a fixed number of foundations—the 1,000 largest, 100 largest, and 50 largest. The graphs reveal that assets are concentrated among even fewer large foundations than are total grants. For example, the 1,000 largest foundations by asset size control seven out of ten asset dollars, while the 1,000 largest by size of giving distribute roughly two-thirds of all grant dollars. The 100 largest by asset size control more than two-fifths of asset dollars, yet the 100 largest ranked by total giving pay out just over one-third of grant dollars. Finally, the 50 largest foundations by assets hold more than one-third (37.1 percent) of assets, while the 50 largest foundations by total giving distribute less than three-tenths (28.3 percent) of grant dollars.

Because they control a substantial portion of funds, the largest foundations merit close scrutiny. The grant programs of the 1,000 largest foundations by giving are tracked in the Foundation Center's *Foundation 1000*. Giving patterns of the 100 largest foundations and of more than 900 representative foundations are analyzed in *Foundation Giving Trends*, part of the *Foundations Today Series* of annual research reports. Finally, rankings of the 50 largest foundations by giving, assets, and gifts received are presented in Tables 13 through 15.

There are significant differences between these few larger foundations and the vast majority of private foundations, most importantly:

Local vs. National Giving. The overwhelming majority of the nation's 56,582 active foundations limit their giving to their local community. Of the 20,964 foundations with assets of at least $1 million or grant programs of $100,000 or over, only about one out of eight

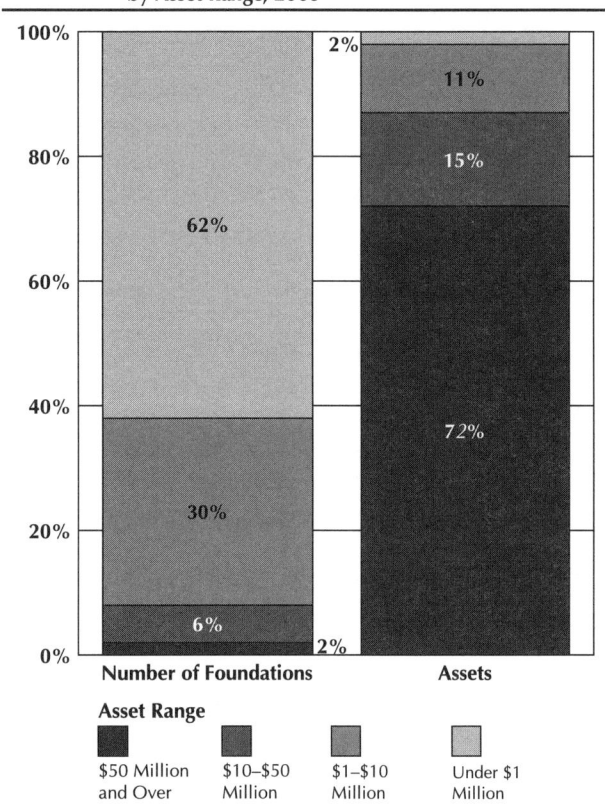

FIGURE 8. Distribution of Foundations and Foundation Assets by Asset Range, 2000

Source: *Foundation Yearbook*, 2002.

TABLE 11. Analysis of Foundations by Asset Size, 2000*

Asset Range	Number of Foundations	%	Assets	%	Total Giving[1]	%
$1 billion+	47	0.1	$177,437,054	36.5	$ 6,881,248	25.0
$250 million–$1 billion	170	0.3	80,153,432	16.5	4,097,243	14.9
$50 million–$250 million	908	1.6	92,898,096	19.1	5,056,267	18.3
$10 million–$50 million	3,446	6.1	72,466,896	14.9	4,811,243	17.5
$1 million–$10 million	16,770	29.6	53,298,538	11.0	4,473,967	16.2
Under $1 million	35,241	62.3	9,831,294	2.0	2,243,200	8.1
Total	56,582	100.0	$486,085,311	100.0	$27,563,166	100.0

Source: *Foundation Yearbook*, 2002.
*Dollar amounts in thousands. Due to rounding, figures may not add up.
[1] Includes grants, scholarships, and employee matching gifts; excludes set–asides, loans, PRIs, and program expenses.

(2,459) give on a national or international basis, and they are usually the largest independent and operating foundations, or corporate foundations whose sponsoring companies operate nationally or internationally. Although few in number, national foundations held 40.4 percent of the assets of the larger foundations and were responsible for 36.9 percent of giving.

TABLE 12. Analysis of Foundations by Total Giving Range, 2000*

Total Giving Range	Number of Foundations	%	Total Giving[1]	%
$100 million+	24	0.0	$ 5.8	21.2
$25 million–$100 million	109	0.2	5.0	18.0
$10 million–$25 million	228	0.4	3.4	12.4
$1 million–$10 million	2,935	5.2	7.9	28.7
$100,000–$1 million	14,321	25.3	4.3	15.7
Under $100,000	38,965	68.9	1.1	3.9
Total	56,582	100.0	$27.6	100.0

Source: *Foundation Yearbook*, 2002.
*Dollars in billions; due to rounding, figures may not add up.
[1] Includes grants, scholarships, and employee matching gifts; excludes set-asides, loans, PRIs, and program expenses.

Broad Giving vs. Defined Programs. Many of the largest foundations organize their giving through announced programs that may be limited to a specific subject or field (e.g., the Robert Wood Johnson Foundation concentrates on the health field), or cover a wide range of interests. Small foundations that give locally tend to support a broad range of activities. Information about their programs is generally not as widely available to the public. Nevertheless, these funders remain an important source of grants for community service agencies, cultural organizations, schools, and other locally-based nonprofit organizations.

Public Reporting. Nearly all of the 56,582 grantmaking foundations are required by law to file IRS Form 990-PF and must make that document available to the public. In addition, 3,239 foundations issue statements of their program interests or guidelines for grant applications, and 1,479—mainly the larger staffed foundations—state that they publish annual or biennial reports. Of the smaller grantmakers publishing reports, many are community trusts. Community trusts are not classified as private foundations by the IRS and

FIGURE 9. Largest Foundations by Total Giving and Percentage of 2000 Giving

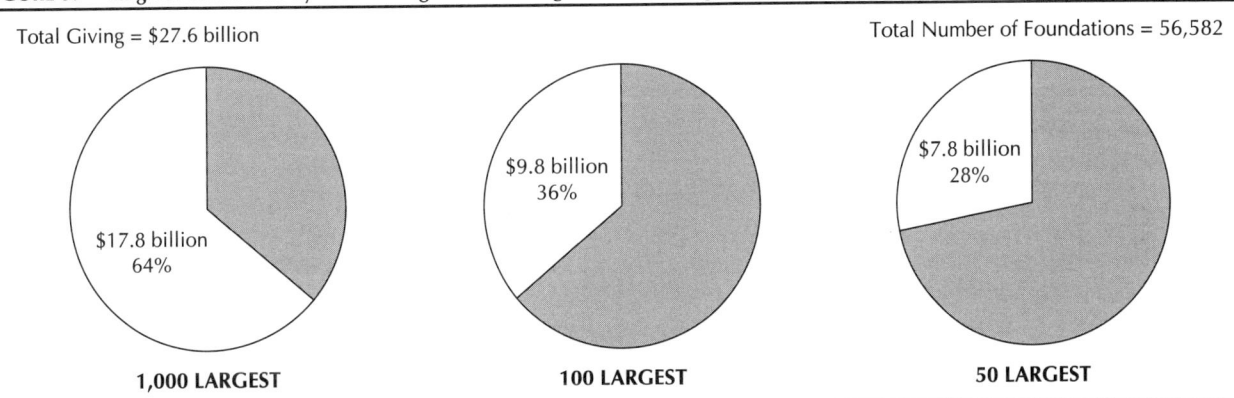

Total Giving = $27.6 billion

1,000 LARGEST: $17.8 billion 64%
100 LARGEST: $9.8 billion 36%
50 LARGEST: $7.8 billion 28%

Total Number of Foundations = 56,582

Source: *Foundation Yearbook*, 2002.

FIGURE 10. Largest Foundations by Asset Size and Percentage of 2000 Assets

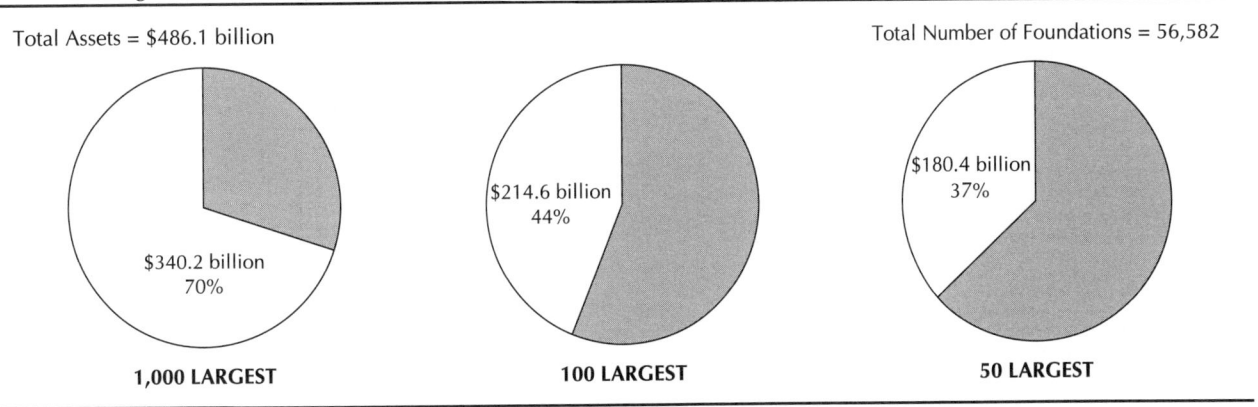

Total Assets = $486.1 billion

1,000 LARGEST: $340.2 billion 70%
100 LARGEST: $214.6 billion 44%
50 LARGEST: $180.4 billion 37%

Total Number of Foundations = 56,582

Source: *Foundation Yearbook*, 2002.

TABLE 13. 50 Largest Foundations by Total Giving, 2000*

	Foundation	State	Foundation Type[1]	Total Giving[2]	Qualifying Distributions[3]	Assets	Fiscal Date
1.	Bill & Melinda Gates Foundation	WA	IN	**$994,900,000**	$994,900,000	$21,149,100,000	12/31/00
2.	Ford Foundation	NY	IN	**652,091,000**	652,091,000	14,659,683,000	9/30/00
3.	Lilly Endowment	IN	IN	**583,890,521**	588,943,280	15,591,737,808	12/31/00
4.	David and Lucile Packard Foundation	CA	IN	**533,589,987**	605,793,134	9,793,212,529	12/31/00
5.	Robert Wood Johnson Foundation	NJ	IN	**351,683,796**	444,128,246	8,793,792,000	12/31/00
6.	Andrew W. Mellon Foundation	NY	IN	**205,870,150**	205,870,150	4,888,237,000	12/31/00
7.	Starr Foundation	NY	IN	**192,502,039**	194,246,442	6,257,848,627	12/31/00
8.	California Endowment	CA	IN	**189,663,220**	211,000,000	3,490,256,407	2/28/01
9.	Pew Charitable Trusts	PA	IN	**187,853,822**	243,841,247	4,800,776,253	12/31/00
10.	W. K. Kellogg Foundation	MI	IN	**178,739,742**	196,651,170	5,719,735,520	8/31/01
11.	Ford Motor Company Fund	MI	CS	**169,100,475**	170,268,431	247,625,772	12/31/00
12.	John D. and Catherine T. MacArthur Foundation	IL	IN	**164,022,738**	198,205,781	4,479,153,951	12/31/00
13.	Rockefeller Foundation	NY	IN	**163,391,841**	202,375,330	3,619,028,000	12/31/00
14.	Robert W. Woodruff Foundation	GA	IN	**149,979,270**	150,387,356	3,139,654,481	12/31/00
15.	New York Community Trust	NY	CM	**143,950,743**	143,950,743	1,930,370,263	12/31/00
16.	Charles Stewart Mott Foundation	MI	IN	**139,480,791**	154,952,273	2,881,802,805	12/31/00
17.	William and Flora Hewlett Foundation	CA	IN	**135,748,270**	131,802,992	3,930,366,990	12/31/00
18.	Annenberg Foundation	PA	IN	**132,384,109**	132,384,109	2,932,205,767	6/30/01
19.	Open Society Institute[4]	NY	OP	**116,342,544**	160,496,757	135,447,900	12/31/00
20.	Kresge Foundation	MI	IN	**107,956,140**	107,956,140	2,770,530,893	12/31/00
21.	Robert R. McCormick Tribune Foundation	IL	IN	**106,830,351**	112,200,000	1,855,000,000	12/31/00
22.	Duke Endowment	NC	IN	**106,030,389**	106,000,000	2,874,017,045	12/31/00
23.	Annie E. Casey Foundation	MD	IN	**101,012,809**	127,380,064	3,001,942,131	12/31/00
24.	Searle Patients in Need Foundation[4]	NJ	OP	**95,975,582**	96,311,112	10,163,451	12/31/00
25.	Bristol-Myers Squibb Patient Assistance Foundation[4]	NJ	OP	**94,805,585**	98,269,671	1,675,064	12/31/00
26.	McKnight Foundation	MN	IN	**93,954,410**	97,687,834	2,006,436,000	12/31/00
27.	Richard King Mellon Foundation	PA	IN	**91,699,221**	97,898,818	1,907,473,636	12/31/00
28.	Lilly Cares Foundation[4]	IN	OP	**86,650,335**	87,695,970	2,861,597	12/31/00
29.	Doris Duke Charitable Foundation	NY	IN	**86,310,650**		1,574,746,419	12/31/00
30.	San Francisco Foundation	CA	CM	**86,000,000**	86,710,000	741,000,000	6/30/01
31.	Bank of America Foundation	NC	CS	**85,755,841**	85,755,841	2,212,307	12/31/00
32.	Greater Kansas City Community Foundation and Affiliated Trusts	MO	CM	**85,426,000**	85,426,000	719,476,000	12/31/00
33.	W. M. Keck Foundation	CA	IN	**81,745,562**	81,745,562	1,533,721,000	12/31/00
34.	Janssen Ortho Patient Assistance Foundation[4]	NJ	OP	**81,294,984**	81,294,984	895,057	12/31/00
35.	California Community Foundation	CA	CM	**78,300,000**	78,277,336	547,793,000	6/30/01
36.	Harry and Jeanette Weinberg Foundation	MD	IN	**77,329,311**	78,504,235	2,063,325,086	2/28/01
37.	John S. and James L. Knight Foundation	FL	IN	**70,746,766**	77,965,065	2,198,985,122	12/31/00
38.	Donald W. Reynolds Foundation	NV	IN	**69,363,245**	81,849,880	1,269,083,024	12/31/00
39.	SBC Foundation	TX	CS	**68,678,574**	68,630,454	328,100,000	12/31/00
40.	Freeman Foundation	NY	IN	**68,256,173**	68,888,913	2,113,688,541	12/31/00
41.	Houston Endowment	TX	IN	**66,061,151**	69,000,000	1,506,627,708	12/31/00
42.	William Penn Foundation	PA	IN	**64,898,490**	65,598,706	1,170,193,129	12/31/00
43.	Peninsula Community Foundation	CA	CM	**64,243,451**	64,243,451	449,062,871	12/31/00
44.	Ewing Marion Kauffman Foundation	MO	IN	**63,741,000**	63,741,000	2,034,722,000	6/30/01
45.	Wal-Mart Foundation	AR	CS	**62,617,641**	62,964,540	359,724	1/31/01
46.	Brown Foundation	TX	IN	**62,446,805**	62,236,020	1,323,153,103	6/30/01
47.	Carnegie Corporation of New York	NY	IN	**60,803,959**	73,457,872	1,929,598,812	9/30/00
48.	James Irvine Foundation	CA	IN	**58,223,073**	66,375,159	1,509,641,006	12/31/00
49.	Columbus Foundation and Affiliated Organizations	OH	CM	**57,605,631**	57,605,631	677,889,306	12/31/00
50.	Cleveland Foundation	OH	CM	**57,030,931**	57,030,931	1,600,206,255	12/31/00

Source: *Foundation Yearbook*, 2002.

*Aggregate foundation fiscal information is based on data provided to the Center as of February 2, 2002; fiscal data on individual foundations included in this table may be more current.

Note: Due to the unavailability of 2000 year-end fiscal information for the Arthur S. DeMoss Foundation, it has been excluded from this list.

[1] IN = Independent; CS = Corporate; CM = Community; OP = Operating.

[2] Includes grants, scholarships, and employee matching gifts; excludes set-asides, loans, PRIs, and program expenses. For some operating foundations, program expenses are included.

[3] Qualifying distributions is the amount used in calculating the required 5 percent payout; includes total giving, as well as reasonable administrative expenses, set-asides, PRIs, operating program expenses, and amount paid to acquire assets used directly for charitable purposes.

[4] For some operating foundations, total giving amount includes grants and program expenses; for others, total giving amount includes only grants. Most operating foundations' qualifying distributions are paid out for administration of operating programs and not for grants.

TABLE 14. 50 Largest Foundations by Assets, 2000*

	Foundation	State	Foundation Type[1]	Assets	Total Giving[2]	Qualifying Distributions[3]	Fiscal Date
1.	Bill & Melinda Gates Foundation	WA	IN	$21,149,100,000	$994,900,000	$994,900,000	12/31/00
2.	Lilly Endowment	IN	IN	15,591,737,808	583,890,521	588,943,280	12/31/00
3.	Ford Foundation	NY	IN	14,659,683,000	652,091,000	652,091,000	9/30/00
4.	J. Paul Getty Trust[4]	CA	OP	10,929,809,811	17,344,634	279,747,018	6/30/00
5.	David and Lucile Packard Foundation	CA	IN	9,793,212,529	533,589,987	605,793,134	12/31/00
6.	Robert Wood Johnson Foundation	NJ	IN	8,793,792,000	351,683,796	444,128,246	12/31/00
7.	Starr Foundation	NY	IN	6,257,848,627	192,502,039	194,246,442	12/31/00
8.	W. K. Kellogg Foundation	MI	IN	5,719,735,520	178,739,742	196,651,170	8/31/01
9.	Andrew W. Mellon Foundation	NY	IN	4,888,237,000	205,870,150	205,870,150	12/31/00
10.	Pew Charitable Trusts	PA	IN	4,800,776,253	187,853,822	243,841,247	12/31/00
11.	John D. and Catherine T. MacArthur Foundation	IL	IN	4,479,153,951	164,022,738	198,205,781	12/31/00
12.	William and Flora Hewlett Foundation	CA	IN	3,930,366,990	135,748,270	131,802,992	12/31/00
13.	Rockefeller Foundation	NY	IN	3,619,028,000	163,391,841	202,375,330	12/31/00
14.	California Endowment	CA	IN	3,490,256,407	189,663,220	211,000,000	2/28/01
15.	Robert W. Woodruff Foundation	GA	IN	3,139,654,481	149,979,270	150,387,356	12/31/00
16.	Annie E. Casey Foundation	MD	IN	3,001,942,131	101,012,809	127,380,064	12/31/00
17.	Annenberg Foundation	PA	IN	2,932,205,767	132,384,109	132,384,109	6/30/01
18.	Charles Stewart Mott Foundation	MI	IN	2,881,802,805	139,480,791	154,952,273	12/31/00
19.	Duke Endowment	NC	IN	2,874,017,045	106,030,389	106,000,000	12/31/00
20.	Casey Family Programs[4]	WA	OP	2,811,000,726	1,824,177	136,683,045	12/31/00
21.	Kresge Foundation	MI	IN	2,770,530,893	107,956,140	107,956,140	12/31/00
22.	John S. and James L. Knight Foundation	FL	IN	2,198,985,122	70,746,766	77,965,065	12/31/00
23.	Freeman Foundation	NY	IN	2,113,688,541	68,256,173	68,888,913	12/31/00
24.	Harry and Jeanette Weinberg Foundation	MD	IN	2,063,325,086	77,329,311	78,504,235	2/28/01
25.	Ewing Marion Kauffman Foundation	MO	IN	2,034,722,000	63,741,000	63,741,000	6/30/01
26.	McKnight Foundation	MN	IN	2,006,436,000	93,954,410	97,687,834	12/31/00
27.	New York Community Trust	NY	CM	1,930,370,263	143,950,743	143,950,743	12/31/00
28.	Carnegie Corporation of New York	NY	IN	1,929,598,812	60,803,959	73,457,872	9/30/00
29.	Richard King Mellon Foundation	PA	IN	1,907,473,636	91,699,221	97,898,818	12/31/00
30.	Robert R. McCormick Tribune Foundation	IL	IN	1,855,000,000	106,830,351	112,200,000	12/31/00
31.	Wallace-Reader's Digest Funds	NY	IN	1,619,344,210	40,678,318	52,173,570	12/31/00
32.	Cleveland Foundation	OH	CM	1,600,206,255	57,030,931	57,030,931	12/31/00
33.	Doris Duke Charitable Foundation	NY	IN	1,574,746,419	86,310,650	84,676,886	12/31/00
34.	W. M. Keck Foundation	CA	IN	1,533,721,000	81,745,562	81,745,562	12/31/00
35.	James Irvine Foundation	CA	IN	1,509,641,006	58,223,073	66,375,159	12/31/00
36.	Houston Endowment	TX	IN	1,506,627,708	66,061,151	69,000,000	12/31/00
37.	Alfred P. Sloan Foundation	NY	IN	1,373,141,818	52,367,329	57,659,423	12/31/00
38.	Brown Foundation	TX	IN	1,323,153,103	62,446,805	62,236,020	6/30/01
39.	Packard Humanities Institute[4]	CA	OP	1,302,804,659	20,655,346	35,022,214	12/31/00
40.	Chicago Community Trust and Affiliates	IL	CM	1,302,626,633	41,243,732	41,243,732	9/30/00
41.	Donald W. Reynolds Foundation	NV	IN	1,269,083,024	69,363,245	81,849,880	12/31/00
42.	William Penn Foundation	PA	IN	1,170,193,129	64,898,490	65,598,706	12/31/00
43.	Marin Community Foundation	CA	CM	1,150,556,205	50,524,713	52,624,713	6/30/01
44.	Henry Luce Foundation	NY	IN	1,059,392,814	48,786,289	53,351,479	12/31/00
45.	Freedom Forum	VA	OP	1,037,110,607	36,320,040	N/A	12/31/00
46.	California Wellness Foundation	CA	IN	1,029,461,012	44,715,936	49,793,244	12/31/00
47.	Howard Heinz Endowment	PA	IN	1,028,810,621	45,810,679	48,778,695	12/31/00
48.	Joyce Foundation	IL	IN	999,530,958	39,596,622	42,908,225	12/31/00
49.	Walton Family Foundation	AR	IN	973,255,920	52,379,873	58,701,564	12/31/00
50.	Samuel Roberts Noble Foundation[4]	OK	OP	971,672,378	17,554,773	41,290,165	10/31/00

Source: *Foundation Yearbook*, 2002.

*Aggregate foundation fiscal information is based on data provided to the Center as of February 2, 2002; fiscal data on individual foundations included in this table may be more current.

Note: Due to the unavailability of 2000 year-end fiscal information for the Arthur S. DeMoss Foundation, it has been excluded from this list.

[1]IN = Independent; CS = Corporate; CM = Community; OP = Operating.

[2]Includes grants, scholarships, and employee matching gifts; excludes set-asides, loans, PRIs, and program expenses. For some operating foundations, program expenses are included.

[3]Qualifying distributions is the amount used in calculating the required 5 percent payout; includes total giving, as well as reasonable administative expenses, set-asides, PRIs, operating program expenses, and amount paid to acquire assets used directly for charitable purposes.

[4]For some operating foundations, total giving amount includes grants and program expenses; for others, total giving amount includes only grants. Most operating foundations' qualifying distributions are paid out for administration of operating programs and not for grants.

TABLE 15. 50 Largest Foundations by Gifts Received, 2000*

	Foundation	State	Foundation Type[1]	Gifts Received	Assets	Fiscal Date
1.	Bill & Melinda Gates Foundation	WA	IN	$5,068,000,000	$21,149,100,000	12/31/00
2.	Wallace H. Coulter Foundation	FL	IN	454,354,473	508,683,997	9/30/00
3.	William and Flora Hewlett Foundation	CA	IN	394,835,000	3,930,366,990	12/31/00
4.	Open Society Institute	NY	OP	363,639,131	135,447,900	12/31/00
5.	General Motors Foundation	MI	CS	286,867,500	401,916,997	12/31/00
6.	California Endowment	CA	IN	262,680,840	3,490,256,407	2/28/01
7.	AVI CHAI Foundation	NY	IN	242,195,811	427,293,174	12/31/00
8.	Peninsula Community Foundation	CA	CM	230,268,777	449,062,871	12/31/00
9.	Walton Family Foundation	AR	IN	226,820,614	973,255,920	12/31/00
10.	Daniels Fund	CO	IN	204,327,857	170,097,179	12/31/00
11.	Goldman, Sachs Foundation	NY	CS	200,000,000	230,721,571	6/30/00
12.	Broad Foundation	CA	IN	194,414,188	222,308,387	12/31/00
13.	Community Foundation Silicon Valley	CA	CM	170,231,708	463,637,185	6/30/00
14.	Communities Foundation of Texas	TX	CM	148,932,294	657,906,999	6/30/00
15.	Kresge Foundation	MI	IN	148,879,353	2,770,530,893	12/31/00
16.	Anschutz Foundation	CO	IN	144,691,103	1,050,694,662	11/30/00
17.	New York Community Trust	NY	CM	126,156,270	1,930,370,263	12/31/00
18.	Greater Kansas City Community Foundation and Affiliated Trusts	MO	CM	119,047,000	719,476,000	12/31/00
19.	Maybelle Clark Macdonald Fund	OR	IN	118,550,375	125,581,289	6/30/00
20.	Davee Foundation	IL	IN	111,789,137	125,677,642	12/31/00
21.	Waitt Family Foundation	CA	IN	111,190,015	207,252,015	12/31/00
22.	Flora Family Foundation	CA	IN	108,260,903	148,348,802	12/31/00
23.	Citigroup Foundation	NY	CS	107,812,500	179,182,168	12/31/00
24.	California Community Foundation	CA	CM	103,996,063	547,793,000	6/30/01
25.	San Francisco Foundation	CA	CM	103,000,000	741,000,000	6/30/01
26.	Cisco Systems Foundation	CA	CS	91,024,874	132,211,438	7/31/00
27.	Oregon Community Foundation	OR	CM	81,322,109	471,989,656	12/31/00
28.	Community Foundation for National Capital Region	DC	CM	80,994,401	153,896,592	3/31/01
29.	Baton Rouge Area Foundation	LA	CM	79,713,000	229,406,000	12/31/00
30.	Community Foundation for Southeastern Michigan	MI	CM	71,834,623	309,173,270	12/31/00
31.	Verizon Foundation	NY	CS	70,688,063	80,214,080	12/30/00
32.	Columbus Foundation and Affiliated Organizations	OH	CM	70,417,959	677,889,306	12/31/00
33.	Ford Motor Company Fund	MI	CS	70,000,000	247,625,772	12/31/00
34.	Hartford Foundation for Public Giving	CT	CM	65,883,751	647,516,680	9/30/00
35.	Buffett Foundation	NE	IN	65,003,505	57,195,568	6/30/00
36.	Oklahoma City Community Foundation	OK	CM	62,423,801	400,661,819	6/30/01
37.	McKnight Brain Research Foundation	FL	IN	61,336,287	52,851,612	6/30/00
38.	Richard M. Fairbanks Foundation	IN	IN	61,103,075	117,429,860	12/31/00
39.	Community Foundation of Middle Tennessee	TN	CM	60,588,238	125,518,170	12/31/00
40.	Gilo Family Foundation	CA	IN	59,351,141	61,375,884	8/31/00
41.	Seattle Foundation	WA	CM	58,138,462	305,644,179	12/30/00
42.	Community Foundation Serving Richmond & Central Virginia	VA	CM	57,700,000	379,000,000	12/31/00
43.	Alpha Foundation	AL	OP	57,412,500	22,185,545	12/31/00
44.	Gill Foundation	CO	IN	55,056,399	177,613,525	12/31/00
45.	Mississippi Common Fund Trust	MS	IN	52,964,828	92,039,425	6/30/00
46.	Weill Family Foundation	NY	IN	51,932,121	203,339,618	12/31/00
47.	Dennis M. Jones Family Foundation	MO	OP	51,409,300	51,839,301	12/31/00
48.	Coca-Cola Foundation	GA	CS	51,302,278	68,176,408	12/31/00
49.	Avon Products Foundation	NY	CS	50,667,895	38,437,478	12/31/00
50.	San Diego Foundation	CA	CM	49,263,000	401,000,000	6/30/01

Source: *Foundation Yearbook*, 2002.

*Aggregate foundation fiscal information is based on data provided to the Center as of February 2, 2002; fiscal data on individual foundations included in this table may be more current.

[1] IN = Independent; CS = Corporate; CM = Community; OP = Operating.

are therefore not required to follow the same public reporting requirements as private foundations. Instead, most report their giving voluntarily. Finally, in addition to published reports, more than 2,200 private and public foundations currently maintain Web sites, which are accessible via the Center's Web site at *www.fdncenter.org*. (For detailed comparisons of reporting patterns by foundation size, type, and regional location, see *Foundation Reporting*, part of the *Foundations Today Series* of annual research reports.)

Staffing. Only the largest foundations are likely to have paid staff to review and investigate proposals, develop projects, and work with the public. From a survey mailed to nearly 19,000 larger foundations by the Foundation Center in 2001, only 3,123 respondents (one-in-six) reported paid staff. Moreover, of those with assets lower than $5 million, only about one-in-thirteen reported paid staff. Few, if any, of the more than 37,000 small foundations not included in the Foundation Center's survey are able to employ paid staff. Instead, their programs are typically administered by lawyers, bank trustees, and family members on a part-time basis. (For detailed comparisons of staffing patterns by foundation size, type, and regional location, see *Foundation Staffing*, part of the *Foundations Today Series* of annual research reports.)

Foundations' Share of Private Philanthropy, 2000

Sources of Private Contributions

- Individuals provide more than four-fifths of private contributions
- Foundations account for highest share of private contributions on record
- Excluding giving for religion, foundations account for more than one-sixth of private contributions

Given the large number of foundations, and the attention paid to a few highly visible grantmaker programs, grantseekers and journalists often overestimate the role that foundations play in the nonprofit sector. In fact, foundation giving represents a modest portion of all private contributions, which in turn account for a relatively small percentage of the overall income of America's nonprofits.

According to estimates published in *Giving USA*, private contributions from all sources totaled $203.5 billion in 2000 (Figure P1 and Table P1), representing 2.0 percent of the Gross Domestic Product.[1] The largest portion of these contributions—$168.1 billion or 82.8 percent—came from individual donors either through gifts (75.0 percent) or bequests (7.8 percent). Independent, community, and grantmaking operating foundations were responsible for another 12.0 percent of total estimated private giving—the highest share on record—while the remaining 5.3 percent came from corporations and corporate foundations. (If corporate foundation grant dollars are added to those of

1. Brown, M., *Giving USA 2001: The Annual Report on Philanthropy for the Year 2000,*. Indianapolis, IN: AAFRC Trust for Philanthropy, 2001.

FIGURE P1. Distribution of Private Philanthropic Giving, 2000*

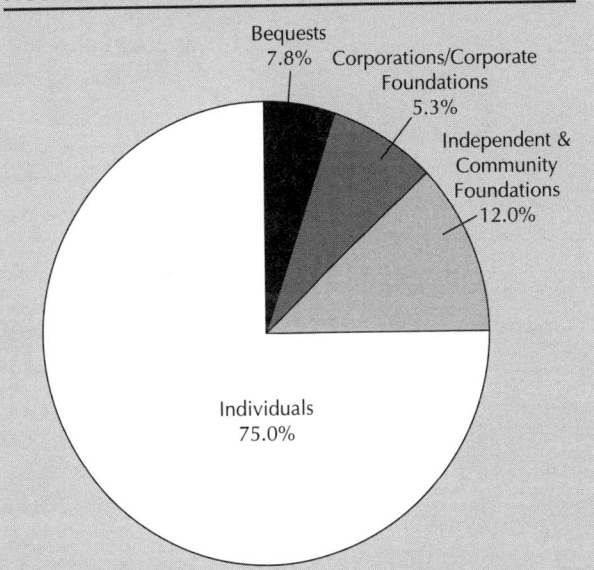

- Bequests 7.8%
- Corporations/Corporate Foundations 5.3%
- Independent & Community Foundations 12.0%
- Individuals 75.0%

Source: *Giving USA*, New York: AAFRC Trust for Philanthropy, 2001.
*Figures based on estimates. Corporate data include corporate foundation giving.

TABLE P1. 2000 Private Philanthropic Giving (Dollars in billions)*

Source	Amount	%
Individuals	$152.1	75.0
Independent and Community Foundations	24.5	12.0
Bequests	16.0	7.8
Corporations/Corporate Foundations	10.9[1]	5.3
Total	**$203.5**	**100.0**

Source: *Giving USA*, Indianapolis, IN: AAFRC Trust for Philanthropy, 2001. Figures based on estimates.
*Due to rounding, figures may not add up.
[1]Of total estimated corporate giving for 2000, $3.0 billion (27.4%) was paid through corporate foundations (see Table 2).

other foundations, the share rises to 13.5 percent for foundations.)

Individuals thus provide the vast majority of private donations, roughly five times that provided by foundations and businesses combined. Yet these proportions are somewhat misleading. It bears noting that well over two-fifths of giving from individuals is for the benefit of religious congregations, primarily, although far from exclusively, for sacramental purposes. Consequently, if religion is excluded from the private giving denominator, foundations' and corporations' share of support for the nonprofit public-benefit service sector increases significantly.[2]

For example, *Giving USA* estimates that 36.5 percent of private contributions in 2000—$74.3 billion—went to religion, most of it in gifts from individuals to their congregations. If religion is excluded, then independent and community foundations' share of the remaining $129.1 billion in contributions jumps to 17.4 percent. While still relatively modest, this proportion nevertheless presents a far more accurate measure of all U.S. foundation support as a percent of overall private funding in the fields in which they are most active (e.g., education, human services, health, and the arts).

Foundation giving as a proportion of the whole philanthropic pie grew rapidly during the 1960s and then reached a peak in 1970 (9.0 percent). Throughout the 1970s, restrictive government regulations, inflation, and a shrinking asset base effectively reduced the role of foundations. By 1979, foundation's share of giving had dropped to 5.0 percent. With the easing of some government restrictions in the 1980s, a soaring stock market, and thousands of new foundations helping to raise asset values, foundation giving as a share of private contributions inched back up and continued to rise in the 1990s. In fact, between 1975 and 2000, inflation-adjusted growth in giving by independent and community foundations far outpaced increases reported for other types of private giving (Figure P2). As a result, independent and community foundations raised their share of all private philanthropic giving to a record 12.0 percent, up from 10.7 percent in 1999 (Figure P3).

Corporate contributions, including corporate foundation giving, grew quickly between 1975 and 1986 and then experienced several years of decline. While support offered through corporate giving programs and corporate foundations grew in the 1990s (see the "Corporate Foundations" analysis in Chapter 4), this growth often did not match increases reported by non-corporate foundations and individuals. Still, between 1975 and 2000, growth in corporate giving exceeded the overall increases reported for individuals and bequests during this period.

As a share of all private support, corporate philanthropy surpassed non-corporate foundations in 1984 (6.0 percent versus 5.7 percent). However, the 1987 stock market crash, corporate downsizing, deep losses in some industries during the recession of the early 1990s, numerous mergers, and continued challenges to corporate giving (often deemed by stockholders as too controversial or

---

2. Salamon, L., *America's Nonprofit Sector: A Primer*, New York: Foundation Center, 1999.

FIGURE P2. Growth of Private Philanthropic Giving by Source, 1975 to 2000*

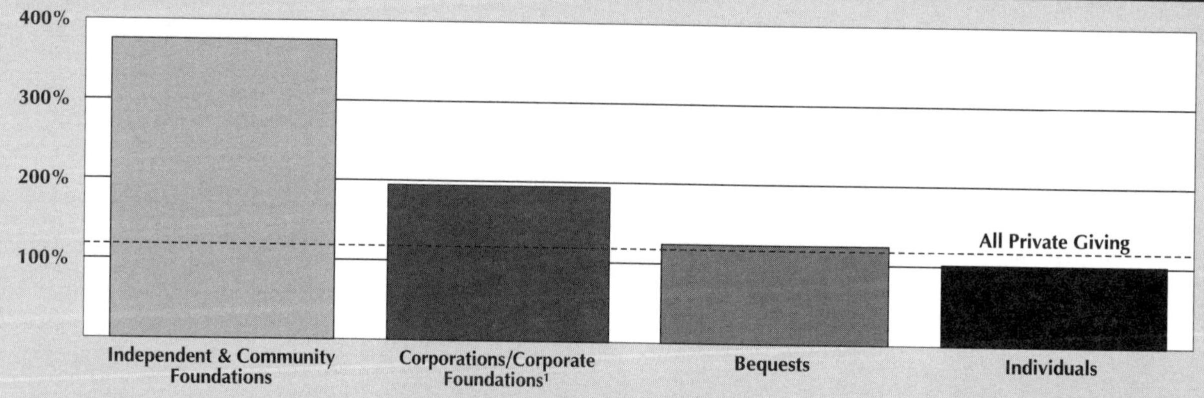

Source: *Giving USA*. New York: AAFRC Trust for Philanthropy, 2001. Figures for 2000 based on estimates.
*Figures based on adjusted dollars using Consumer Price Index, all urban consumers, U.S. Department of Labor, Bureau of Labor Statistics.
[1] Figures include direct corporate giving as well as giving by corporate foundations.

outside of the company's interests) pointed to a reduced role for business in American philanthropy. In addition, corporations are channeling an increasing share of their charitable support through corporate sponsorships and other forms of corporate marketing, which are not reflected in figures for charitable giving. (However, charitable giving does include in-kind giving, as well as cash support.)

Based on 2000 estimates, corporate contributions increased to 5.3 percent of total private giving, up from 5.1 percent in 1999 (Figure P3). Despite this increase, slower growth in corporate foundation giving estimated for 2001 suggests that corporations' share of all private philanthropy is unlikely to increase further.

Sources of Income by Subsector

- Private contributions account for less than one-fifth of nonprofits' income
- Private support most important for arts and civic affairs organizations

Private giving from all sources—individuals, foundations, and corporations—accounts for only a fraction of overall nonprofit income. In 1998, nonprofit income (including church revenues), was estimated at $692.8 billion.[3] Of that total, one-eighth (12.5 percent) came from private contributions, compared to nearly four-fifths (79.5 percent) from earned income, including fees and other charges for services, income from endowments, and other receipts. The final one-twelfth (8.0 percent) came from federal, state, and local governments.

The proportion of annual income—both operating and capital—derived from these major sources of revenue differed widely by sector. For example, private donations in 1997 (the latest year for which comparable figures were available) accounted for 4 percent of health agencies' income, more than 13 percent for educational organizations, 20 percent for social service agencies, 36 percent for civic affairs organizations, and 44 percent for arts organizations. In the arts subsector, however, the high proportion of private contributions as a percent of income included gifts of expensive art objects donated at current market value to museums and other large capital gifts. If those gifts were excluded, private donations would represent a smaller share of income. Still, foundation giving, as one source of private support, is likely to be far more important to the average arts organization than to the average health organization.

3. See Table 5.5 in Weitzman, M. et al., *The New Nonprofit Almanac and Desk Reference: The Essential Facts and Figures for Managers, Researchers, and Volunteers*, Washington, DC: INDEPENDENT SECTOR, 2002.

FIGURE P3. Giving by Independent and Community Foundations and Corporations/Corporate Foundations as a Share of All Private Giving, 1975 to 2000*

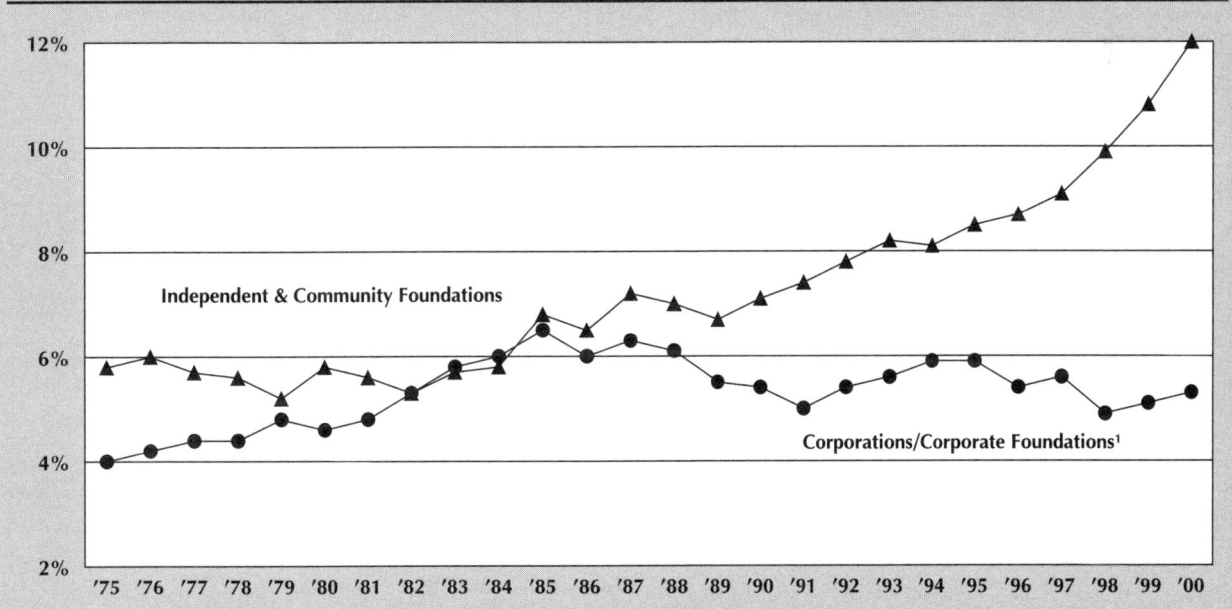

Source: *Giving USA*. New York: AAFRC Trust for Philanthropy, 2001. Figures for 2000 based on estimates.
*At least four out of five private philanthropic dollars are provided each year by living donors and through bequests.
[1] Figures include direct corporate giving as well as giving by corporate foundations.

CHAPTER 3

Foundations by Region and State

Regional Trends, 1975 to 2000

Since the earliest days of philanthropy, the Northeast has held a disproportionate share of foundations and their resources. Beginning in the 1970s and accelerating in the 1980s, however, population shifts and strong economic growth in the South and West regions altered the philanthropic map. During the first half of the 1990s, change was more gradual. But the rapid growth of foundations in the West near decade's end and the above-average growth in the South's foundation community contributed to an increasing balance of foundation resources across regions. The following analysis examines changes in foundation number, giving, and assets over the latest year and since 1975 that have led to the current allocation of foundation resources across the four major U.S. regions (Table 16).

Foundation Number by Region

- **West experiences fastest growth in number of foundations in 2000**
- **South reports largest gain in actual number of foundations since 1975**

Growth of Number of Foundations, 1975 to 2000. The number of U.S. grantmaking foundations grew by a record 12.7 percent in 2000, far surpassing the prior year's 7.2 percent gain. Growth was extremely robust across all regions. Still, Figure 11 shows that the West, with growth of 17.3 percent, led in terms of increase in active grantmakers reported in the latest year, followed by the South (15.9 percent). The Midwestern and Northeastern foundation communities grew at a moderately slower pace—10.2 percent and 10.1 percent, respectively—but exceeded the rate of increase reported annually for all U.S. foundations throughout the 1980s and 1990s.

Beyond experiencing the fastest growth in the latest year, the West also realized the highest growth rate in number of foundations since 1975. The number of active foundations in the region grew by close to three and one-half times (242.3 percent) since the mid-1970s, compared to slightly more than three times (211.2 percent) for foundations in the South (Figure 12). Among all U.S. foundations, their number grew more than two and one-half times (158.5 percent) during this period, which slightly exceeded gains reported for the Midwest (146.2 percent) and far surpassed growth in the Northeast (111.9 percent).

Growth of Actual Number of Foundations. An examination of the growth rate of a foundation community provides a useful measure of the strength of philanthropy in a region. However, regions with larger and more established foundation communities, such as the Northeast and Midwest, may experience increases in actual foundation resources that surpass faster growing regions with a smaller philanthropic base. For example, Figure 13 shows that, while the Northeast experienced the slowest rate of growth in number of active foundations between 1975 and 2000, this region still accounted for the second largest number of new foundations (9,533). By comparison, the rapidly growing West reported the lowest number of actual foundations added during this period (6,669). Interestingly, the South, which began with a relatively smaller foundation base, surpassed the Northeast in actual number of additional foundations counted (9,698). In the latest year alone, the South reported an increase of 1,963 active foundations, bringing the regional total to 14,289 (Table 16). The Northeast recorded the second largest increase in actual number of active foundations in 2000 (1,657), followed by the West (1,392) and Midwest (1,368) regions.

TABLE 16. Fiscal Data of Grantmaking Foundations by Region and State, 2000*

Region[1]	Number of Foundations	%	Assets	%	Gifts Received	%	Qualifying Distributions[2]	%	Total Giving[3]	%
NORTHEAST	18,052	31.9	$155,772,107	32.0	$ 7,208,274	26.1	$10,118,045	33.2	$ 9,281,578	33.7
New England	5,174	9.1	22,237,364	4.6	1,235,772	4.5	1,433,361	4.7	1,321,031	4.8
Connecticut	1,256	2.2	6,315,930	1.3	364,872	1.3	427,824	1.4	386,666	1.4
Maine	266	0.5	792,229	0.2	100,324	0.4	48,917	0.2	46,617	0.2
Massachusetts	2,556	4.5	11,665,383	2.4	640,325	2.3	746,056	2.4	707,647	2.6
New Hampshire	259	0.5	944,243	0.2	55,650	0.2	61,192	0.2	47,025	0.2
Rhode Island	648	1.1	2,133,533	0.4	48,387	0.2	122,161	0.4	114,688	0.4
Vermont	189	0.3	386,046	0.1	26,214	0.1	27,211	0.1	18,388	0.1
Middle Atlantic	12,878	22.8	133,534,743	27.5	5,972,502	21.6	8,684,684	28.5	7,960,547	28.9
New Jersey	1,920	3.4	16,509,534	3.4	950,191	3.4	1,438,910	4.7	1,295,802	4.7
New York	7,824	13.8	89,914,543	18.5	4,472,149	16.2	5,674,737	18.6	5,248,198	19.0
Pennsylvania	3,134	5.5	27,110,666	5.6	550,162	2.0	1,571,037	5.2	1,416,546	5.1
MIDWEST	14,811	26.2	111,097,136	22.9	4,919,290	17.8	6,865,087	22.5	6,443,319	23.4
East North Central	10,476	18.5	85,336,139	17.6	3,603,317	13.0	5,042,845	16.5	4,751,148	17.2
Illinois	3,343	5.9	22,976,314	4.7	869,634	3.1	1,409,143	4.6	1,302,315	4.7
Indiana	1053	1.9	21,286,596	4.4	427,906	1.5	993,433	3.3	964,839	3.5
Michigan	1,741	3.1	22,136,388	4.6	1,007,458	3.6	1,302,220	4.3	1,201,304	4.4
Ohio	2,783	4.9	13,542,216	2.8	830,033	3.0	947,228	3.1	908,083	3.3
Wisconsin	1,556	2.7	5,394,625	1.1	468,287	1.7	390,821	1.3	374,607	1.4
West North Central	4,335	7.7	25,760,997	5.3	1,315,973	4.8	1,822,242	6.0	1,692,172	6.1
Iowa	784	1.4	2,320,576	0.5	149,053	0.5	208,910	0.7	150,347	0.5
Kansas	598	1.1	1,701,435	0.4	120,820	0.4	116,922	0.4	109,099	0.4
Minnesota	1,130	2.0	10,239,523	2.1	401,303	1.5	706,556	2.3	666,409	2.4
Missouri	1,206	2.1	8,951,988	1.8	402,851	1.5	572,589	1.9	556,922	2.0
Nebraska	435	0.8	2,094,229	0.4	193,634	0.7	191,425	0.6	186,061	0.7
North Dakota	85	0.2	128,196	0.0	13,564	0.0	6,730	0.0	5,859	0.0
South Dakota	97	0.2	325,051	0.1	34,747	0.1	19,111	0.1	17,475	0.1
SOUTH	14,289	25.3	99,528,744	20.5	4,998,153	18.1	6,586,094	21.6	5,924,155	21.5
South Atlantic	8,426	14.9	58,772,908	12.1	3,056,632	11.1	3,963,387	13.0	3,518,798	12.8
Delaware	261	0.5	2,840,234	0.6	88,461	0.3	158,604	0.5	156,608	0.6
District of Columbia	358	0.6	4,559,925	0.9	282,037	1.0	402,885	1.3	276,488	1.0
Florida	2,632	4.7	13,631,403	2.8	1,178,083	4.3	925,865	3.0	830,826	3.0
Georgia	1,150	2.0	9,989,265	2.1	375,992	1.4	661,067	2.2	623,045	2.3
Maryland	1,130	2.0	9,818,998	2.0	258,792	0.9	551,620	1.8	495,788	1.8
North Carolina	1,207	2.1	10,135,063	2.1	487,995	1.8	688,146	2.3	666,336	2.4
South Carolina	333	0.6	1,252,567	0.3	45,489	0.2	77,654	0.3	73,293	0.3
Virginia	1,157	2.0	5,868,554	1.2	315,253	1.1	465,737	1.5	367,004	1.3
West Virginia	198	0.3	676,898	0.1	24,531	0.1	31,808	0.1	29,410	0.1
East South Central	1,798	3.2	7,705,822	1.6	525,300	1.9	562,675	1.8	520,530	1.9
Alabama	575	1.0	1,755,887	0.4	124,006	0.4	131,009	0.4	119,520	0.4
Kentucky	409	0.7	1,595,221	0.3	79,053	0.3	102,283	0.3	97,613	0.4
Mississippi	200	0.4	757,689	0.2	90,062	0.3	44,605	0.1	38,303	0.1
Tennessee	614	1.1	3,597,026	0.7	232,178	0.8	284,778	0.9	265,094	1.0
West South Central	4,065	7.2	33,050,014	6.8	1,416,221	5.1	2,060,032	6.8	1,884,827	6.8
Arkansas	221	0.4	2,021,419	0.4	231,557	0.8	192,020	0.6	178,743	0.6
Louisiana	380	0.7	1,976,335	0.4	159,338	0.6	107,902	0.4	101,220	0.4
Oklahoma	495	0.9	4,968,930	1.0	210,341	0.8	252,909	0.8	210,830	0.8
Texas	2,969	5.2	24,083,329	5.0	814,986	3.0	1,507,201	4.9	1,394,034	5.1
WEST	9,421	16.7	119,639,232	24.6	10,479,963	38.0	6,925,102	22.7	5,910,888	21.4
Mountain	2,607	4.6	15,676,337	3.2	968,361	3.5	983,480	3.2	892,208	3.2
Arizona	468	0.8	1,929,780	0.4	155,647	0.6	112,767	0.4	102,653	0.4
Colorado	854	1.5	5,004,656	1.0	494,432	1.8	307,966	1.0	277,802	1.0
Idaho	153	0.3	965,385	0.2	30,537	0.1	60,255	0.2	58,342	0.2
Montana	166	0.3	311,204	0.1	17,187	0.1	15,192	0.0	13,918	0.1
Nevada	330	0.6	3,365,981	0.7	92,980	0.3	236,726	0.8	216,081	0.8
New Mexico	158	0.3	1,122,731	0.2	23,810	0.1	81,579	0.3	65,046	0.2
Utah	323	0.6	2,228,364	0.5	32,021	0.1	121,783	0.4	114,754	0.4
Wyoming	155	0.3	748,236	0.2	121,747	0.4	47,212	0.2	43,610	0.2
Pacific	6,814	12.0	103,962,895	21.4	9,511,602	34.4	5,941,623	19.5	5,018,680	18.2
Alaska	58	0.1	111,910	0.0	54,182	0.2	8,095	0.0	6,973	0.0
California	4,948	8.7	70,125,281	14.4	3,638,410	13.2	4,054,048	13.3	3,432,247	12.5
Hawaii	241	0.4	1,765,371	0.4	17,024	0.1	82,488	0.3	64,801	0.2
Oregon	600	1.1	3,405,039	0.7	417,567	1.5	196,316	0.6	178,172	0.6
Washington	967	1.7	28,555,295	5.9	5,384,419	19.5	1,600,675	5.2	1,336,487	4.8
CARIBBEAN[4]	7	0.0	46,944	0.0	8,110	0.0	3,179	0.0	3,177	0.0
Puerto Rico	3	0.0	40,579	0.0	2,654	0.0	2,872	0.0	2,871	0.0
Virgin Islands	4	0.0	6,364	0.0	5,456	0.0	307	0.0	306	0.0
SOUTH PACIFIC[4]	2	0.0	1,150	0.0	5	0.0	53	0.0	50	0.0
American Samoa	2	0.0	1,150	0.0	5	0.0	53	0.0	50	0.0
Total	56,582	100.0	$486,085,311	100.0	$27,613,795	100.0	$30,497,560	100.0	$27,563,166	100.0

Source: *Foundation Yearbook*, 2002.
*Dollars in thousands; due to rounding, figures may not add up.
[1] Geographic regions as defined by the U.S. Bureau of the Census.
[2] Qualifying distributions is the amount used in calculating the required payout; includes total giving, as well as reasonable administrative expenses, set-asides, PRIs, operating program expenses, and amount paid to acquire assets used directly for charitable purposes.
[3] Includes grants, scholarships, and employee matching gifts; excludes set-asides, loans, PRIs, and program expenses. For some operating foundations, program expenses are included.
[4] Private foundations in Puerto Rico, the Virgin Islands, and American Samoa are not required to file Form 990-PF. Only a few voluntary reporters are represented.

Giving by Region

- West experiences fastest growth in giving since 1975
- Northeast shows largest increase in actual grant dollars in 2000
- West poised to surpass South in share of giving in next few years

Growth of Giving. U.S. foundations overall increased their giving by 18.2 percent between 1999 and 2000 (Figure 11). Grantmakers in the West exceeded this growth, with gains in giving totaling a remarkable 31.1 percent. The foundation community in Washington State experienced by far the biggest percentage gain in giving (66.4 percent) in the latest year, while foundations in Nevada and Wyoming also realized increases of more than 30 percent. Foundations in the Northeast also reported slightly above-average growth in giving in 2000, with funding up 18.9 percent. By comparison, giving by Southern foundations grew 13.9 percent; and for Midwestern foundations, the increase totaled 11.0 percent, following an 18.9 percent rise in 1999.

FIGURE 11. Growth of Foundation Number, Giving, and Assets by Region, 1999 to 2000

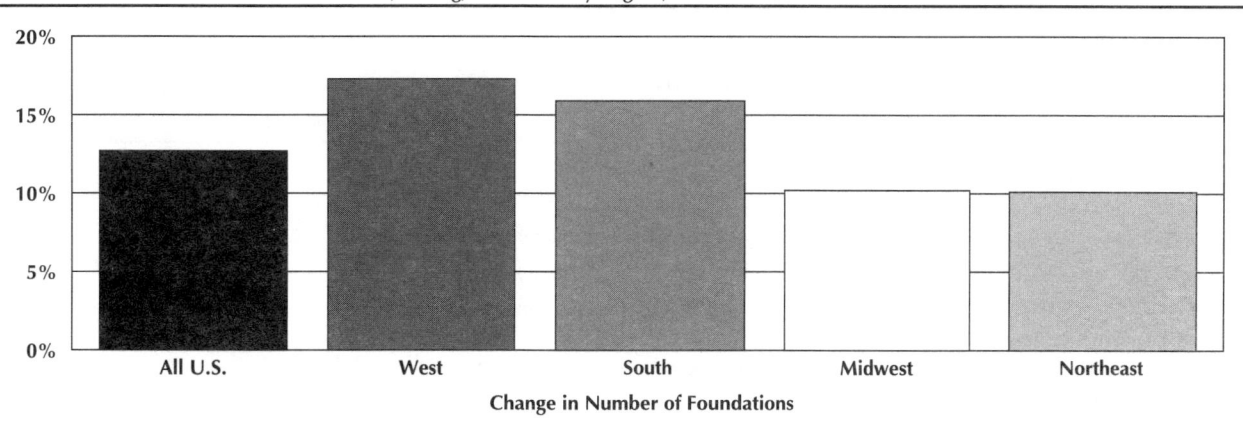

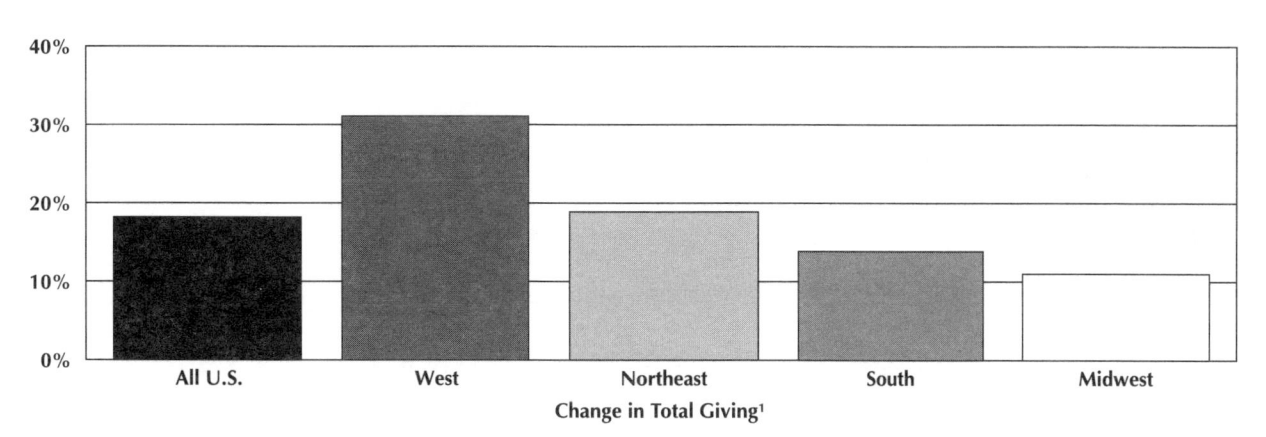

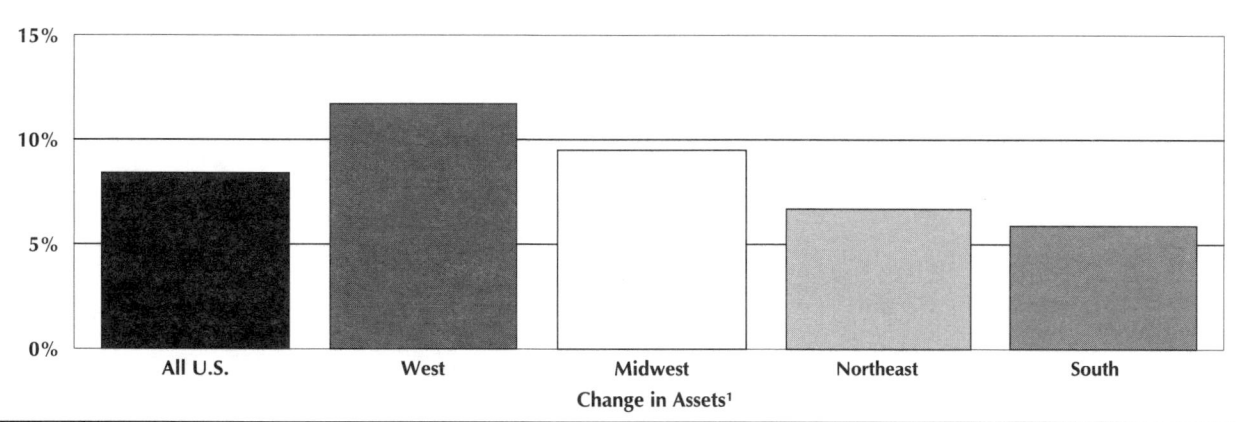

Source *Foundation Yearbook*, 2002.
[1] Percent change based on unadjusted dollars.

Growth of Actual Grant Dollars. Although the West reported the fastest rate of growth in giving in 2000, in terms of actual grant dollars, the Northeast reported a larger increase. Northeastern grantmakers raised their giving by $1.5 billion, to nearly $9.3 billion in the latest year. Foundations in the West ranked second with giving up $1.4 billion to $5.9 billion. Two foundations in the West—Gates and Packard—accounted for over two-thirds (41.9 percent) of the region's gain. Southern foundations increased giving by $724.3 million to $5.9 billion, while giving in the Midwest increased by $640.8 million to more than $6.4 billion.

Growth of Giving, 1975 to 2000. Since 1975, the West has led in the growth of foundation giving (Figure 14). Grantmaking by foundations in the region has increased close to eleven times (976.9 percent) after inflation during this period, far surpassing growth reported by foundations in the South (463.0 percent) and U.S. foundations overall (343.9 percent). With giving up almost four times (296.1 percent) since the mid-1970s, funders based in the Midwest region approached the average growth in U.S. foundation giving. Grantmakers based in the Northeast raised giving more than three times (209.7 percent), but this nonetheless placed the region well below average growth across the country.

As a result of differing rates of growth in foundation giving since 1975, giving has become far more evenly distributed by region. Figure 15 shows that in 1975, foundations in the South accounted for about one-in-six grant dollars (16.9 percent) awarded by U.S. foundations. By 2000, their share had increased to over one-in-five (21.5 percent). Among grantmakers in the West, their share of all grant dollars has risen from less than one-in-eleven (8.8 percent) to more than one-in-five (21.4 percent). Despite recent downturns in the technology sector (an important source of support for the West's foundation community), prospects for continued growth in giving by Western foundations remain strong. As a result, the West can be expected to surpass the South in share of all U.S. foundation giving in the next few years.

In contrast to rapid growth in the South and West, the Midwest managed to maintain a roughly one-quarter share of giving over the past quarter century. However, Northeastern foundation's share of giving declined from close to half (48.1 percent) to about one-third (33.7 percent) during this period. Despite the

FIGURE 13. Increase in Number of Grantmaking Foundations by Region, 1975 to 2000*

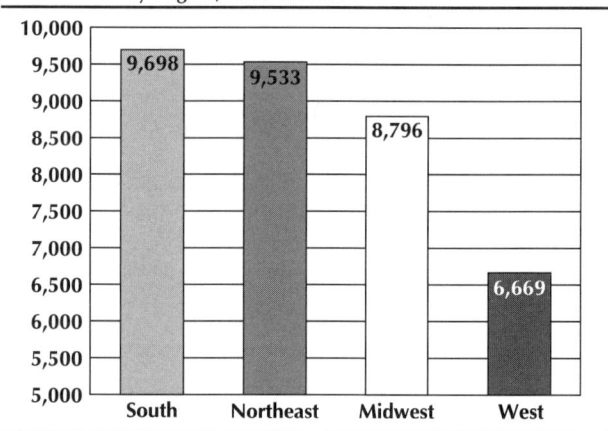

Source: *Foundation Yearbook,* 2002.
*Overall, the Northeast reported 18,052 active foundations in 2000, followed by the Midwest (14,811), South (14,289), and West (9,421).

FIGURE 12. Growth of Foundation Number by Region, 1975 to 2000

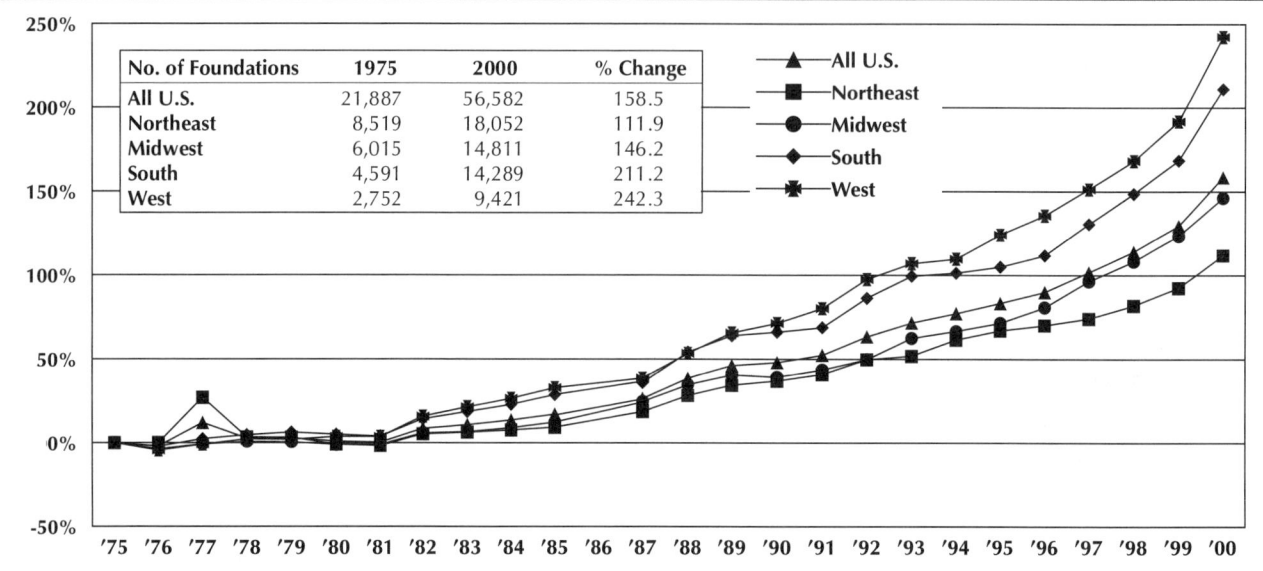

No. of Foundations	1975	2000	% Change
All U.S.	21,887	56,582	158.5
Northeast	8,519	18,052	111.9
Midwest	6,015	14,811	146.2
South	4,591	14,289	211.2
West	2,752	9,421	242.3

Source: *Foundation Yearbook,* 2002. Dates approximate; reporting years varied. 1986 figures not available.

loss in share of giving represented by Northeastern foundations, funders in the region continued to provide the dominant share of support and over one and one-half times the share provided by Western foundations. Moreover, although giving grew far more rapidly in the West and South, growth in giving was strong across the U.S., with the benefits of this increased support reaching many more parts of the country.

Assets by Region

- Led by Gates Foundation, West ranks first in growth of assets and actual dollar gains for third consecutive year

- West increases share of all U.S. foundation assets

Growth of Assets. U.S. foundation assets grew 8.4 percent overall in 2000 (Figure 11). With assets up by close to one-eighth (11.7 percent), grantmakers in the West surpassed gains in every other region during the latest year. Within the region, Alaska, Wyoming, and Washington State led in percentage growth in assets. In contrast, while the Midwest (up 9.5 percent), Northeast (up 6.7 percent), and South (up 5.9 percent) all experienced positive asset growth, only the Midwest exceeded the average U.S. increase.

Growth of Actual Asset Dollars. The Western region's continued growth translated into the largest rise in foundation assets reported for any region between 1999 and 2000. Overall, the assets of foundations in the West increased $12.6 billion to $119.6 billion—the third consecutive year in which the West's asset gains have surpassed the other regions.

FIGURE 15. Foundation Giving by Region, 1975 and 2000*

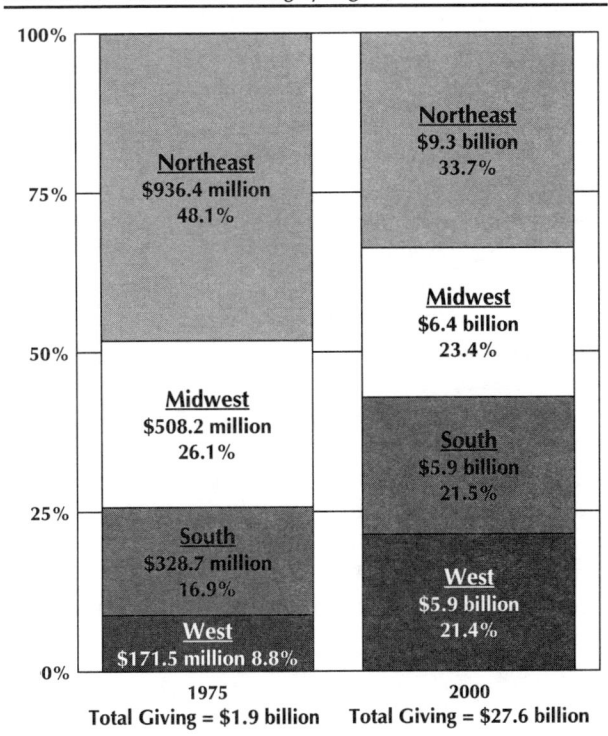

Region	1975	2000
Northeast	$936.4 million / 48.1%	$9.3 billion / 33.7%
Midwest	$508.2 million / 26.1%	$6.4 billion / 23.4%
South	$328.7 million / 16.9%	$5.9 billion / 21.5%
West	$171.5 million / 8.8%	$5.9 billion / 21.4%
Total Giving	$1.9 billion	$27.6 billion

Source: *Foundation Yearbook,* 2002.
*Figures based on unadjusted dollars. Due to rounding, percentages may not total 100. Excludes foundations based in the Caribbean and South Pacific, which accounted for 0.0 percent of total foundation giving in 1975 and 2000.

FIGURE 14. Growth of Foundation Giving by Region, 1975 to 2000*

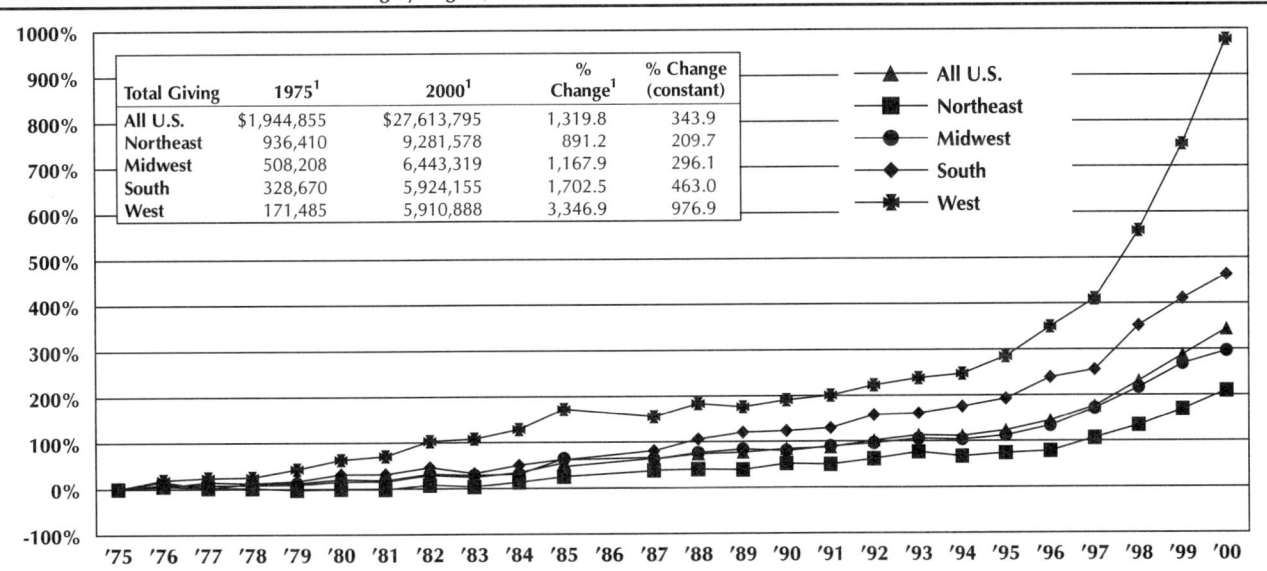

Total Giving	1975[1]	2000[1]	% Change[1]	% Change (constant)
All U.S.	$1,944,855	$27,613,795	1,319.8	343.9
Northeast	936,410	9,281,578	891.2	209.7
Midwest	508,208	6,443,319	1,167.9	296.1
South	328,670	5,924,155	1,702.5	463.0
West	171,485	5,910,888	3,346.9	976.9

Source: *Foundation Yearbook,* 2002. Dates approximate; reporting years varied. 1986 figures not available.
*Dollar figures in thousands. Constant 1975 dollars based on annual average Consumer Price Index, all urban consumers, U.S. Department of Labor, Bureau of Labor Statistics, as of March 2002.
[1]Figures based on current dollars.

Northeastern foundations experienced the second highest gain in actual dollars—a $9.7 billion rise to $155.8 billion. Grantmakers in the Midwest realized a $9.6 billion increase to $111.1 billion. Finally, assets of Southern foundations grew by $5.6 billion, to $99.5 billion.

Growth of Assets, 1975 to 2000. Similar to findings based on growth in giving by region, the assets of foundations in the West grew far faster than those of any other region since 1975 (Figure 16). In fact, while giving by Western foundations jumped close to elevenfold (976.9 percent), assets climbed just over fourteen and one-half-fold (1,351.7 percent) in inflation-adjusted dollars. (However, this discrepancy can be expected to diminish as foundation payout catches up with increased asset values.)

A substantial share of the asset growth in the West over the last quarter century came from bequests received in the late 1970s or early 1980s, such as the endowment of the J. Paul Getty Trust in California. In 1996, California experienced a major burst of new growth coming from two principal sources, one established and one new. First, the Packard Foundation received its principal endowment from its founder in two bequests valued at $5.7 billion. Second, the California Endowment, a "new health" foundation, was formed with an initial endowment of $1.3 billion. Finally, in the late 1990s, the Bill & Melinda Gates Foundation (established in 1994 as the William H. Gates Foundation) began receiving several multi-billion-dollar gifts from Bill and Melinda Gates. The foundation held assets totaling $21.1 billion in 2000.

A close to six-fold (487.0 percent) increase in the real value of assets of foundations based in the South also surpassed the national average (404.0 percent) during the period 1975 to 2000. Foundation growth in this region accelerated in the mid-1980s along with regional economic growth and continued into the 1990s. Several established foundations received important additions to endowments (e.g., Burroughs Wellcome Fund and Walton Family Foundation), large new foundations were formed (e.g., Freedom Forum and Goizeuta Foundation), a few leading foundations relocated to the South (e.g., Arthur S. DeMoss Foundation and John S. and James L. Knight Foundation), and corporate foundation activity increased. As of 2000, the South claimed eight of the nation's 47 "billion-dollar" foundations, led by the Georgia-based Robert W. Woodruff Foundation.

FIGURE 16. Growth of Foundation Assets by Region, 1975 to 2000*

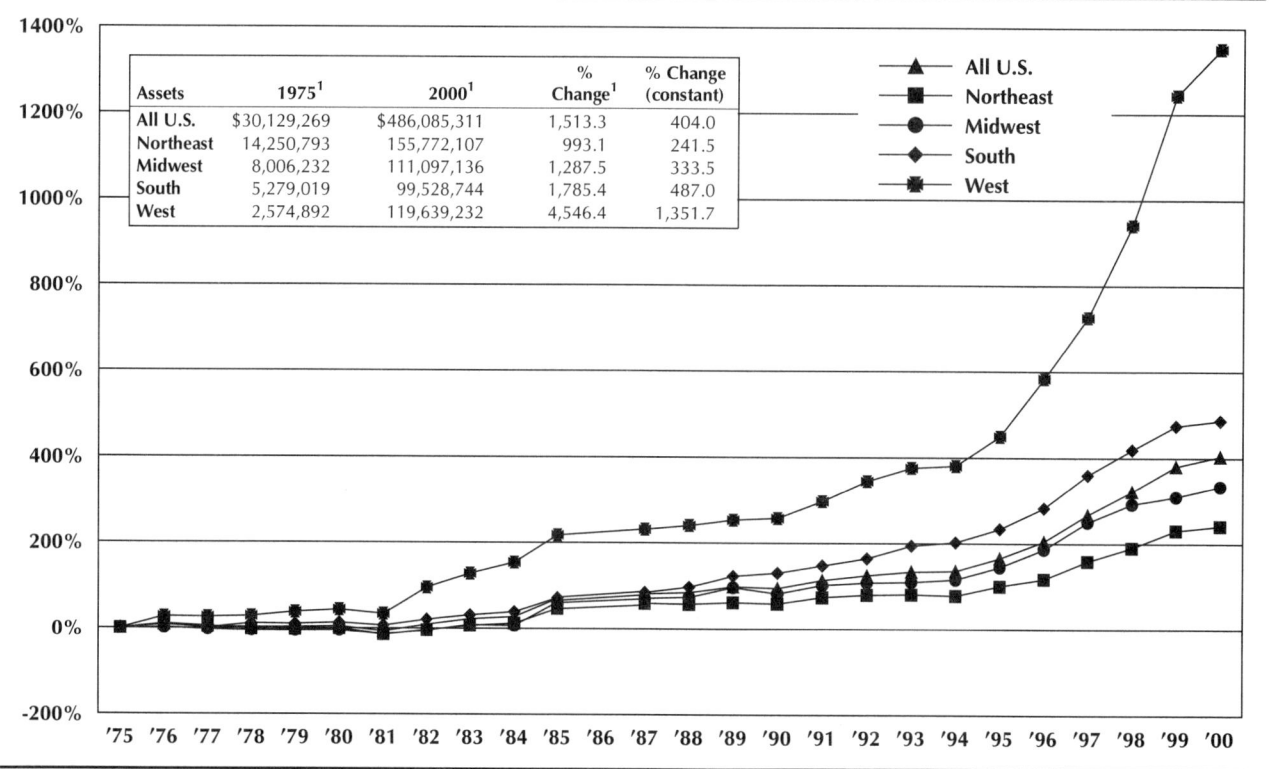

Assets	1975[1]	2000[1]	% Change[1]	% Change (constant)
All U.S.	$30,129,269	$486,085,311	1,513.3	404.0
Northeast	14,250,793	155,772,107	993.1	241.5
Midwest	8,006,232	111,097,136	1,287.5	333.5
South	5,279,019	99,528,744	1,785.4	487.0
West	2,574,892	119,639,232	4,546.4	1,351.7

Source: *Foundation Yearbook*, 2002. Dates approximate; reporting years varied. 1986 figures not available.
*Dollar figures in thousands. Constant 1975 dollars based on annual average Consumer Price Index, all urban consumers, U.S. Department of Labor, Bureau of Labor Statistics, as of March 2002.
[1]Figures based on current dollars.

Finally, adjusted asset growth of grantmakers in the Midwest (333.5 percent) and Northeast (241.5 percent) fell well below the average increase in U.S. foundation assets overall since 1975.

The significant growth of foundation assets in the West has led to pronounced changes in the distribution of foundation resources by region. In 1999, for example, the West surpassed the South and the Midwest in share of all foundation assets for the first time. Overall, between 1975 and 2000 the West close to tripled its share of foundation assets from 8.6 percent to 22.9 percent (Figure 17). As an additional $2 billion gift to the Bill & Melinda Gates Foundation, William Hewlett's more than $3 billion bequest to the William and Flora Hewlett Foundation, and the $5 billion pledge from Gordon Moore to the Gordon E. and Betty I. Moore Foundation (CA) are accounted for, the West will likely further increase its share of foundation assets.

Following the West, the Southern region increased its share of all foundation assets from less than one-sixth (17.6 percent) to nearly one-fourth (24.6 percent). In contrast, the Midwest slipped from just over one-quarter (26.5 percent) to well under one-quarter (22.9 percent) of all U.S. foundation assets, while the Northeast region dropped from close to half (47.3 percent) to under one-third (32.0 percent).

Nonetheless, all regions benefited from strong growth in foundation assets since the mid-1970s, and grantmakers in the Northeast continued to control by far the largest share of foundation resources.

State-Level Trends, 1975 to 2000

The preceding analysis examined variations in the growth of foundation number, giving, and assets for the four major regions of the U.S. Among individual states, most realized strong growth in the latest year. Still, there have been notable variations in the growth and distribution of foundation resources at the state level.

Giving by State

- **Washington State experiences most rapid growth in giving in 2000**

- **New York and California lead in actual grant dollar gains**

Growth of Giving. Nationally, foundation giving grew by 18.2 percent between 1999 and 2000. At the state level, 21 states and the District of Columbia reported faster than average growth in giving. Washington State showed by far the fastest increase, a roughly two-thirds (66.4 percent) gain in grant dollars, from $803.2 million to $1.3 billion (Figure 18). Continued growth in giving by the Gates Foundation accounted for most of this increase, with an 81.1 percent jump in giving to $994.0 million. New Jersey followed with a more than two-fifths (42.0 percent) increase in giving by foundations in the state. The start of giving by the Bristol-Myers Squibb Patient Assistance Foundation and increased grantmaking by the Searle Patients in Need Foundation and the Robert Wood Johnson Foundation—the state's largest funder—provided for three-fifths of the increase.

In contrast to those states showing above-average gains in giving, foundations in five states registered decreases in giving in 2000: Idaho, with giving dropping 17.5 percent to $58.3 million; South Dakota, with giving off 14.9 percent to $17.5 million; Virginia, with giving down by 13.9 percent to $367.0 million; Iowa, with giving slipping by 2.4 percent to $150.3 million; and Arkansas, with giving off just 0.9 percent to $178.7 million. A reduction in giving by the J.A. & Kathryn Albertson Foundation accounted for most of the change in funding by Idaho grantmakers. In 2000, the foundation paid grants totaling $34.9 million, down

FIGURE 17. Foundation Assets by Region, 1975 and 2000*

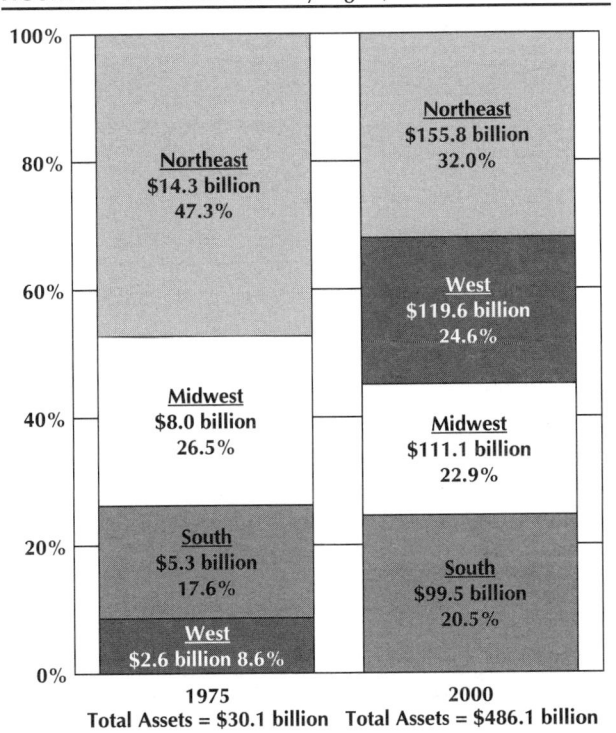

Region	1975	2000
Northeast	$14.3 billion (47.3%)	$155.8 billion (32.0%)
Midwest	$8.0 billion (26.5%)	$111.1 billion (22.9%)
South	$5.3 billion (17.6%)	$99.5 billion (20.5%)
West	$2.6 billion (8.6%)	$119.6 billion (24.6%)
Total Assets	**$30.1 billion**	**$486.1 billion**

Source: *Foundation Yearbook*, 2002.
*Figures based on unadjusted dollars. Excludes assets of foundations based in the Caribbean and South Pacific, which accounted for 0.0 percent of total foundation assets in 1975 and 2000.

from $44.1 million in 1999. Over the same period, the foundation's assets declined from $664.2 million to $497.2 million.

Growth of Actual Grant Dollars. As noted earlier in the analysis by regions, states with larger or more established foundation communities may not show as rapid growth in foundation resources. Yet these states may exceed faster growing states in terms of the increase in actual grant dollars. Thus, while Washington State reported the fastest *rate* of growth in foundation giving between 1999 and 2000, rankings differed considerably based on actual dollar gains. The states showing the largest rise in actual grant dollars in the latest year were: New York ($748.2 million), California ($654.5 million), Washington State ($533.3 million), New Jersey ($383.1 million), and Texas ($221.4 million). In all, 11 states reported increased giving of at least $100 million.

Giving: Average, Per Capita, and as a Share of GSP. Average giving by all 56,582 active U.S. foundations equaled $487,137 in 2000. Only 13 states reported higher levels of average foundation giving. Washington State ($1,382,096) realized the highest average foundation giving in the latest year, followed by Indiana ($916,276) and Arkansas ($808,792). Still, the overall number of foundations in each of these states tended to be small, and a single or small number of relatively large foundations accounted for the vast majority of giving. By comparison, New York, which is home to more than 7,800 foundations, albeit nine of the 50 largest foundations by total giving, showed lower average giving of $670,782.

Other interesting comparisons of giving across states take into account such relative measurements as state population and Gross State Product (GSP). Rankings of giving based on these criteria show that, while New York foundations ranked first by overall giving and by giving as a percentage of GSP, they ranked second based on giving per capita (Table 17). Funders in the District of Columbia ranked first based on giving per capita, probably because of the small size of the population relative to other metropolitan areas and also due to the presence of a few large national and international funders.

Distribution of Giving by State, 1975 and 2000. Varying patterns of foundation development across the U.S. have resulted in dramatic changes in the regional and state-level distribution of foundation resources. For example, while New York ranked first by foundation giving in both 1975 and 2000, Figure 19 shows that its share of all grant dollars declined from roughly one-in-three (32.1 percent) to just under one-in-five (19.0 percent). In contrast, California increased its share of all U.S. foundation grant dollars during this period from roughly one-in-seventeen (5.8 percent) to one-in-eight (12.5 percent). Still, just five states accounted for close to half (46.5 percent) of all foundation giving in 2000, although this share was down from the close to three-fifths (57.5 percent) of giving reported in 1975.

An examination of the ten largest states by foundation giving in 2000 showed that, with the exception of Washington State, all ranked among the top ten in 1975 (Table 18). Moreover, grantmakers in just those ten

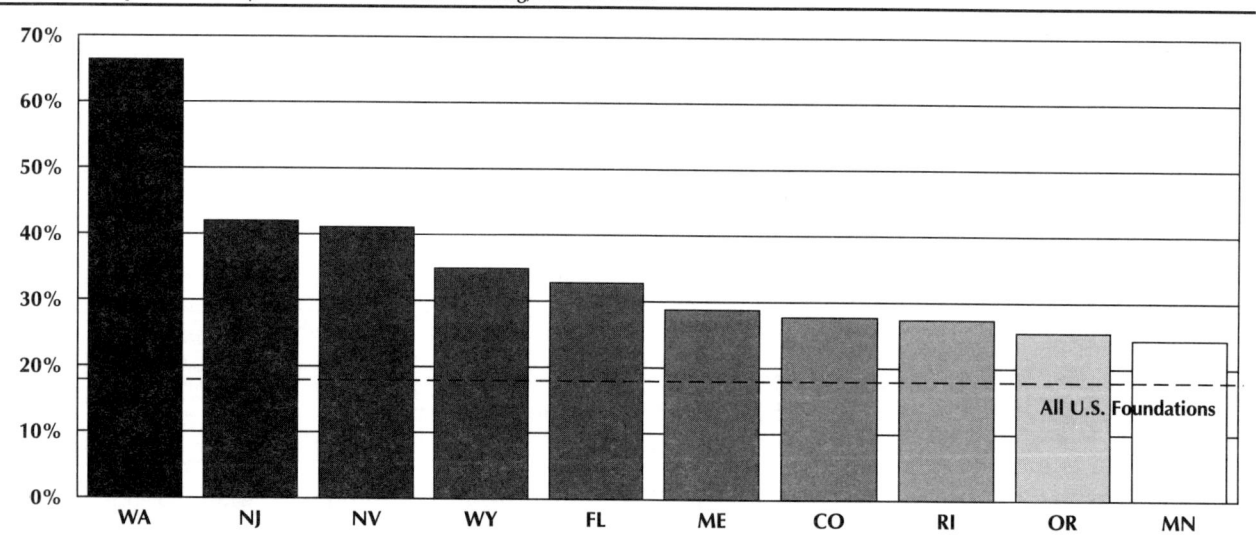

FIGURE 18. Top Ten States by Growth of Foundation Giving, 1999 to 2000*

Source: *Foundation Yearbook,* 2002.
*Percent change based on unadjusted dollars.

TABLE 17. Foundation Giving Per Capita and as a Share of Gross State Product, 2000

Region*	Total Giving[1]	Rank	Giving Per Capita[2]	Rank	Giving as a % of Gross State Product[3]	Rank
NORTHEAST	$ 9,281,578		$172.50		0.461	
New England	1,321,031		94.21		0.244	
Connecticut	386,666	18	112.89	10	0.255	21
Maine	46,617	43	36.23	39	0.137	36
Massachusetts	707,647	12	110.93	11	0.270	19
New Hampshire	47,025	42	37.35	38	0.106	41
Rhode Island	114,688	33	108.31	13	0.352	10
Vermont	18,388	47	29.99	41	0.107	40
Middle Atlantic	7,960,547		200.10		0.542	
New Jersey	1,295,802	7	152.73	6	0.391	6
New York	5,248,198	1	276.06	2	0.696	1
Pennsylvania	1,416,546	3	115.29	9	0.370	9
MIDWEST	6,443,319		99.61		0.312	
East North Central	4,751,148		104.74		0.324	
Illinois	1,302,315	6	104.33	14	0.292	15
Indiana	964,839	9	157.79	5	0.530	3
Michigan	1,201,304	8	120.24	8	0.390	7
Ohio	908,083	10	79.84	21	0.251	22
Wisconsin	374,607	19	69.35	24	0.225	25
West North Central	1,692,172		87.57		0.281	
Iowa	150,347	30	51.43	29	0.176	31
Kansas	109,099	34	40.49	36	0.135	37
Minnesota	666,409	13	134.02	7	0.385	8
Missouri	556,922	16	98.93	17	0.327	12
Nebraska	186,061	26	108.60	12	0.346	11
North Dakota	5,859	51	9.23	51	0.034	50
South Dakota	17,475	48	23.10	44	0.082	43
SOUTH	5,924,1555		59.29		0.205	
South Atlantic	3,518,798		66.69		0.230	
Delaware	156,608	29	196.70	4	0.464	5
District of Columbia	276,488	22	483.52	1	0.511	4
Florida	830,826	11	50.67	32	0.198	27
Georgia	623,045	15	74.31	22	0.246	24
Maryland	495,788	17	92.24	18	0.301	14
North Carolina	666,336	14	81.40	20	0.283	17
South Carolina	73,293	38	18.04	46	0.073	47
Virginia	367,004	20	51.06	31	0.159	34
West Virginia	29,410	46	16.32	47	0.074	46
East South Central	520,530		30.39		0.119	
Alabama	119,520	31	26.77	42	0.109	39
Kentucky	97,613	37	24.01	43	0.091	42
Mississippi	38,303	45	13.40	49	0.062	49
Tennessee	265,094	43	46.18	34	0.166	32
West South Central	1,884,827		62.77		0.205	
Arkansas	178,743	27	70.06	23	0.290	16
Louisiana	101,220	36	37.60	37	0.078	44
Oklahoma	210,830	25	60.93	27	0.258	20
Texas	1,394,034	4	65.37	25	0.216	26
WEST	5,910,888		91.68		0.276	
Mountain	892,208		47.84		0.169	
Arizona	102,653	35	19.34	45	0.077	45
Colorado	277,802	21	62.88	26	0.196	28
Idaho	58,342	41	44.16	35	0.189	29
Montana	13,918	49	15.39	48	0.070	48
Nevada	216,081	24	102.60	15	0.309	13
New Mexico	65,046	39	35.56	40	0.127	38
Utah	114,754	32	50.56	33	0.183	30
Wyoming	43,610	44	88.20	19	0.250	23
Pacific	5,018,680		109.53		0.311	
Alaska	6,973	50	10.98	50	0.026	51
California	3,432,247	2	99.48	16	0.279	18
Hawaii	64,801	40	52.92	28	0.158	35
Oregon	178,172	28	51.30	30	0.162	33
Washington	1,336,487	5	223.20	3	0.639	2
TOTAL[4]	**$27,563,166**		**$ 97.44**		**0.303**	

Source: *Foundation Yearbook*, 2002.
*Geographic regions as defined by the U.S. Bureau of the Census.
[1]Giving figures in thousands.
[2]Per capita giving figures in actual dollar amounts. Based on July 1, 2001 population estimates (U.S. Census Bureau).
[3]Based on 1999 Gross State Product figures (U.S. Department of Commerce, Bureau of Economic Analysis, Regional Economic Analysis Division, June 2001).
[4]Includes giving by nine foundations based in the Caribbean and South Pacific.

states provided over two-thirds (67.1 percent) of grant dollars awarded by U.S. foundations overall.

Assets by State

- Alaska ranks first by growth in assets in 2000
- New York tops all states in actual dollar gain

Similar to the analysis of changes in foundation giving by state, most states showed growth in the value of their foundations' endowments over the past year. Still, considerable variation occurred among the states realizing the strongest growth in giving and assets.

Growth of Assets. Across the U.S., foundation assets grew by 8.4 percent between 1999 and 2000. At the state level, 23 states surpassed this average growth in endowment values. Alaska led with a close to nine-tenths (86.8 percent) jump in foundation resources, due largely to the receipt of a $39.0 million gift by the Rasmuson Foundation (Figure 20). Based in Anchorage, the foundation's assets climbed to $46.3 million in 2000, making it the state's largest foundation.

Indiana reported the second fastest growth in foundation assets in 2000, with a 48.2 percent increase in endowment values. The Lilly Endowment accounted for three-quarters of this rise, after its assets increased by $5.2 billion as a result of gains in the value of Eli Lilly & Co. stock, the foundation's principal holding. Overall, eight states reported assets gains of at least one-fifth in 2000, compared to 16 states in 1999.

In the latest year, six states registered decreased foundation assets—up from three the year before. South Dakota's foundation assets experienced a 21.8 percent decline, from $415.6 million to $325.1 million, following the relocation of the Waitt Family Foundation to California. Idaho foundations' assets decreased by 14.2 percent to $965.4 million as a result of a drop

FIGURE 19. Distribution of Foundation Giving by State, 1975 and 2000

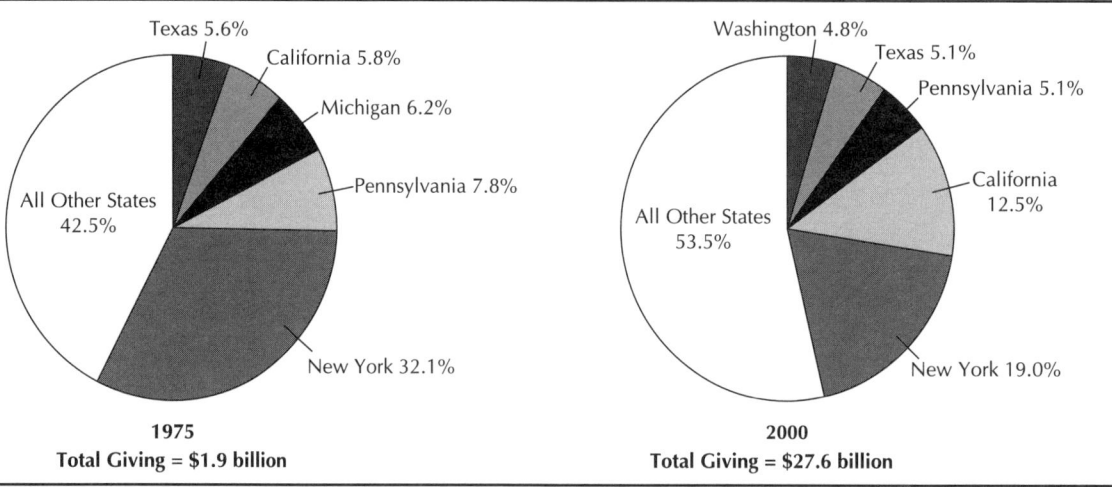

1975 — Total Giving = $1.9 billion
- Texas 5.6%
- California 5.8%
- Michigan 6.2%
- Pennsylvania 7.8%
- New York 32.1%
- All Other States 42.5%

2000 — Total Giving = $27.6 billion
- Washington 4.8%
- Texas 5.1%
- Pennsylvania 5.1%
- California 12.5%
- New York 19.0%
- All Other States 53.5%

Source: *Foundation Yearbook*, 2002.

TABLE 18. Top Ten States by Total Giving Reported, 2000*

State	No. of Foundations	%	Total Giving[1]	%	Average Giving Per Foundation	Rank 1975
1. New York	7,824	13.8	$ 5,248,198	19.0	$ 671	1
2. California	4,948	8.7	3,432,247	12.5	694	4
3. Pennsylvania	3,134	5.5	1,416,546	5.1	452	2
4. Texas	2,969	5.2	1,394,034	5.1	470	5
5. Washington	967	1.7	1,336,487	4.8	1,382	—
6. Illinois	3,343	5.9	1,302,315	4.7	390	6
7. New Jersey	1,920	3.4	1,295,802	4.7	675	9
8. Michigan	1,741	3.1	1,201,304	4.4	690	3
9. Indiana	1,053	1.9	964,839	3.5	916	8
10. Ohio	2,783	4.9	908,083	3.3	326	7
Subtotal	30,682	54.1	$18,499,855	67.1	$ 603	
All other states	25,900	45.9	$9,063,311	32.9	$ 350	
Total	56,582	100.0	$27,563,166	100.0	$ 487	

Source: *Foundation Yearbook*, 2002.

*Dollars in thousands; due to rounding, figures may not add up. Total Giving equals total dollars paid out by foundations in each state and not dollars received by organizations in these states.

[1] Includes grants, scholarships, and employee matching gifts; excludes set-asides, loans, PRIs, and program expenses.

in the J.A. & Kathryn Albertson Foundation's assets. Other states showing decreases in their asset values in 2000 included Maine (down 4.4 percent), Maryland (down 3.0 percent), Pennsylvania (down 1.9 percent), and Illinois (down 1.1 percent).

Growth of Actual Asset Dollars. While states with relatively smaller foundation communities generally dominated based on percentage growth in assets in the latest year, all of the top five states by growth in actual asset values also ranked among the top ten states by foundation assets overall. New York led with a total of $8.2 billion added to the value of its foundations' endowments between 1999 and 2000. Indiana followed with $6.9 billion in additional dollars. Washington State, which jumped from sixth to third place by total assets, gained $6.6 billion in asset value. California ($4.1 billion) and Florida ($1.6 billion) rounded out the top group. In all, six states reported at least $1 billion in additional foundation assets in the latest year, down from 14 in 1999.

Distribution of Assets by State, 1975 and 2000. The more rapid rate of foundation growth outside of the more established Northeast and Midwest regions has resulted in pronounced shifts in foundation resources by state. Figure 21 shows that, while New York ranked first by assets in both 1975 and 2000, its share of all asset dollars dropped from more than three-tenths (31.3 percent) to less than one-fifth (18.5 percent). Conversely, California's share of all U.S. foundation assets close to tripled from one-eighteenth (5.5 percent) to roughly one-seventh (14.4 percent). Still, as was the case with giving, nearly half of foundation assets (49.4 percent) were concentrated in just five states, although this share was down from nearly three-fifths (58.3 percent) in 1975.

FIGURE 20. Top Ten States by Growth of Foundation Assets, 1999 to 2000*

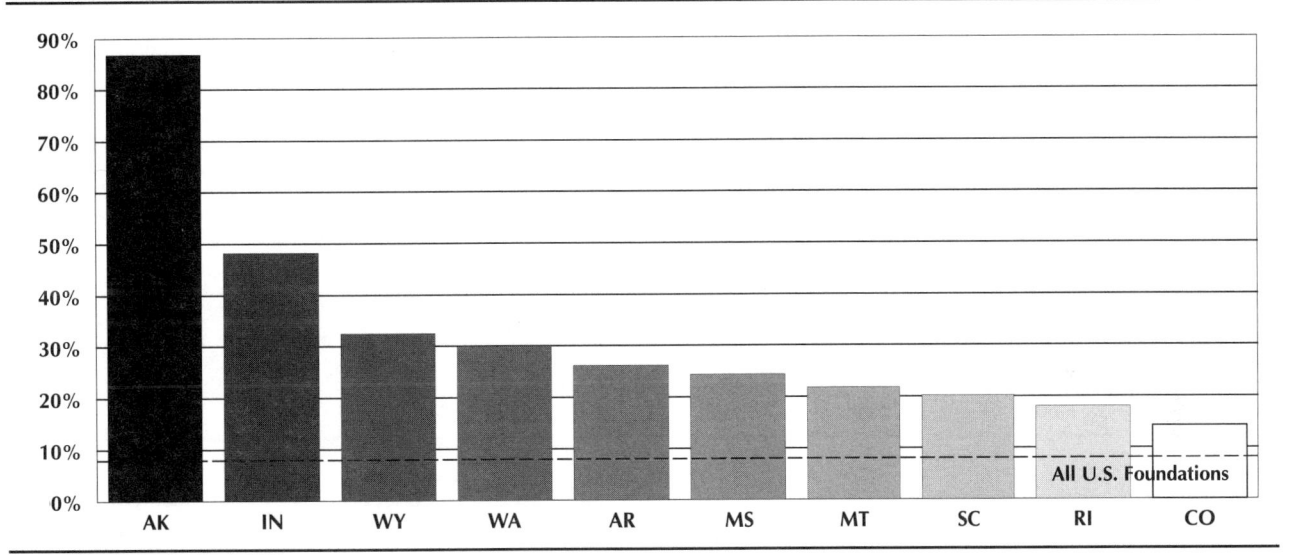

Source: *Foundation Yearbook*, 2002.
*Percent change based on unadjusted dollars.

FIGURE 21. Distribution of Foundation Assets by State, 1975 and 2000

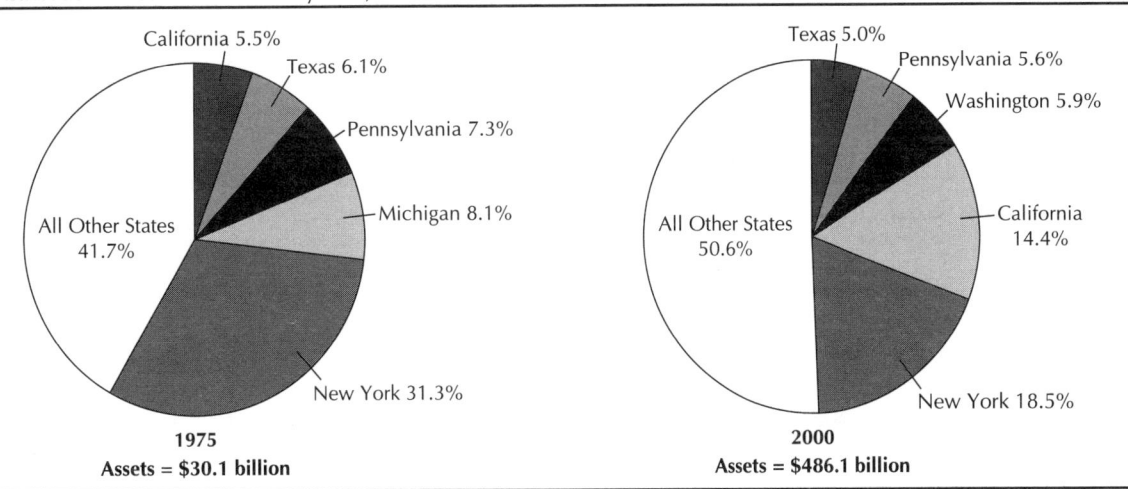

1975
Assets = $30.1 billion

- California 5.5%
- Texas 6.1%
- Pennsylvania 7.3%
- Michigan 8.1%
- New York 31.3%
- All Other States 41.7%

2000
Assets = $486.1 billion

- Texas 5.0%
- Pennsylvania 5.6%
- Washington 5.9%
- California 14.4%
- New York 18.5%
- All Other States 50.6%

Source: *Foundation Yearbook*, 2002.

Regional and State-Level Distribution by Foundation Type, 2000

Just as overall foundation resources are differentially concentrated across the four major regions of the U.S., foundation communities in these regions showed marked variations in the distribution of number and resources by foundation type. The following analysis provides a brief overview of the resources of independent foundations by region, followed by more detailed regional examinations of the resources of corporate and community foundations.

Independent Foundations

- **Independent foundations in the West and Northeast account for largest share of giving by region in 2000**

Across regions, independent foundations represented by far the largest share of the U.S. foundation community. These funders, which include family and new health foundations, accounted for roughly nine out of ten foundations in each of the four major regions in 2000 (Table 19). Still, their share of grant dollars ranged from about seven-in-ten to more than eight-in-ten, with independents in the West (83.0 percent) and the Northeast (78.7 percent) regions reporting the largest shares of giving (Figure 22). By assets, independent grantmakers in the Northeast held about nine-tenths (89.7 percent) of assets in the region, followed by independents in the South (84.0 percent), Midwest (82.8 percent), and West (78.1 percent).

Corporate Foundations

- **Midwest holds largest number of corporate foundations in 2000**
- **Corporate foundations in Midwest account for largest share of giving by region**
- **New York leads in number of corporate foundations by state**

More corporate foundations are located in the Midwest than in any other region. In 2000, close to two-fifths (38.5 percent) of the 2,018 active U.S. business-sponsored foundations were based in the twelve-state region (Table 20). These funders also accounted for a

TABLE 19. 2000 Fiscal Data by Region and Foundation Type (Dollars in thousands)*

NORTHEAST

Foundation Type	Number of Foundations	%	Assets	%	Gifts Received	%	Qualifying Distributions[1]	%	Total Giving[2]	%
Independent	16,376	90.7	$139,695,316	89.7	$4,858,436	67.4	$ 7,922,864	78.3	$7,305,661	78.7
Corporate	552	3.1	5,453,559	3.5	1,040,216	14.4	1,013,585	10.0	986,690	10.6
Community	79	0.4	6,449,308	4.1	527,335	7.3	404,461	4.0	399,335	4.3
Operating	1045	5.8	4,173,923	2.7	782,288	10.9	777,135	7.7	589,892	6.4
Total	18,052	100.0	$155,772,107	100.0	$7,208,274	100.0	$10,118,045	100.0	$9,281,578	100.0

MIDWEST

Foundation Type	Number of Foundations	%	Assets	%	Gifts Received	%	Qualifying Distributions[1]	%	Total Giving[2]	%
Independent	13,029	88.0	$ 91,991,844	82.8	$2,696,874	54.8	$4,936,646	71.9	$4,647,375	72.1
Corporate	777	5.2	5,173,776	4.7	914,416	18.6	1,021,479	14.9	999,474	15.5
Community	270	1.8	11,457,573	10.3	1,045,463	21.3	679,721	9.9	662,660	10.3
Operating	735	5.0	2,473,943	2.2	262,537	5.3	227,242	3.3	133,810	2.1
Total	14,811	100.0	$111,097,136	100.0	$4,919,290	100.0	$6,865,087	100.0	$6,443,319	100.0

SOUTH

Foundation Type	Number of Foundations	%	Assets	%	Gifts Received	%	Qualifying Distributions[1]	%	Total Giving[2]	%
Independent	12,799	89.6	$83,647,049	84.0	$2,873,082	57.5	$4,752,499	72.2	$4,483,963	75.7
Corporate	435	3.0	3,505,094	3.5	577,366	11.6	822,620	12.5	732,320	12.4
Community	125	0.9	6,227,712	6.3	1,184,579	23.7	513,346	7.8	509,552	8.6
Operating	930	6.5	6,148,889	6.2	363,125	7.3	497,629	7.6	198,319	3.3
Total	14,289	100.0	$99,528,744	100.0	$4,998,153	100.0	$6,586,094	100.0	$5,924,155	100.0

WEST

Foundation Type	Number of Foundations	%	Assets	%	Gifts Received	%	Qualifying Distributions[1]	%	Total Giving[2]	%
Independent	8,322	88.3	$ 93,391,937	78.1	$ 8,721,707	83.2	$5,240,062	75.7	$4,908,044	83.0
Corporate	254	2.7	1,766,660	1.5	370,210	3.5	272,489	3.9	266,161	4.5
Community	85	0.9	6,304,348	5.3	1,068,520	10.2	606,045	8.8	592,775	10.0
Operating	760	8.1	18,176,286	15.2	319,525	3.0	806,506	11.6	143,908	2.4
Total	9,421	100.0	$119,639,232	100.0	$10,479,963	100.0	$6,925,102	100.0	$5,910,888	100.0

Source: *Foundation Yearbook*, 2002.

*Due to rounding, figures may not add up. Geographic regions as defined by U.S. Bureau of the Census. Table excludes seven foundations based in the Caribbean and two based in the South Pacific.

[1] Qualifying distributions is the amount used in calculating the required 5 percent payout for private foundations; includes total giving, as well as reasonable administrative expenses, set-asides, PRIs, operating program expenses, and the amount paid to acquire assets used directly for charitable purposes.

[2] Includes grants, scholarships, and employee matching gifts; excludes set-asides, loans, PRIs, and program expenses.

larger share of overall giving within the Midwest region (15.5 percent) than did corporate foundations in the South (12.4 percent), Northeast (10.6 percent), and West (4.5 percent) (Figure 22).

Within the Midwest region, over seven out of ten (70.7 percent) corporate funders were located in the East North Central subregion (IL, IN, MI, OH, and WI) and they provided a nearly equal share (70.8 percent) of corporate giving across the Midwest region. In the Northeast, corporate foundations in the Middle Atlantic subregion (NJ, NY, and PA) accounted for close to seven out of ten (68.5 percent) of Northeastern corporate funders and more than four out of five (82.9 percent) corporate grant dollars. Similarly, corporate foundations in the relatively large South Atlantic subregion (DE, DC, FL, GA, MD, NC, SC, VA, and WV) dominated in the South. In the West, corporate foundations in the Pacific subregion provided a much larger share of support. However, giving by corporate foundations in only one state—California—represented three-fifths (60.1 percent) of all corporate giving across the West.

While the Midwest held the largest number of corporate foundations by region, at the state-level New York led in number of corporate foundations (204). Moreover, these foundations provided close to one-in-six U.S. corporate foundation grant dollars (15.7 percent), more than double the shares accounted for by New Jersey and Michigan, the second- and third-ranked states by giving. Following these states by share of all corporate foundation giving were Texas (6.7 percent) and Illinois (6.4 percent).

Finally, several states that did not rank near the top in terms of their share of all U.S. corporate foundation resources nonetheless counted on these funders for a relatively large share of their state's foundation support. The top five states based on corporate foundation giving as a share of all 2000 foundation giving in the state included Arkansas (35.7 percent), Alaska (32.9 percent), North Carolina (25.9 percent), Minnesota (21.3 percent), and Ohio (19.6 percent).

Community Foundations

- **Close to half of U.S. community foundations based in Midwest in 2000**

- **Community foundations in Midwest and West provide largest shares of giving by region**

- **California ranks first by share of all U.S. community foundation giving**

Community foundations are far more concentrated in the Midwest than in the other major regions. Close to half (48.2 percent) of the 560 grantmaking U.S. community foundations were based in the 12-state region (Table 20). In addition, Figure 22 shows that Midwestern community funds accounted for a larger share of overall giving within their region (10.3 percent). Still, community foundations in the West provided 10.0 percent of giving in that region, nearly matching the Midwest's share. By comparison, community foundations in the South awarded 8.6 percent of grant dollars, while Northeastern community foundations accounted for a much more modest 4.3 percent of giving.

Almost four-fifths (79.6 percent) of Midwestern community foundations were located in the East North Central subregion (IL, IN, MI, OH, and WI) in 2000, and they provided close to two-thirds (65.6 percent) of the region's community foundation giving. In the Northeast, community foundations in the Middle Atlantic subregion (NJ, NY, and PA) accounted for close to three-fifths (57.0 percent) of the number of funds in the region and a similar share (59.1 percent) of Northeast community foundation giving. Led by the New York Community Trust—the nation's largest community foundation—New York community foundations alone provided over two-fifths (43.5 percent)

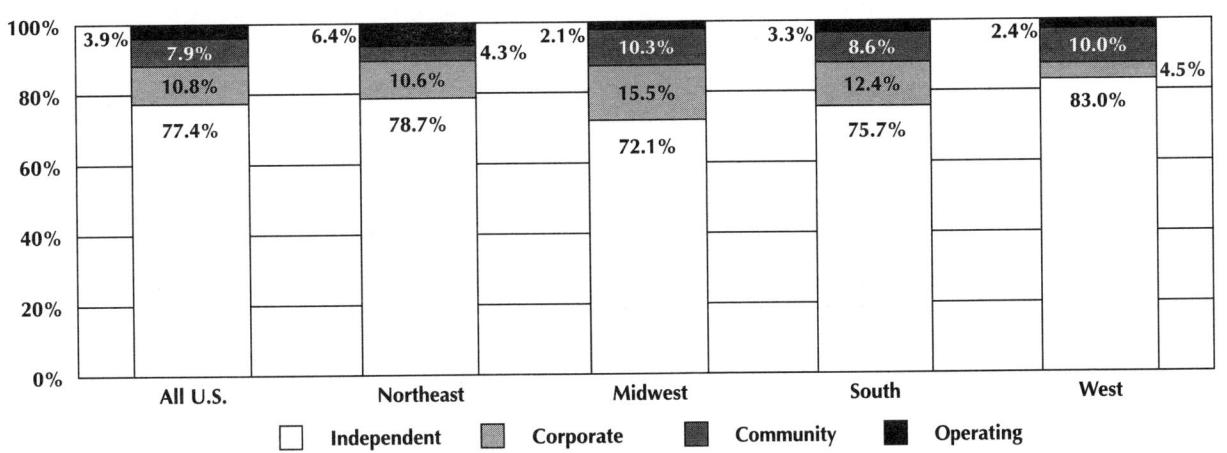

FIGURE 22. Distribution of Foundation Giving by Type and Region, 2000*

Region	Independent	Corporate	Community	Operating
All U.S.	77.4%	10.8%	7.9%	3.9%
Northeast	78.7%	10.6%	6.4%	4.3%
Midwest	72.1%	15.5%	10.3%	2.1%
South	75.7%	12.4%	8.6%	3.3%
West	83.0%	4.5%	10.0%	2.4%

Source: *Foundation Yearbook*, 2002.
*Due to rounding, percentages may not total 100.

TABLE 20. 2000 Fiscal Data of Corporate and Community Grantmaking Foundations by Region and State (Dollars in thousands)*

Region[1]	Corporate Foundations						Community Foundations					
	No.	%	Assets	%	Total Giving[2]	%	No.	%	Assets	%	Total Giving[2]	%
NORTHEAST	552	27.4	$ 5,453,559	34.3	$ 986,690	33.1	79	14.1	$ 6,449,308	21.2	$ 399,335	18.4
New England	174	8.6	1,166,271	7.3	169,095	5.7	34	6.1	2,784,753	9.1	163,425	7.5
Connecticut	43	2.1	271,654	1.7	71,078	2.4	16	2.9	1,055,051	3.5	46,808	2.2
Maine	12	0.6	16,230	0.1	4,572	0.2	1	0.2	95,872	0.3	6,789	0.3
Massachusetts	84	4.2	799,731	5.0	79,940	2.7	13	2.3	937,513	3.1	68,520	3.2
New Hampshire	12	0.6	16,465	0.1	969	0.0	2	0.4	237,742	0.8	12,679	0.6
Rhode Island	19	0.9	53,532	0.3	11,034	0.4	1	0.2	391,199	1.3	22,330	1.0
Vermont	4	0.2	8,660	0.1	1,504	0.1	1	0.2	67,375	0.2	6,300	0.3
Middle Atlantic	378	18.7	4,287,288	27.0	817,595	27.4	45	8.0	3,664,555	12.0	235,910	10.9
New Jersey	61	3.0	751,175	4.7	234,197	7.8	4	0.7	98,548	0.3	7,951	0.4
New York	204	10.1	2,520,494	15.9	468,200	15.7	16	2.9	2,449,485	8.0	173,750	8.0
Pennsylvania	113	5.6	1,015,619	6.4	115,198	3.9	25	4.5	1,116,522	3.7	54,209	2.5
MIDWEST	777	38.5	5,173,776	32.5	999,474	33.5	270	48.2	11,457,573	37.6	662,660	30.6
East North Central	549	27.2	3,844,229	24.2	707,995	23.7	215	38.4	8,548,668	28.1	434,402	20.1
Illinois	151	7.5	955,603	6.0	190,912	6.4	12	2.1	1,417,819	4.7	48,939	2.3
Indiana	55	2.7	306,845	1.9	45,484	1.5	65	11.6	1,036,266	3.4	67,094	3.1
Michigan	73	3.6	1,135,010	7.1	231,517	7.8	59	10.5	1,534,956	5.0	79,365	3.7
Ohio	148	7.3	967,515	6.1	178,064	6.0	58	10.4	3,881,854	12.7	197,762	9.1
Wisconsin	122	6.0	479,256	3.0	62,047	2.1	21	3.8	677,773	2.2	41,242	1.9
West North Central	228	11.3	1,329,547	8.4	291,479	9.8	55	9.8	2,908,904	9.5	228,258	10.5
Iowa	48	2.4	273,928	1.7	21,311	0.7	11	2.0	101,467	0.3	10,212	0.5
Kansas	22	1.1	29,200	0.2	12,404	0.4	7	1.3	70,007	0.2	5,970	0.3
Minnesota	80	4.0	533,829	3.4	141,855	4.8	12	2.1	1,311,188	4.3	61,185	2.8
Missouri	59	2.9	465,609	2.9	96,483	3.2	6	1.1	827,096	2.7	93,671	4.3
Nebraska	16	0.8	22,877	0.1	18,940	0.6	13	2.3	470,443	1.5	49,863	2.3
North Dakota	2	0.1	2,644	0.0	456	0.0	2	0.4	50,191	0.2	2,129	0.1
South Dakota	1	0.0	1,460	0.0	29	0.0	4	0.7	78,512	0.3	5,228	0.2
SOUTH	435	21.6	3,505,094	22.0	732,320	24.5	125	22.3	6,227,712	20.4	509,552	23.5
South Atlantic	278	13.8	1,869,944	11.8	406,768	13.6	74	13.2	3,212,340	10.5	252,170	11.6
Delaware	5	0.2	73,117	0.5	2,162	0.1	1	0.2	111,647	0.4	10,975	0.5
District of Columbia	12	0.6	321,433	2.0	39,620	1.3	1	0.2	153,897	0.5	26,729	1.2
Florida	35	1.7	221,071	1.4	27,330	0.9	17	3.0	591,252	1.9	39,642	1.8
Georgia	40	2.0	474,627	3.0	81,821	2.7	9	1.6	377,976	1.2	34,508	1.6
Maryland	33	1.6	170,077	1.1	27,332	0.9	7	1.3	170,602	0.6	15,258	0.7
North Carolina	74	3.7	308,867	1.9	172,559	5.8	13	2.3	849,514	2.8	70,224	3.2
South Carolina	18	0.9	48,600	0.3	5,969	0.2	5	0.9	228,248	0.7	21,492	1.0
Virginia	52	2.6	246,406	1.5	49,571	1.7	12	2.1	584,680	1.9	28,593	1.3
West Virginia	9	0.4	5,747	0.0	403	0.0	9	1.6	144,524	0.5	4,749	0.2
East South Central	63	3.1	549,319	3.5	49,440	1.7	22	3.9	828,546	2.7	97,536	4.5
Alabama	21	1.0	228,221	1.4	21,733	0.7	7	1.3	154,545	0.5	15,945	0.7
Kentucky	16	0.8	93,711	0.6	10,936	0.4	5	0.9	202,539	0.7	10,378	0.5
Mississippi	5	0.2	14,235	0.1	1,341	0.0	5	0.9	34,416	0.1	3,338	0.2
Tennessee	21	1.0	213,152	1.3	15,429	0.5	5	0.9	437,046	1.4	67,875	3.1
West South Central	94	4.7	1,085,831	6.8	276,112	9.3	29	5.2	2,186,826	7.2	159,846	7.4
Arkansas	8	0.4	8,631	0.1	63,856	2.1	2	0.4	39,614	0.1	3,346	0.2
Louisiana	10	0.5	18,439	0.1	2,366	0.1	3	0.5	357,768	1.2	13,608	0.6
Oklahoma	14	0.7	76,564	0.5	8,533	0.3	3	0.5	432,821	1.4	35,421	1.6
Texas	62	3.1	982,197	6.2	201,357	6.7	21	3.8	1,356,623	4.5	107,471	5.0
WEST	254	12.6	1,766,660	11.1	266,161	8.9	85	15.2	6,304,348	20.7	592,775	27.4
Mountain	74	3.7	175,064	1.1	31,486	1.1	25	4.5	792,019	2.6	63,050	2.9
Arizona	15	0.7	59,427	0.4	5,416	0.2	2	0.4	371,840	1.2	21,774	1.0
Colorado	18	0.9	40,969	0.3	18,888	0.6	11	2.0	232,329	0.8	19,326	0.9
Idaho	4	0.2	20,217	0.1	1,424	0.0	1	0.2	47,823	0.2	1,942	0.1
Montana	5	0.2	17,668	0.1	2,539	0.1	1	0.2	32,460	0.1	574	0.0
Nevada	7	0.3	4,654	0.0	1,290	0.0	4	0.7	15,638	0.1	7,198	0.3
New Mexico	13	0.6	12,068	0.1	758	0.0	3	0.5	48,054	0.2	2,754	0.1
Utah	10	0.5	17,780	0.1	955	0.0	1	0.2	3,296	0.0	129	0.0
Wyoming	2	0.1	2,282	0.0	216	0.0	2	0.4	40,578	0.1	9,352	0.4
Pacific	180	8.9	1,591,596	10.0	234,675	7.9	60	10.7	5,512,329	18.1	529,725	24.5
Alaska	13	0.6	26,914	0.2	2,296	0.1	3	0.5	6,903	0.0	1,353	0.1
California	109	5.4	1,248,930	7.9	160,075	5.4	40	7.1	4,306,836	14.1	424,263	19.6
Hawaii	14	0.7	28,918	0.2	5,513	0.2	1	0.2	237,578	0.8	9,742	0.4
Oregon	19	0.9	209,955	1.3	31,336	1.0	5	0.9	482,454	1.6	36,767	1.7
Washington	25	1.2	76,879	0.5	35,455	1.2	11	2.0	478,557	1.6	57,600	2.7
CARIBBEAN[3]	0	0.0	0	0.0	0	0.0	1	0.2	24,734	0.1	2,021	0.1
Puerto Rico	0	0.0	0	0.0	0	0.0	1	0.2	24,734	0.1	2,021	0.1
Virgin Islands	0	0.0	0	0.0	0	0.0	0	0.0	0	0.0	0	0.0
SOUTH PACIFIC[3]	0	0.0	0	0.0	0	0.0	0	0.0	0	0.0	0	0.0
American Samoa	0	0.0	0	0.0	0	0.0	0	0.0	0	0.0	0	0.0
Total	2,018	100.0	$15,899,090	100.0	$2,984,645	100.0	560	100.0	$30,463,674	100.0	$2,166,343	100.0

Source: *Foundation Yearbook*, 2002.
*Due to rounding, figures may not add up.
[1]Geographic regions are those defined by the U.S. Bureau of Census.
[2]Includes grants, scholarships, and employee matching gifts; excludes set-asides, loans, PRIs, and program expenses.
[3]Private foundations in Puerto Rico, the Virgin Islands and American Samoa are not required to file Form 990-PF. Only a few voluntary reporters are represented.

of all community foundation giving in the Northeast region. The South Atlantic subregion (DE, DC, FL, GA, MD, NC, SC, VA, and WV) held the largest share of community foundations in the South by number (59.2 percent) and giving (49.5 percent). Finally, California, located in the Pacific subregion of the West, alone accounted for close to half (47.1 percent) of the number of Western community foundations and over seven-tenths (71.6 percent) of their giving in the region.

The Midwest held the largest number of community foundations by region and also was home to the three largest states by number of U.S. community foundations: Indiana (65), Michigan (59), and Ohio (58). California ranked fourth by number (40), but first by share of all community foundation giving. Overall, California-based community funds gave almost one-in-five (19.6 percent) U.S. community foundation grant dollars in 2000. Ohio ranked second, accounting for nearly one-in-eleven (9.1 percent) community foundation grant dollars, followed by New York (8.0 percent), Texas (5.0 percent), and Missouri (4.3 percent).

Several states counted on community foundations for a relatively large share of their state's foundation funding, although they did not rank near the top in terms of their share of all U.S. community foundation resources. The top five states based on community foundation giving as a share of all 2000 foundation giving in the state included North Dakota (36.3 percent), Vermont (34.3 percent), South Dakota (29.9 percent), South Carolina (29.3 percent), and New Hampshire (27.0 percent).

New Foundation Creation

The development of new foundations exerts a profound impact on asset growth patterns, and thus on the grantmaking potential of the foundation community. Individuals who establish foundations during their lifetimes may opt to transfer into their foundations only the amount they choose to pay out in grants each year, much as any individual making a private contribution. Alternatively, they may transfer a share of their personal wealth into a permanent endowment for future charitable use, thereby committing the foundation to a more predictable level of spending. In many cases, foundations that begin as the former—also known as "pass-through" foundations—will become fully endowed later in their existence, often as a result of a donor's bequest.

Figure 23 presents the establishment of mid-size and larger foundations by decade and shows that the creation of philanthropies in the West and South lagged behind the Northeast and the Midwest until the 1970s, when foundations in every region experienced a pronounced decline in new creation. Much of this decline can be attributed to more restrictive foundation regulations and to a stagnant economy. New formation rebounded in the 1980s, with 21.6 percent of larger active U.S. foundations created during the decade, and similar shares reported for the Midwest (23.0 percent), South (21.6 percent), West (21.1 percent), and Northeast (21.0 percent).

While information on foundation establishment in the 1990s remains incomplete, close to half (48.2 percent) of larger active Western foundations have been established in this decade, followed by the South (42.1 percent). By comparison, just over two-fifths (40.9 percent) of all U.S. foundations were established in the 1990s, with smaller shares reported for Northeastern (38.5 percent) and Midwestern (37.6 percent) grantmakers. (For a detailed analysis of foundation creation, see Chapter 5.)

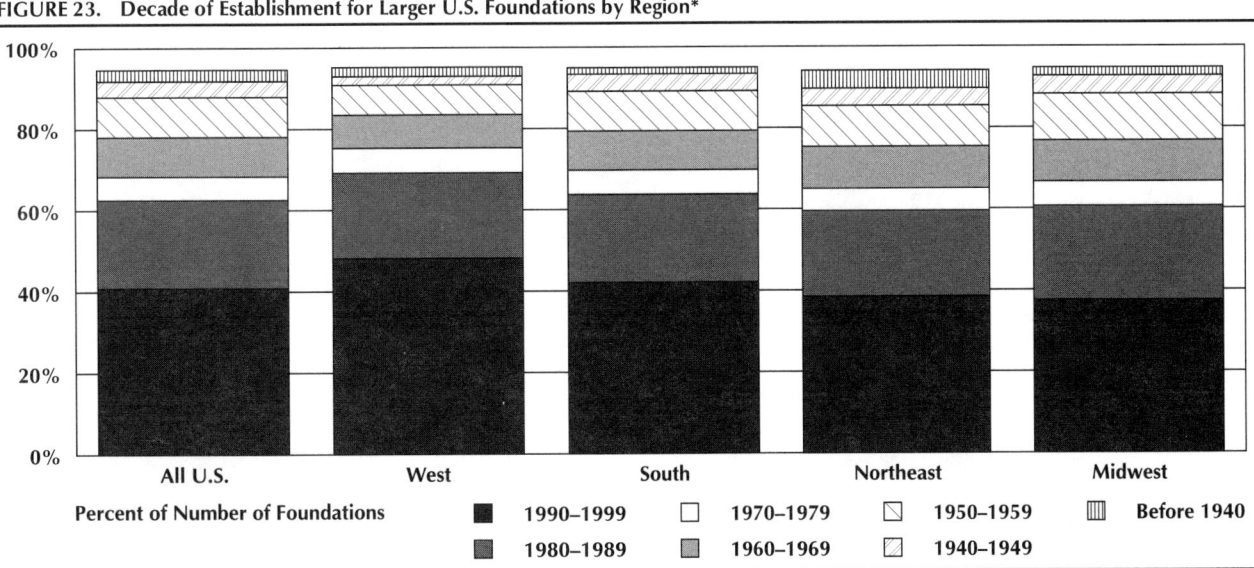

FIGURE 23. Decade of Establishment for Larger U.S. Foundations by Region*

Source: *Foundation Yearbook*, 2002.
Note: Based on Foundation Center survey of 20,964 grantmaking foundations with assets of at least $1 million or making grants of $100,000 or more in 1999–2000. Not represented are 35 active foundations established in 2000, including six in the West, ten in the South, three in the Midwest, and sixteen in the North.
*Establishment data was not available for 1,099 foundations, including 167 in the West, 264 in the South, 397 in the North, and 271 in the Midwest.

CHAPTER 4

Giving and Growth of Independent, Corporate, and Community Foundations

The use of the name foundation can sometimes prove confusing to the public and even to grantmakers themselves. Not only are there important operational and legal distinctions between private foundations and other types of charitable programs, but sharp contrasts exist between different types of private foundations (Figure 24). Foundation type, as much as foundation size, strongly determines patterns of giving and growth.

In general, the Foundation Center defines a private foundation as a nonprofit, nongovernmental organization with a principal endowment of its own that maintains or aids charitable, educational, religious, or other activities serving the public good, primarily by making grants to other nonprofit organizations. Private foundations derive their funds from a single source, such as an individual, a family, or a corporation, and their activities are governed by specific rules and regulations set in the tax code (see Appendix B, "Regulation of Private Foundations").[1]

Some private foundations are organized as operating foundations, which conduct their own research programs or provide a direct service. Although it is not their primary function, some operating foundations occasionally make grants to other nonprofit organizations. In general, however, only a very few maintain grant programs of any size.

Community foundations function in much the same way as private foundations, but because their funds are drawn from many donors, they are usually classified as public charities.

The Center's analysis of trends since 1975 has been primarily concerned with three types of foundations: independent,

corporate, and community. The emergence in the 1990s of several large grantmaking operating foundations prompted the expansion of this analysis to include these foundations, beginning with 1995 data.

Growth in Giving, 2001 and 2000

U.S. foundations increased their giving by an estimated 5.1 percent in 2001, following an 18.2 percent gain in 2000 (Figure 25). Economic recession, continuing stock market declines, and national uncertainty in the wake of the 9/11 terrorist attacks brought an end to five straight years of double-digit growth in foundation giving. Still, the following analysis shows notable variations in the growth of foundation giving by independent, corporate, and community foundations during this period.

Independent Foundations. Total giving by independent foundations, including family foundations and "new health" foundations, rose an estimated 5.4 percent in 2001, following an 18.7 percent actual gain in 2000. This represented the slowest annual growth in independent foundation giving reported since 1994. Overall, independent foundations gave an estimated $22.5 billion in grants in 2001, up $1.2 billion from 2000 and $3.4 billion from 1999. Despite slower growth in the latest year, since 1991 giving by independent foundations has grown nearly two and one-half times (146.2 percent) after inflation (Figure 26).

Independent foundations must pay out each year at least 5 percent of the value of their investments in the preceding year. (Foundations may carry forward payout in excess of 5 percent over several years.) In 2001, estimated giving represented 5.5 percent of

---

1. For a more detailed summary of the differences between various types of foundations and the federal regulations that govern them, see the Foundation Center's *Foundation Fundamentals*; see also *First Steps in Starting a Foundation* (Washington, D.C.: Council on Foundations, 1997).

independent foundation assets at the close of 2000. This share was down slightly from 5.6 in the prior year.[2]

Corporate Foundations. Giving by America's 2,018 corporate foundations grew an estimated 2.6 percent in 2001, falling below 2000's already modest 6.1 percent rise and amounting to one-seventh the record 18.4 percent gain reported for 1998. This lower rate of growth in giving compared to other types of foundations reflects the greater vulnerability of corporate foundations to reduced profits. Balancing out this negative force, however, was the tremendous outpouring of support by corporate foundations in response to the 9/11 attacks.

2. The estimated giving amount includes grants to organizations and individuals. In addition to these grants, charitable loans and other qualifying expenditures also apply toward the 5 percent payout requirement. These disbursements are combined in the figure for "qualifying distributions." For additional background on foundation payout requirements and qualifying distributions, see "Measures of Foundation Support, 2000" in Chapter 2 and "Regulation of Private Foundations" in Appendix B.

Overall, corporate foundations contributed an estimated $3.1 billion in grants in 2001, up $78 million from 2000. Corporate foundation giving represented well over one-quarter of overall 2000 corporate contributions, estimated at $10.9 billion by the AAFRC Trust for Philanthropy. Excluding in-kind contributions, the share of cash gifts from corporate foundations was higher. (For additional details, see "Foundations' Share of Private Philanthropy, 2000" in Chapter 2).

Community Foundations. Giving by community foundations rose an estimated 4.6 percent in 2001, following a 17.1 percent increase in 2000 and a record 26.8 percent jump in 1999. This more modest gain represented the slowest growth in community foundation giving since 1994 and reflected the sensitivity of their tens of thousands of individual donors to changes in the economy. Overall, community foundation giving reached an estimated $2.3 billion in the latest year, up from $2.2 billion in 2000 and $1.8 billion in 1999. Moreover, despite the slowdown, community foundation giving has increased more than three-fold after inflation since 1991.

FIGURE 24. General Characteristics of Four Types of Foundations

Foundation Type	Description	Source of Funds	Decision-Making Activity	Grantmaking Parameters	Reporting
Independent	An independent grantmaking organization established to aid social, educational, religious, or other charitable activities.	Endowment generally derived from a single source such as an individual, a family, or a group of individuals. Contributions to endowment limited as to tax deductibility.	Decisions may be made by donor or members of the donor's family; by an independent board of directors or trustees; or by a bank or trust officer acting on the donor's behalf.	Broad discretionary giving allowed but may have specific guidelines and give only in a few specific fields. About three out of four limit their giving to local area.	Annual information returns (990-PF) filed with IRS must be made available to public. A small percentage issue separately printed annual reports.
Corporate	Legally an independent grantmaking organization with close ties to the corporation providing funds.	Endowment and annual contributions from a profit-making corporation. May maintain small endowment and pay out most of contributions received annually in grants, or may maintain endowment to cover contributions in years when corporate profits are down.	Decisions made by board of directors often composed of corporate officials, but which may include individuals with no corporate affiliation. Decisions may also be made by local company officials.	Giving tends to be in fields related to corporate activities or in communities where corporation operates. Usually give more grants but in smaller dollar amounts than independents with comparable giving.	Same as above.
Operating	An organization that uses its resources to conduct research or provide a direct service.	Endowment usually provided from a single source, but eligible for maximum deductible contributions from public.	Decisions generally made by independent board of directors.	Makes few, if any grants. Grants generally related directly to the foundation's program.	Same as above.
Community	A publicly sponsored organization that makes grants for social, educational, religious, or other charitable purposes in a specific community or region.	Contributions received from many donors. Usually eligible for maximum tax deductible contributions from public.	Decisions made by board of directors representing the diversity of the community.	Grants generally limited to charitable organizations in local community.	Annual information returns (990) filed with the IRS must be made available to public. Many publish full guidelines or annual reports.

Source: *Foundation Yearbook*, 2002.

Growth and Distribution by Foundation Type, 2000

The following analyses examine changes in foundation resources by foundation type—independent, corporate, community, and grantmaking operating—through 2000. They include comparisons by number of foundations (Figure 27 and Table 21), total giving (Figure 28 and Table 22), assets (Figure 29 and Table 23), and gifts received (Figure 30 and Table 24). For a comparison of foundation creation since 1975 by foundation type, see Chapter 5, "Foundation Development."

Independent Foundations

Independent foundations comprise the largest and perhaps most diverse segment of the foundation universe and include family-sponsored and new health foundations. Because most of the top-ranking foundations by assets and giving are independent or family-sponsored, trends described in Chapter 2 relating to large foundations apply equally to independents.

FIGURE 25. Growth of Foundation Giving by Type, 1999 to 2001*

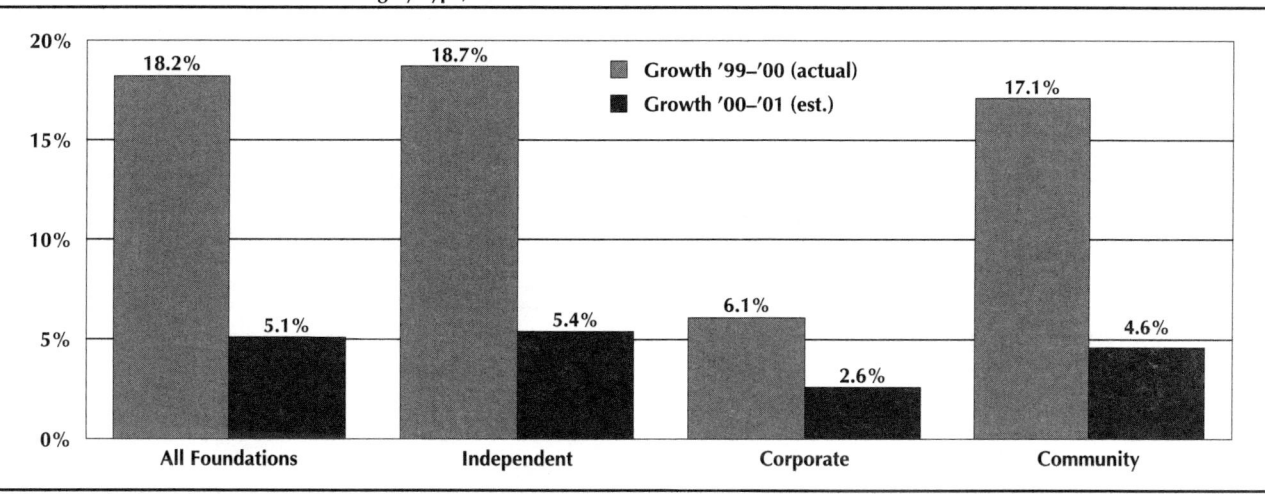

	Growth '99–'00 (actual)	Growth '00–'01 (est.)
All Foundations	18.2%	5.1%
Independent	18.7%	5.4%
Corporate	6.1%	2.6%
Community	17.1%	4.6%

Source: *Foundation Yearbook,* 2002.
*All figures based on unadjusted dollars.

FIGURE 26. Growth of Foundation Giving by Type, 1991 to 2001*

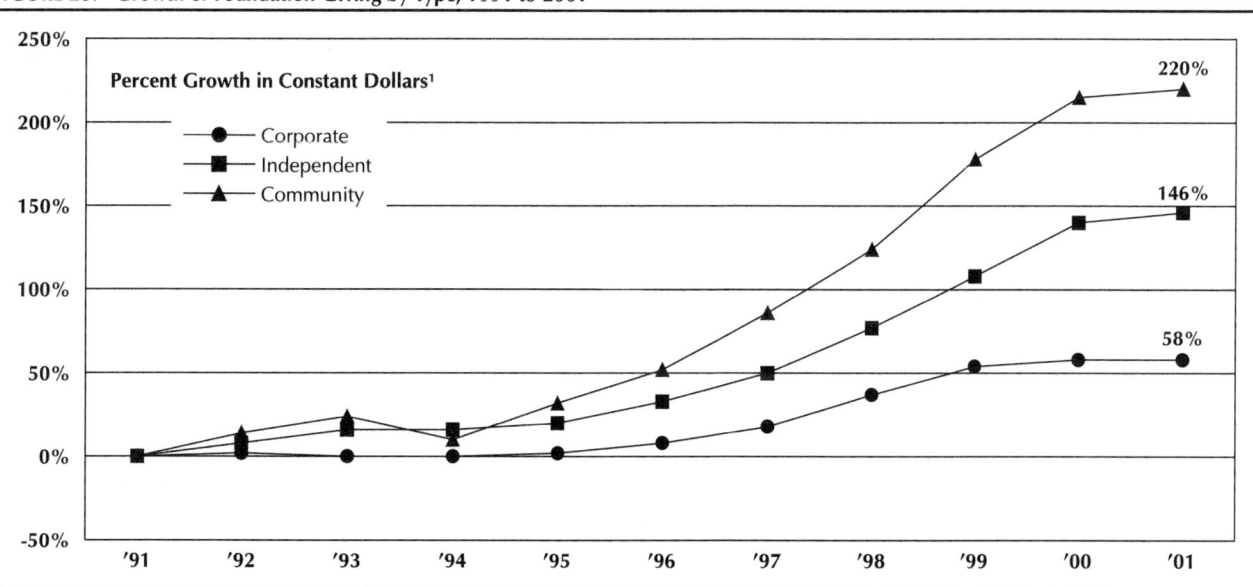

Percent Growth in Constant Dollars[1]

Year	Corporate	Independent	Community
'01	58%	146%	220%

Source: *Foundation Yearbook,* 2002.
*Figures estimated for 2001.
[1] Percent change in constant 1991 dollars based on year average Consumer Price Index, all urban consumers, U.S. Department of Labor, Bureau of Labor Statistics, as of March 2001.

FIGURE 27. 2000 Number of Foundations by Foundation Type

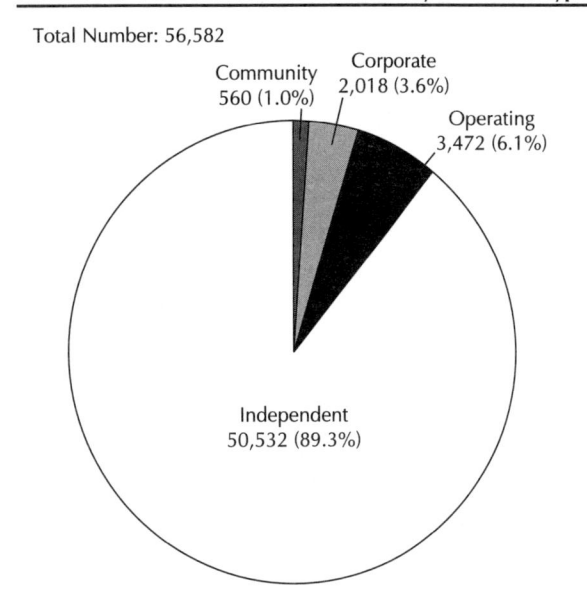

Total Number: 56,582

- Community 560 (1.0%)
- Corporate 2,018 (3.6%)
- Operating 3,472 (6.1%)
- Independent 50,532 (89.3%)

Source: *Foundation Yearbook*, 2002.

FIGURE 28. 2000 Giving by Foundation Type

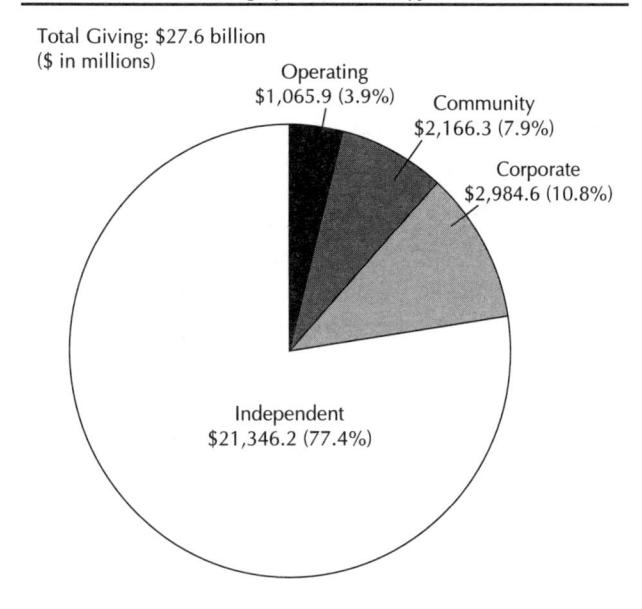

Total Giving: $27.6 billion ($ in millions)

- Operating $1,065.9 (3.9%)
- Community $2,166.3 (7.9%)
- Corporate $2,984.6 (10.8%)
- Independent $21,346.2 (77.4%)

Source: *Foundation Yearbook*, 2002.

TABLE 21. Comparison of 2000 to 1999 Total Number of Foundations

Foundation Type	1999	2000	% change
Independent	44,824	50,532	12.7
Corporate	2,019	2,018	0.0
Community	519	560	7.9
Operating	2,839	3,472	22.3
Total	50,201	56,582	12.7

Source: *Foundation Yearbook*, 2002.

TABLE 22. Comparison of 2000 to 1999 Total Giving*

Foundation Type	1999	2000	% change
Independent	$17,989.4	$21,346.2	18.7
Corporate	2,813.6	2,984.6	6.1
Community	1,849.4	2,166.3	17.1
Operating	669.1	1,065.9	59.2
Total	$23,321.5	$27,563.2	18.2

Source: *Foundation Yearbook*, 2002.
*Dollars in millions; total giving includes all charitable contributions except loans and program expenses. Due to rounding, figures may not add up. Percent change represents current dollars.

2000 Giving

- Giving by independent foundations grows 18.7 percent
- Independent foundations account for more than three-quarters of grant dollars
- Giving increases faster among larger independent foundations

Growth in Number of Independent Foundations. 50,532 independent foundations reported grant activity in 2000, up a record 12.7 percent from the previous year (Figure 27 and Table 21). The actual number of independent foundations grew by 5,708—the largest single-year increase ever recorded. In fact, the overwhelming majority of new foundations formed since the mid-1980s have been family-sponsored or independent, reflecting strong interest in the foundation vehicle among wealthy individuals. Overall, the number of independent foundations has doubled since 1987 (see Table 47 in Chapter 5).

Independent Foundations as a Share of All Grant Dollars. Independent foundations accounted for almost 90 percent of the total number of grantmaking foundations (Figure 27) and were responsible for over 77 percent of the foundation grant dollars awarded in 2000 (Figure 28).

Giving by Large vs. Small Independent Foundations. Of the 50,532 active independent foundations, only 15,442 or roughly 31 percent awarded grants totaling $100,000 or more (Table 25). Yet these foundations distributed $20.4 billion or about 95 percent of the grant dollars paid in 2000 by all independent foundations. Moreover, while giving jumped 18.7 percent among independents, faster growth in giving among the larger independent foundations tended to skew the overall increase. For example, giving by foundations awarding grants totaling $25 million or more grew by 23.0 percent. In contrast, giving by foundations awarding grants totaling less than $100,000 increased by 12.7 percent.

Giving and Growth of Independent, Corporate, and Community Foundations

FIGURE 29. 2000 Assets by Foundation Type

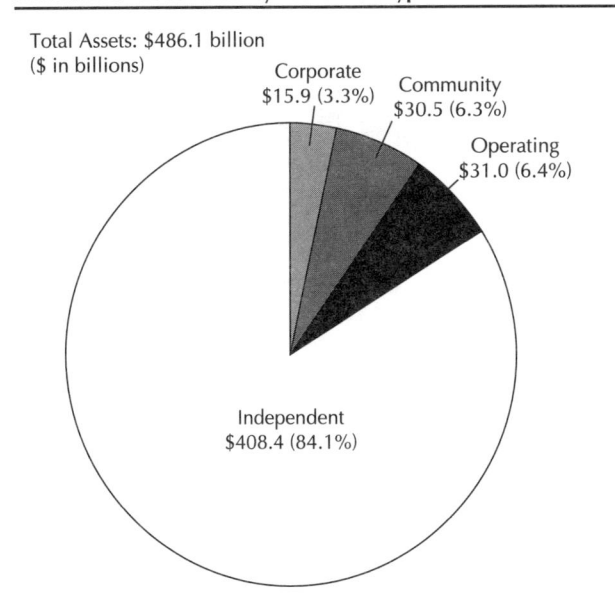

Total Assets: $486.1 billion
($ in billions)
- Corporate $15.9 (3.3%)
- Community $30.5 (6.3%)
- Operating $31.0 (6.4%)
- Independent $408.4 (84.1%)

Source: *Foundation Yearbook*, 2002.

FIGURE 30. 2000 Gifts Received by Foundation Type

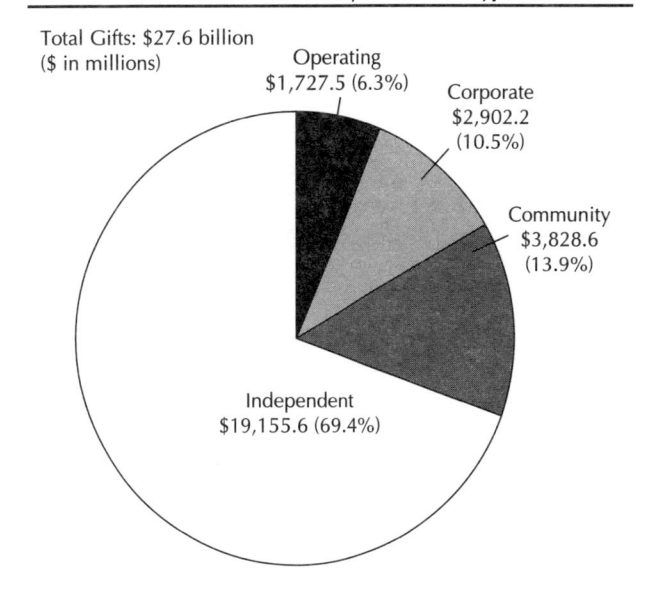

Total Gifts: $27.6 billion
($ in millions)
- Operating $1,727.5 (6.3%)
- Corporate $2,902.2 (10.5%)
- Community $3,828.6 (13.9%)
- Independent $19,155.6 (69.4%)

Source: *Foundation Yearbook*, 2002.

TABLE 23. Comparison of 2000 to 1999 Assets*

Foundation Type	1999	2000	% change
Independent	$381.4	$408.7	7.2
Corporate	15.3	15.9	4.2
Community	27.6	30.5	10.2
Operating	24.3	31.0	27.3
Total	$448.6	$486.1	8.4

Source: *Foundation Yearbook*, 2002.
*Dollars in billions; assets at market value. Due to rounding, figures may not add up. Percent change represents current dollars.

TABLE 24. Comparison of 2000 to 1999 Gifts Received*

Foundation Type	1999	2000	% change
Independent	$24,097.4	$19,155.6	-20.5
Corporate	3,313.2	2,902.2	-12.4
Community	3,295.4	3,828.6	16.2
Operating	1,370.6	1,727.5	26.0
Total	$32,076.7	$27,613.8	-13.9

Source: *Foundation Yearbook*, 2002.
*Dollars in millions; due to rounding, figures may not add up. Percent change represents current dollars.

Established vs. New Independent Foundations' Support. Established funders accounted for most of the increase in giving in 2000. Still, the 6,194 newly-reporting independents provided $533.6 million or 15.9 percent of the $3.4 billion in increased giving reported by independent foundations. Excluding the grants of newly reporting independent foundation, giving by established funders grew 15.7 percent.

Funding by the Top 50 Independent Foundations. Giving by the nation's top 50 independent foundations (Table 26) increased 21.1 percent in 2000, down from 34.5 percent in 1999. Three foundations, the Bill & Melinda Gates Foundation (WA), the David and Lucile Packard Foundation (CA), and the Ford Foundation (NY) were responsible for close to three-fifths of this increase. If these foundations were excluded from the top 50 in both years, giving by the remaining top independents would have increased 11.6 percent. To qualify for ranking among the top 50 independents,

the minimum spending level was $39.2 million, compared to the maximum of $994.9 million distributed by the Gates Foundation. In addition to Gates, five other funders distributed at least $200 million—the Ford, Packard, Robert Wood Johnson (NJ), and A.W.

TABLE 25. Analysis of Independent Foundations by Total Giving Range, 2000*

Total Giving Range	Number of Foundations	%	Total Giving[1]	%
$100 million+	20	0.0	$ 5,377,621	25.2
$25 million–$100 million	63	0.1	2,732,566	12.8
$10 million–$25 million	157	0.3	2,350,825	11.0
$1 million–$10 million	2,322	4.6	6,062,147	28.4
$100,000–$1 million	12,880	25.5	3,839,801	18.0
Under $100,000	35,090	69.4	983,272	4.6
Total	50,532	100.0	$21,346,232	100.0

Source: *Foundation Yearbook*, 2002.
*Dollars in thousands.
[1] Includes grants, scholarships, and employee matching gifts; excludes set-asides, loans, PRIs, and program expenses.

Mellon (NY) foundations and the Lilly Endowment (IN). An additional fourteen funders distributed at least $100 million, one more than the number of funders in this giving range in 1999. Among the top ten funders, the threshold for giving increased to $178.7 million from last year's $161.5 million.

Top 50 Independent Foundations with Increased Funding. Forty of the top 50 independent foundations by giving increased funding in 2000. Among the top ten funders, the Gates Foundation raised its giving by more than four-fifths over 1999, while the Packard and Starr foundations increased their giving by more than one-third. The Gates Foundation's giving jumped from $549.4 million to $994.9 million in 2000. The foundation benefited from an additional gift of $5.1 billion in the latest year, which raised its assets to $21.1 billion. The Gates Foundation's priorities include: improving global health through its programs in children's health, reproductive health, vaccine development, and disease eradication; and funding a variety of organizations in the Pacific Northwest, especially in the areas of learning and human services.

The David and Lucile Packard Foundation increased its giving in 2000 to $533.6 million, from $391.6 million in 1999. The foundation—which funds in the areas of environmental conservation, population,

TABLE 26. 50 Largest Independent Foundations by Total Giving, 2000*

	Foundation	State	Total Giving[1]	Qualifying Distributions[2]	Assets	Fiscal Date
1.	Bill & Melinda Gates Foundation	WA	**$994,900,000**	$994,900,000	$21,149,100,000	12/31/00
2.	Ford Foundation	NY	**652,091,000**	652,091,000	14,659,683,000	9/30/00
3.	Lilly Endowment	IN	**583,890,521**	588,943,280	15,591,737,808	12/31/00
4.	David and Lucile Packard Foundation	CA	**533,589,987**	605,793,134	9,793,212,529	12/31/00
5.	Robert Wood Johnson Foundation	NJ	**351,683,796**	444,128,246	8,793,792,000	12/31/00
6.	Andrew W. Mellon Foundation	NY	**205,870,150**	205,870,150	4,888,237,000	12/31/00
7.	Starr Foundation	NY	**192,502,039**	194,246,442	6,257,848,627	12/31/00
8.	California Endowment	CA	**189,663,220**	211,000,000	3,490,256,407	2/28/01
9.	Pew Charitable Trusts	PA	**187,853,822**	243,841,247	4,800,776,253	12/31/00
10.	W. K. Kellogg Foundation	MI	**178,739,742**	196,651,170	5,719,735,520	8/31/01
11.	John D. and Catherine T. MacArthur Foundation	IL	**164,022,738**	198,205,781	4,479,153,951	12/31/00
12.	Rockefeller Foundation	NY	**163,391,841**	202,375,330	3,619,028,000	12/31/00
13.	Robert W. Woodruff Foundation	GA	**149,979,270**	150,387,356	3,139,654,481	12/31/00
14.	Charles Stewart Mott Foundation	MI	**139,480,791**	154,952,273	2,881,802,805	12/31/00
15.	William and Flora Hewlett Foundation	CA	**135,748,270**	131,802,992	3,930,366,990	12/31/00
16.	Annenberg Foundation	PA	**132,384,109**	132,384,109	2,932,205,767	6/30/01
17.	Kresge Foundation	MI	**107,956,140**	107,956,140	2,770,530,893	12/31/00
18.	Robert R. McCormick Tribune Foundation	IL	**106,830,351**	112,200,000	1,855,000,000	12/31/00
19.	Duke Endowment	NC	**106,030,389**	106,000,000	2,874,017,045	12/31/00
20.	Annie E. Casey Foundation	MD	**101,012,809**	127,380,064	3,001,942,131	12/31/00
21.	McKnight Foundation	MN	**93,954,410**	97,687,834	2,006,436,000	12/31/00
22.	Richard King Mellon Foundation	PA	**91,699,221**	97,898,818	1,907,473,636	12/31/00
23.	Doris Duke Charitable Foundation	NY	**86,310,650**	84,676,886	1,574,746,419	12/31/00
24.	W. M. Keck Foundation	CA	**81,745,562**	81,745,562	1,533,721,000	12/31/00
25.	Harry and Jeanette Weinberg Foundation	MD	**77,329,311**	78,504,235	2,063,325,086	2/28/01
26.	John S. and James L. Knight Foundation	FL	**70,746,766**	77,965,065	2,198,985,122	12/31/00
27.	Donald W. Reynolds Foundation	NV	**69,363,245**	81,849,880	1,269,083,024	12/31/00
28.	Freeman Foundation	NY	**68,256,173**	68,888,913	2,113,688,541	12/31/00
29.	Houston Endowment	TX	**66,061,151**	69,000,000	1,506,627,708	12/31/00
30.	William Penn Foundation	PA	**64,898,490**	65,598,706	1,170,193,129	12/31/00
31.	Ewing Marion Kauffman Foundation	MO	**63,741,000**	63,741,000	2,034,722,000	6/30/01
32.	Brown Foundation[2]	TX	**62,446,805**	62,236,020	1,323,153,103	6/30/01
33.	Carnegie Corporation of New York	NY	**60,803,959**	73,457,872	1,929,598,812	9/30/00
34.	James Irvine Foundation	CA	**58,223,073**	66,375,159	1,509,641,006	12/31/00
35.	Walton Family Foundation	AR	**52,379,873**	58,701,564	973,255,920	12/31/00
36.	Alfred P. Sloan Foundation	NY	**52,367,329**	57,659,423	1,373,141,818	12/31/00
37.	Henry Luce Foundation	NY	**48,786,289**	53,351,479	1,059,392,814	12/31/00
38.	Atlantic Foundation of New York	NY	**48,320,467**	48,320,467	100,563,696	12/31/00
39.	Whitaker Foundation	VA	**47,213,220**	47,213,220	370,095,910	12/31/00
40.	Ahmanson Foundation	CA	**46,574,905**	46,372,356	964,422,000	10/31/00
41.	Howard Heinz Endowment	PA	**45,810,679**	48,778,695	1,028,810,621	12/31/00
42.	Barr Foundation	MA	**44,902,736**	44,902,736	865,000,000	11/30/00
43.	Bush Foundation	MN	**44,852,609**	47,003,147	836,335,488	11/30/00
44.	California Wellness Foundation	CA	**44,715,936**	49,793,244	1,029,461,012	12/31/00
45.	Lynde and Harry Bradley Foundation	WI	**44,559,466**	44,559,466	626,124,000	12/31/00
46.	Turner Foundation	GA	**44,441,523**	47,802,254	209,515,569	12/31/00
47.	Longwood Foundation	DE	**43,090,837**	42,064,210	800,060,048	9/30/00
48.	Wallace-Reader's Digest Funds	NY	**40,678,318**	52,173,570	1,619,344,210	12/31/00
49.	Joyce Foundation	IL	**39,596,622**	42,908,225	999,530,958	12/31/00
50.	Hall Family Foundation	MO	**39,174,044**	40,081,568	861,619,838	12/31/00

Source: *Foundation Yearbook*, 2002.
*Aggregate foundation fiscal information is based on data provided to the Center as of February 2, 2002; fiscal data on individual foundations included in this table may be more current.
Note: Due to the unavailability of 2000 year-end fiscal information for the Arthur S. DeMoss Foundation, it has been excluded from this list.
[1] Includes grants, scholarships, and employee matching gifts; excludes set-asides, loans, PRIs, and program expenses.
[2] Qualifying distributions is the amount used in calculating the required 5 percent payout; includes total giving, as well as reasonable administrative expenses, set-asides, PRIs, operating program expenses, and amount paid to acquire assets used directly for charitable purposes.

science, children, families, and communities, the arts, organizational effectiveness, and philanthropy—awarded the largest environmental grant in the latest year: $50.0 million to the California-based Peninsula Open Space Trust for a plan to complete the protection of the San Mateo coast. Still, the foundation experienced a one-quarter decline in the value of its endowment in 2000, and its overall giving is likely to be lower in coming years.

Finally, the New York-based Starr Foundation raised giving by just over one-third in the latest year to $192.5 million. Growth in grant payments by the foundation in 2000 coincided with a nearly two-fifths gain in the foundation's assets. The foundation primarily funds in the area of education, with a focus on higher education, and also makes grants for culture, health, welfare, and the social sciences.

Among other top funders, the Doris Duke Charitable Foundation (NY) more than tripled its giving (up 228.8 percent) to $86.3 million. The foundation primarily supports the performing arts, environmental conservation and preservation, and medical research, including the fields of AIDS, cancer, heart disease, and sickle-cell anemia.

Independent Foundations New to the Top 50. Seven foundations were new to the top 50 independents by total giving. In addition to the twenty-third-ranked Doris Duke Charitable Foundation (noted above), the Houston Endowment (TX), ranked twenty-ninth, more than doubled giving to $66.1 million. The Endowment funds in the areas of arts, education, health, and human services within the state of Texas. Other foundations new to the top 50 included the Atlantic Foundation of New York (NY), with giving up 96.3 percent to $48.3 million; Barr Foundation (MA), with giving up 63.2 percent to $44.9 million; Bush Foundation (MN), with giving up 52.3 percent to $44.9 million; Turner Foundation (GA), with giving up 132.1 percent to $44.4 million; and Hall Family Foundation, with giving up 98.2 percent to $39.2 million.

Top 50 Independent Foundations with Reduced Giving. Fully one-fifth of the top foundations reduced their grant payments in 2000. The largest decline was reported by the Wallace-Reader's Digest Funds (NY), which decreased funding from $72.9 million in 1999 to $40.7 million. The decline came despite a more than one-tenth gain in the value of the foundation's assets in the latest year.

Among other top 50 foundations that reduced their paid grants in 2000 were: the Pew Charitable Trusts (PA), with giving down 11.0 percent to $187.9 million; W.K. Kellogg Foundation (MI), with giving down 4.2 percent to $178.7 million; Robert W. Woodruff Foundation (GA), with giving down 21.6 percent to $150.0 million; Annenberg Foundation (PA), with giving down 0.8 percent to $132.4 million; Kresge Foundation (MI), with giving down 4.2 percent to $108.0 million; Annie E. Casey Foundation (MD), with giving down 2.8 percent to $101.0 million; Walton Family Foundation (AR), with giving down 21.2 percent to $52.4 million; Whitaker Foundation (VA), with giving down 17.9 percent to $47.2 million; and Longwood Foundation (PA), with giving down 1.6 percent to $43.1 million.

2000 Assets

- Independent foundation assets grow 7 percent
- 39 "billion-dollar" independent foundations reported
- Bill & Melinda Gates Foundation experiences largest increase in asset dollars among top funders for third consecutive year

Assets of Large vs. Small Independent Foundations. The 50,532 active independent foundations held assets totaling $408.7 billion in 2000, a 7.2 percent rise over 1999 (Table 23). This increase fell well below last year's 16.6 percent growth, reflecting the start of the economic downturn after mid-2000. Still, independent foundation assets have more than doubled since 1995. In addition, while less than two-fifths of these funders reported assets of at least $1 million, together they held 98 percent of the assets of all independent foundations (Table 27).

TABLE 27. Analysis of Independent Foundations by Asset Range, 2000*

Asset Range	Number of Foundations	%	Assets	%	Total Giving[1]	%
$1 billion+	39	0.1	$155,286,742	38.0	$ 6,515,341	30.5
$250 million–$1 billion	124	0.2	59,439,195	14.5	2,691,914	12.6
$50 million–$250 million	728	1.5	75,074,049	18.4	3,562,183	16.7
$10 million–$50 million	2,957	5.9	61,977,309	15.2	3,576,364	16.8
$1 million–$10 million	15,237	30.1	47,992,052	11.8	3,400,589	15.9
Under $1 million	31,447	62.1	8,980,044	2.2	1,599,839	7.5
Total	50,532	100.0	$408,749,391	100.0	$21,346,232	100.0

Source: *Foundation Yearbook*, 2002.
*Dollars in thousands; due to rounding, figures may not add up.
[1]Includes grants, scholarships, and employee matching gifts; excludes set-asides, loans, PRIs, and program expenses.

Assets of the Top 50 Independent Foundations. Assets of the 50 largest independent foundations rose 8.3 percent in 2000, consistent with the 8.4 percent overall increase reported. Yet, two foundations—the Bill & Melinda Gates Foundation and the Lilly Endowment—accounted for nearly all of this growth. If these foundations were excluded, assets of the remaining top funders would have increased only 1.5 percent. Moreover, the median change in assets among the top independent foundations in 2000 was –0.7 percent, compared to a 14.6 percent increase in 1999.

Qualifying asset values among the top 50 independents ranged from the Gates Foundation's $21.1 billion to the Moody Foundation's (TX) $815.1 million (Table 28). By comparison, the minimum asset value for the top independent foundations in 1999 was $818.0 million. In addition, thirty-nine independent foundations held assets of at least $1 billion, down from 41 last year. The two foundations to fall below the "billion-dollar" threshold in the latest year were the Joyce Foundation (IL) and the Barr Foundation.

TABLE 28. 50 Largest Independent Foundations by Asset Size, 2000*

	Foundation	State	Assets	Total Giving[1]	Qualifying Distributions[2]	Fiscal Date
1.	Bill & Melinda Gates Foundation	WA	$21,149,100,000	$994,900,000	$994,900,000	12/31/00
2.	Lilly Endowment	IN	15,591,737,808	583,890,521	588,943,280	12/31/00
3.	Ford Foundation	NY	14,659,683,000	652,091,000	652,091,000	9/30/00
4.	David and Lucile Packard Foundation	CA	9,793,212,529	533,589,987	605,793,134	12/31/00
5.	Robert Wood Johnson Foundation	NJ	8,793,792,000	351,683,796	444,128,246	12/31/00
6.	Starr Foundation	NY	6,257,848,627	192,502,039	194,246,442	12/31/00
7.	W. K. Kellogg Foundation	MI	5,719,735,520	178,739,742	196,651,170	8/31/01
8.	Andrew W. Mellon Foundation	NY	4,888,237,000	205,870,150	205,870,150	12/31/00
9.	Pew Charitable Trusts	PA	4,800,776,253	187,853,822	243,841,247	12/31/00
10.	John D. and Catherine T. MacArthur Foundation	IL	4,479,153,951	164,022,738	198,205,781	12/31/00
11.	William and Flora Hewlett Foundation	CA	3,930,366,990	135,748,270	131,802,992	12/31/00
12.	Rockefeller Foundation	NY	3,619,028,000	163,391,841	202,375,330	12/31/00
13.	California Endowment	CA	3,490,256,407	189,663,220	211,000,000	2/28/01
14.	Robert W. Woodruff Foundation	GA	3,139,654,481	149,979,270	150,387,356	12/31/00
15.	Annie E. Casey Foundation	MD	3,001,942,131	101,012,809	127,380,064	12/31/00
16.	Annenberg Foundation	PA	2,932,205,767	132,384,109	132,384,109	6/30/01
17.	Charles Stewart Mott Foundation	MI	2,881,802,805	139,480,791	154,952,273	12/31/00
18.	Duke Endowment	NC	2,874,017,045	106,030,389	106,000,000	12/31/00
19.	Kresge Foundation	MI	2,770,530,893	107,956,140	107,956,140	12/31/00
20.	John S. and James L. Knight Foundation	FL	2,198,985,122	70,746,766	77,965,065	12/31/00
21.	Freeman Foundation	NY	2,113,688,541	68,256,173	68,888,913	12/31/00
22.	Harry and Jeanette Weinberg Foundation	MD	2,063,325,086	77,329,311	78,504,235	2/28/01
23.	Ewing Marion Kauffman Foundation	MO	2,034,722,000	63,741,000	63,741,000	6/30/01
24.	McKnight Foundation	MN	2,006,436,000	93,954,410	97,687,834	12/31/00
25.	Carnegie Corporation of New York	NY	1,929,598,812	60,803,959	73,457,872	9/30/00
26.	Richard King Mellon Foundation	PA	1,907,473,636	91,699,221	97,898,818	12/31/00
27.	Robert R. McCormick Tribune Foundation	IL	1,855,000,000	106,830,351	112,200,000	12/31/00
28.	Wallace-Reader's Digest Funds	NY	1,619,344,210	40,678,318	52,173,570	12/31/00
29.	Doris Duke Charitable Foundation	NY	1,574,746,419	86,310,650	84,676,886	12/31/00
30.	W. M. Keck Foundation	CA	1,533,721,000	81,745,562	81,745,562	12/31/00
31.	James Irvine Foundation	CA	1,509,641,006	58,223,073	66,375,159	12/31/00
32.	Houston Endowment	TX	1,506,627,708	66,061,151	69,000,000	12/31/00
33.	Alfred P. Sloan Foundation	NY	1,373,141,818	52,367,329	57,659,423	12/31/00
34.	Brown Foundation	TX	1,323,153,103	62,446,805	62,236,020	6/30/01
35.	Donald W. Reynolds Foundation	NV	1,269,083,024	69,363,245	81,849,880	12/31/00
36.	William Penn Foundation	PA	1,170,193,129	64,898,490	65,598,706	12/31/00
37.	Henry Luce Foundation	NY	1,059,392,814	48,786,289	53,351,479	12/31/00
38.	California Wellness Foundation	CA	1,029,461,012	44,715,936	49,793,244	12/31/00
39.	Howard Heinz Endowment	PA	1,028,810,621	45,810,679	48,778,695	12/31/00
40.	Joyce Foundation	IL	999,530,958	39,596,622	42,908,225	12/31/00
41.	Walton Family Foundation	AR	973,255,920	52,379,873	58,701,564	12/31/00
42.	Ahmanson Foundation	CA	964,422,000	46,574,905	46,372,356	10/31/00
43.	Lumina Foundation for Education	IN	928,954,681	212,848	1,978,617	12/31/00
44.	Horace W. Goldsmith Foundation	NY	892,935,524	39,014,530	39,116,302	12/31/00
45.	Meadows Foundation	TX	879,029,308	31,784,622	31,784,622	12/31/00
46.	Barr Foundation	MA	865,000,000	44,902,736	44,902,736	11/30/00
47.	Hall Family Foundation	MO	861,619,838	39,174,044	40,081,568	12/31/00
48.	Bush Foundation	MN	836,335,488	44,852,609	47,003,147	11/30/00
49.	Burroughs Wellcome Fund	NC	832,146,472	32,819,704	38,421,218	8/31/00
50.	Moody Foundation	TX	815,100,261	6,034,961	8,522,146	12/31/00

Source: *Foundation Yearbook,* 2002.
*Aggregate foundation fiscal information is based on data provided to the Center as of February 2, 2002; fiscal data on individual foundations included in this table may be more current.
Note: Due to the unavailability of 2000 year-end fiscal information for the Arthur S. DeMoss Foundation, it has been excluded from this list.
[1]Includes grants, scholarships, and employee matching gifts; excludes set-asides, loans, PRIs, and program expenses.
[2]Qualifying distributions is the amount used in calculating the required 5 percent payout; includes total giving, as well as reasonable administrative expenses, set-asides, PRIs, operating program expenses, and amount paid to acquire assets used directly for charitable purposes.

Top 50 Independent Foundations with Asset Gains. The Lilly Endowment outranked all other top foundations by percentage growth in assets in 2000. The Endowment's assets grew by nearly half to $15.6 billion. The foundation benefited from gains in the value of Eli Lilly and Co. stock, its principal holding.

The William and Flora Hewlett Foundation (CA) reported the second fastest growth in independent foundation assets—a more than two-fifths increase from $2.7 billion in 1999 to $3.9 billion in 2000. The Hewlett Foundation has diversified its investments in recent years in anticipation of a multi-billion-dollar bequest consisting of Hewlett-Packard Company stock from the estate of its founder, William Hewlett.

Among other funders showing at least one-third growth in the value of their endowments in 2000, the Starr Foundation's assets grew from $4.5 billion to $6.3 billion, while assets of the Bill & Melinda Gates Foundation rose from $15.5 billion to $21.1 billion. This $5.6 billion increase—the largest gain in actual dollars in the latest year—resulted primarily from a gift totaling $5.1 billion into the foundation from its founders, Bill and Melinda Gates. (In 2001, the foundation received an additional gift of roughly $2 billion, elevating its assets to over $24 billion.)

In all, seven of the 50 largest independents by assets experienced asset growth of at least one-fifth. In addition to the funders noted above, these included the Ford Foundation, Duke Endowment (NC), and Freeman Foundation (NY).

Independent Foundations New to the Top 50. Three foundations were new to the list of top 50 independents by asset size, led by the Lumina Foundation for Education (IN), ranked forty-third with $928.9 million. Established in 2000 with proceeds from the sale of the not-for-profit USA Group—formerly the nation's largest guarantor and administrator of student loans—to a profit-making loan provider, the Lumina Foundation funds on a national basis primarily to support access to post-secondary education. Other independent foundations new to the top 50 in 2000 included the Bush Foundation, ranked forty-eighth with $836.3 million; and the forty-ninth-ranked Burroughs Wellcome Fund, with assets of $832.1 million.

Top 50 Independent Foundations with Reduced Assets. Signaling the start of a major economic downturn, more than half (27) of the top 50 foundations posted asset declines in 2000, up from four in 1999. Among foundations reporting the largest decreases, the Packard Foundation's assets dropped just over one-quarter (25.5 percent), from $13.1 billion to $9.8 billion, due to a fall in the value of Hewlett-Packard Company stock, its principal holding; the Robert R. McCormick Tribune Foundation (IL) experienced a 24.3 percent loss in the value of its assets, from $2.5 billion to $1.9 billion; and the Annie E. Casey Foundation's assets decreased by more than one sixth (17.2 percent), from $3.6 billion to $3.0 billion, due to a decline in the value of United Parcel Service stock, the foundation's principal holding. Other top 50 foundations reporting at least 10 percent decreases in asset values in 2000 included the Barr Foundation (21.0 percent), Ewing Marion Kauffman Foundation (16.7 percent), W.M. Keck Foundation (14.3 percent), Hall Family Foundation (11.5 percent), Charles Stewart Mott Foundation (10.8 percent), and California Endowment (10.1 percent).

2000 Gifts Received

- **154 independent foundations receive gifts of $10 million+**

- **Gates Foundation receives second largest gift on record**

Gifts and Bequests to Independent Foundations. Bequests to independent foundations, combined with gifts from living donors, slipped from a record $24.1 billion in 1999 to $19.2 billion in 2000 (Table 24). In 1999, the Bill & Melinda Gates Foundation received a record $11.5 billion gift. By comparison, in the latest year the foundations received a $5.1 billion gift—less than half the prior year's amount. Nonetheless, this represented the second largest single gift to a foundation on record. Moreover, gifts and bequests in the latest year totaled roughly four times the gifts reported in 1994.

Thirteen foundations received gifts totaling at least $100 million, up from seven in the previous year (Table 29). Yet, while 154 foundations reported gifts totaling $10 million or more, this total was down by 56 from 1999. Thirty-nine New York-based received gifts totaling at least $10 million in 2000, followed by California (21), Illinois (11), Massachusetts (8), New Jersey (7), and Texas (6). None of the remaining states reported more than five foundations with gifts in this range.

Largest Gifts Received. The Bill & Melinda Gates Foundation received the largest gift into an independent foundation in 2000 (Table 29). The $5.1 billion gift from Bill and Melinda Gates increased the foundation's assets by more than one-third to $21.1 billion (noted earlier).

Other Notable Gifts. The Wallace H. Coulter Foundation (FL) received the second largest gift into a foundation in 2000, a $454.4 million gift that raised the foundation's assets to $508.7 million; followed by the William and Flora Hewlett Foundation, which received a $394.8 million gift. In addition, the Hewlett Foundation is expected to receive a bequest totaling approximately $3 billion from the estate of its founder, William Hewlett, over the next several years.

Trends of Independent Foundations, 1987 to Present

To measure the growth of independent foundations over time, the Foundation Center has compiled data on all independent foundations since 1987.[3] An analysis of these foundations reveals the following trends in giving and assets.

---

3. Prior to the 2001 edition of *Foundation Yearbook*, this report presented biennial data on changes in the number of foundations, total giving, and total assets of larger independent foundations, beginning with 1975.

Growth of Independent Foundations. Between 1987 and 2000, the number of independent foundations doubled, from 25,094 to 50,532 (Table 30). In the latest year, the number of foundations climbed a record 12.7 percent. Moreover, roughly 5,700 foundations were added to the set in 2000—including newly-reporting foundations and those that resumed grantmaking—surpassing the 3,073 added in 1999, the previous record year.

Giving by Independent Foundations. Independent foundation giving jumped more than four times since 1987, from $5.1 billion to $21.3 billion. When adjusted for inflation, giving increased two and three-quarters times (175.5 percent). Giving in current dollars grew

TABLE 29. 50 Largest Independent Foundations by Gifts Received, 2000*

	Foundation	State	Gifts Received	Assets	Fiscal Date
1.	Bill & Melinda Gates Foundation	WA	$5,068,000,000	$21,149,100,000	12/31/00
2.	Wallace H. Coulter Foundation	FL	454,354,473	508,683,997	9/30/00
3.	William and Flora Hewlett Foundation	CA	394,835,000	3,930,366,990	12/31/00
4.	Howard Gilman Foundation	NY	364,221,165	349,410,212	12/31/99
5.	California Endowment	CA	262,680,840	3,490,256,407	2/28/01
6.	AVI CHAI Foundation	NY	242,195,811	427,293,174	12/31/00
7.	Daniels Fund	CO	204,327,857	170,097,179	12/31/00
8.	Broad Foundation	CA	194,414,188	222,308,387	12/31/00
9.	Kresge Foundation	MI	148,879,353	2,770,530,893	12/31/00
10.	Maybelle Clark Macdonald Fund	OR	118,550,375	125,581,289	6/30/00
11.	Davee Foundation	IL	111,789,137	125,677,642	12/31/00
12.	Waitt Family Foundation	CA	111,190,015	207,252,015	12/31/00
13.	Flora Family Foundation	CA	108,260,903	148,348,802	12/31/00
14.	Iowa West Foundation	IA	69,497,208	158,160,490	12/31/99
15.	Fred A. Lennon Charitable Trust	OH	68,511,910	67,854,709	11/30/99
16.	Buffett Foundation	NE	65,003,505	57,195,568	6/30/00
17.	Walt and Lilly Disney Foundation	CA	61,743,971	209,154,496	12/31/99
18.	McKnight Brain Research Foundation	FL	61,336,287	52,851,612	6/30/00
19.	Richard M. Fairbanks Foundation	IN	61,103,075	117,429,860	12/31/00
20.	Gilo Family Foundation	CA	59,351,141	61,375,884	8/31/00
21.	Gill Foundation	CO	56,932,822	114,701,485	12/31/99
22.	Anschutz Foundation	CO	54,186,700	370,005,023	11/30/99
23.	Mississippi Common Fund Trust	MS	52,964,828	92,039,425	6/30/00
24.	Weill Family Foundation	NY	51,932,121	203,339,618	12/31/00
25.	Libra Foundation	ME	48,894,715	294,234,550	12/31/00
26.	Charitable Leadership Foundation	NY	47,906,891	54,666,276	12/31/00
27.	Energy Foundation	CA	44,619,176	41,522,154	12/31/99
28.	S & G Foundation	WY	44,554,326	110,967,274	6/30/00
29.	Matan B'Seter Foundation	NJ	43,214,000	43,676,598	11/30/00
30.	Rasmuson Foundation	AK	39,015,000	46,303,950	12/31/00
31.	Technical Training Foundation	MA	35,727,838	82,016,050	8/31/00
32.	Oberkotter Foundation	PA	31,505,476	195,278,685	11/30/00
33.	Lincy Foundation	CA	31,024,977	26,218,145	9/30/00
34.	William I. H. and Lula E. Pitts Foundation	GA	28,787,457	94,790,619	12/31/00
35.	Nancy Lurie Marks Charitable Foundation	MA	25,746,561	52,353,067	10/31/00
36.	Anna Maria & Stephen Kellen Foundation	NY	25,719,657	42,985,053	4/30/00
37.	Leon Levine Foundation	NC	25,429,957	126,990,291	6/30/00
38.	Peter and Elizabeth C. Tower Foundation	NY	25,190,130	52,597,430	12/31/00
39.	John M. O'Quinn Foundation	TX	25,115,237	51,549,713	12/31/99
40.	Bernard L. & Ruth Madoff Foundation	NY	25,000,000	29,940,206	12/31/00
41.	Williams Family Foundation of Georgia	GA	24,048,556	71,466,634	11/30/00
42.	Education for Youth Society	NY	23,871,638	21,202,279	12/31/99
43.	Highland Street Connection	MA	23,371,284	182,154,897	12/31/99
44.	Kemper and Ethel Marley Foundation	AZ	22,877,937	126,341,178	2/28/00
45.	Louis V. Gerstner, Jr. Foundation	NY	22,176,250	31,811,761	12/31/00
46.	Janet H. and T. Henry Wilson, Jr. Foundation	NC	20,806,975	24,798,058	12/31/00
47.	Ridgefield Foundation	NY	20,800,422	54,141,702	2/28/00
48.	Dorrance Family Foundation	AZ	20,343,750	42,370,622	12/31/00
49.	Sunderland Foundation	KS	20,166,300	82,670,427	12/31/00
50.	Greentree Foundation	NY	20,140,150	137,226,814	12/31/99

Source: *Foundation Yearbook*, 2002.

*Aggregate foundation fiscal information is based on data provided to the Center as of Febuary 2, 2002; fiscal data on individual foundations included in this table may be more current.

at between 6.0 percent and 12.0 percent annually between 1987 and 1993, then dropped to 2.0 percent in 1994. Independent foundation giving picked up again in 1995 and began posting strong gains in 1996, with record-high growth of 20.7 percent recorded in 1998.

Assets of Independent Foundations. Assets of independent foundations increased more than four times between 1987 and 2000, from $98.6 billion to $408.7 billion. In constant dollars, assets grew close to two and three-quarters times (173.5 percent). For independent foundations, the 1980s ended and the 1990s began with moderate gains and some losses, reflecting a period of volatility in investment markets. This was especially true in 1994, when many independent foundations suffered losses to their endowments. In contrast, the period 1995 through 1999 witnessed dramatic growth in asset values as most foundations' portfolios benefited from exceptional stock market performance. The beginning of the stock market decline and economic slowdown after mid-2000 reduced asset growth in the latest year. Overall, independent foundations posted only a 3.7 percent gain in real asset values, which followed five straight years of double-digit gains in inflation-adjusted assets.

Corporate Foundations

Like independent foundations, corporate foundations are classified as private foundations and are therefore subject to the same regulatory and reporting requirements applicable to that tax status (see Appendix B). Their basic operations, however, differ substantially. A corporate foundation generally maintains close ties with the parent company that provides its endowment and receives annual or periodic contributions from that corporation based on yearly profits. A corporate foundation's board and staff are usually composed of individuals who also hold positions within the parent company, and its giving program often reflects corporate interests and is targeted to geographic areas in which the parent company operates.

Foundations represent only one of many channels corporations use to make charitable contributions. Corporations may also make both cash and in-kind contributions—e.g., equipment, office space, staff time—through a direct giving program administered wholly within the company and funded from the company's pre-tax earnings. They may also provide support for charitable organizations through their corporate marketing budgets.

The following statistics cover only the 2,018 corporate foundations reporting complete data to the IRS. Key information on these foundations and close to 1,300 direct giving programs is available, however, in the National Directory of Corporate Giving, FC Search, *and* The Foundation Directory Online.

2000 Giving

- **Giving by corporate foundations grows 6.1 percent**
- **Giving by largest corporate funders increases 24 percent**
- **Corporate foundations account for close to one-in-nine grant dollars**

Growth in Number of Corporate Foundations. 2,018 corporate foundations reported giving activity in 2000, down by one from 2,019 in the previous year

TABLE 30. Growth of Independent Foundation Giving and Assets, 1987 to 2000*

			Total Giving (in millions)[1]				Assets (in millions)			
			Current Dollars		Constant Dollars[2]		Current Dollars		Constant Dollars[2]	
Year	Number of Foundations	% Change	Amount	% Change	Amount	% Change	Amount	% Change	Amount	% Change
1987	25,094		$ 5,112		$ 5,112		$ 98,582		$ 98,582	
1988	27,411	9.2	5,590	9.3	5,368	5.0	104,403	5.9	100,256	1.7
1989	28,669	4.6	5,992	7.2	5,489	2.3	117,941	13.0	108,049	7.8
1990	28,743	0.3	6,623	10.5	5,757	4.9	121,597	3.1	105,688	(2.2)
1991	29,476	2.6	7,033	6.2	5,866	1.9	139,335	14.6	116,215	10.0
1992	31,604	7.2	7,844	11.5	6,352	8.3	151,277	8.6	122,488	5.4
1993	33,224	5.1	8,669	10.5	6,816	7.3	162,074	7.1	127,416	4.0
1994	34,319	3.3	8,840	2.0	6,776	(0.6)	167,230	3.2	128,187	0.6
1995	35,602	3.7	9,419	6.5	7,021	3.6	191,700	14.6	142,895	11.5
1996	36,885	3.6	10,714	13.8	7,797	11.1	226,574	18.2	164,887	15.4
1997	39,248	6.4	12,375	15.5	8,781	12.6	282,618	24.7	200,534	21.6
1998	41,751	6.4	14,934	20.7	10,408	18.5	326,949	15.7	227,862	13.6
1999	44,824	7.4	17,989	20.5	12,266	17.9	381,365	16.6	260,042	14.1
2000	50,532	12.7	21,346	18.7	14,082	14.8	408,743	7.2	269,647	3.7

Source: *Foundation Yearbook,* 2002.
*The Foundation Center began tracking separate information on all independent foundations in 1987.
[1]Includes grants, scholarships, and employee matching gifts; excludes set-asides, loans, PRIs, and program expenses.
[2]Constant 1987 dollars based on annual average Consumer Price Index, all urban consumers, U.S. Department of Labor, Bureau of Labor Statistics, as of March 2002.

(Table 21). This small decline was likely due to mergers and acquisitions in the corporate world, which were not fully offset by the creation of new foundations. Despite this decrease, the number of corporate foundations has grown by more than half (55.9 percent) from the 1,295 corporate funders reported in 1987 (see Table 47 in Chapter 5).

Corporate Foundations as a Share of All Giving. Corporate foundations accounted for only 3.6 percent of the total number of U.S. grantmaking foundations (Figure 27) but were responsible for 10.8 percent of grant dollars awarded and 10.5 percent of gifts received by foundations in 2000 (Figure 28). However, corporate foundations represent a diminishing share of foundation philanthropy. In 1988, for example, they accounted for 17 percent of total giving.

Giving by Large vs. Small Corporate Foundations. Of the 2,018 active corporate foundations, 1,197 or 59.3 percent awarded grants totaling $100,000 or more in 2000 (Table 31). This group was responsible for 99.1 percent of all grant dollars paid in 2000 by corporate foundations.

Although giving increased 6.1 percent among corporate foundations, faster growth in giving among the largest funders provided for much of the overall increase. Specifically, giving by foundations making grants totaling $10 million or more increased by 12.5 percent, and those funders (65 in 2000) accounted for all of the increase in grant dollars. In contrast, giving by corporate foundations awarding grants totaling between $1 million and $10 million remained unchanged, and corporate foundations awarding grants totaling less than $1 million decreased their giving by 1.0 percent.

Established vs. New Corporate Foundations' Support. Established funders accounted for most of the increase in giving in 2000. Still, the 60 newly reporting corporate foundations provided $27.9 million or 16.3 percent of the $171.1 million in increased giving reported by all corporate foundations. Excluding the grants of newly reporting corporate foundations, giving by established funders grew 5.1 percent.

Corporate Foundation Support by Industry. A breakdown of 2000 corporate foundation giving by industry showed that banking institutions provided roughly one-in-six (15.8 percent) corporate foundation grant dollars (Table 32). The foundations of telecommunications companies followed with more than one-in-thirteen

Family Foundations

Since the early 1990s, so called "family foundations" have represented a growing area of interest to the grantmaking community, philanthropic research organizations, and the general public. The dramatic increase in the number of new foundations since 1980 has resulted largely from the decisions of living individuals and family members to channel their charitable giving through the organized structure of a private foundation. Moreover, given the involvement of individual donors and/or family members in guiding their foundations' operations, these grantmaking entities are seen as functioning differently from typically larger, endowed independent foundations—e.g., the Ford Foundation—that are run by paid staff under the supervision of a non-donor-family board of directors.

Since there is no legal definition of a family foundation, there is not yet—and there may never be—a precise way to identify all family foundations. While a small independent foundation with a living donor who makes all of the grant decisions would easily qualify as one of these funders, a third-generation billion-dollar foundation with only one or two family members playing a lesser role in governance may fall outside of common perceptions of a family philanthropy.

To begin collecting information on family foundations, in 1995 the Foundation Center added a question to its annual survey of larger foundations, asking them to self-identify as family foundations.[1] Although this "subjective" method captures only a fraction of the total number of foundations that are believed to be operated by individual donors and families, it does provide a starting point for developing more refined methods of identifying these funders.

In addition to this subjective measure, the Center has added three "objective" criteria for identifying family foundations. First, family foundation data include any independent foundation that has identified itself as a family foundation through the use of the term "Family" or "Families" in its name. Second, family foundation data include any independent foundation with a living donor whose

1. In 2001, the Center's annual survey was sent to over 24,000 foundations with assets of at least $1 million or giving of $50,000 or more included in *The Foundation Directory, Foundation Directory, Part 2,* and *Guide to U.S. Foundations.*

surname matches the foundation name, based on the assumption that living donors will take an active role in the governance of a foundation that carries their name. Third, data on family foundations include any independent foundation with at least two trustees whose surnames match a living or deceased donor's name, based on the assumption that a foundation with at least two family members on its board shows meaningful family involvement in governance. (For additional details, see Appendix A.)

The following examination is based on a total of 24,434 independent grantmakers that have been identified as family foundations using the "subjective" and "objective" criteria described above. These foundations accounted for less than one-half (48.4 percent) of all independent foundations. If a more definitive means of identifying family foundations were available, this share would undoubtedly rise.

Family Foundations by Giving. In 2000, family foundations identified by the Center reported giving of $11.3 billion or over one-half (53.0 percent) of all independent foundation grantmaking. Giving by the top 25 family foundations ranged from the Meadows Foundation's $31.8 million to the Bill & Melinda Gates Foundation's $994.9 million (Table F1). Yet while the Gates Foundation ranked first by giving among independent foundations, as well as among all funders, the Meadows Foundation ranked 61st among independent foundations and 102nd overall.[2]

Family Foundations by Assets. Family foundations identified in the sample held assets totaling $197.7 billion in 2000 or close to half (48.4 percent) of all independent foundation assets. The Washington State-based Bill and Melinda Gates Foundation, with assets of $21.1 billion, ranked as the largest family, independent, and U.S. foundation in the latest year.

Family Foundations by Gifts Received. Contributing to the growth of family foundation assets was a $5.1 billion gift from Bill and Melinda Gates to the Gates Foundation—the second largest gift ever reported. Overall, gifts into family foundations in 2000 totaled $13.4 billion or nearly seven-tenths (69.9 percent) of dollars received by all independent foundations.

---

2. For an analysis of the giving patterns of a sample of larger family foundations, see Lawrence, S., and D. Ganguly, *Foundation Giving Trends: Update on Funding Priorities*, New York: Foundation Center, annual.

TABLE F1. 25 Largest Family Foundations by Total Giving, 2000*

	Foundation Name	State	Year Created	Total Giving[1]	Assets	Fiscal Date
1.	Bill & Melinda Gates Foundation	WA	1994	$994,900,000	$21,149,100,000	12/31/00
2.	Lilly Endowment	IN	1937	583,890,521	15,591,737,808	12/31/00
3.	David and Lucile Packard Foundation	CA	1964	533,589,987	9,793,212,529	12/31/00
4.	Pew Charitable Trusts	PA	1948	187,853,822	4,800,776,253	12/31/00
5.	Annenberg Foundation	PA	1989	132,384,109	2,932,205,767	6/30/01
6.	McKnight Foundation	MN	1953	93,954,410	2,006,436,000	12/31/00
7.	Richard King Mellon Foundation	PA	1947	91,699,221	1,907,473,636	12/31/00
8.	W. M. Keck Foundation	CA	1954	81,745,562	1,533,721,000	12/31/00
9.	Freeman Foundation	NY	1978	68,256,173	2,113,688,541	12/31/00
10.	William Penn Foundation	PA	1945	64,898,490	1,170,193,129	12/31/00
11.	Brown Foundation	TX	1951	60,964,045	1,434,297,259	6/30/00
12.	Walton Family Foundation	AR	1987	52,379,873	973,255,920	12/31/00
13.	Henry Luce Foundation	NY	1936	48,786,289	1,059,392,814	12/31/00
14.	Ahmanson Foundation	CA	1952	46,574,905	964,422,000	10/31/00
15.	Howard Heinz Endowment	PA	1941	45,810,679	1,028,810,621	12/31/00
16.	Barr Foundation	MA	1987	44,902,736	865,000,000	11/30/00
17.	Turner Foundation	GA	1990	44,441,523	209,515,569	12/31/00
18.	Longwood Foundation	DE	1937	43,090,837	800,060,048	9/30/00
19.	Hall Family Foundation	MO	1943	39,174,044	861,619,838	12/31/00
20.	Horace W. Goldsmith Foundation	NY	1955	39,014,530	892,935,524	12/31/00
21.	J. A. & Kathryn Albertson Foundation	ID	1966	34,883,820	497,216,909	12/31/00
22.	Goizueta Foundation	GA	1992	33,802,380	686,026,134	12/31/00
23.	Richard & Rhoda Goldman Fund	CA	1951	32,540,477	430,000,000	12/31/00
24.	Rockefeller Brothers Fund	NY	1940	32,139,090	753,327,772	12/31/00
25.	Meadows Foundation	TX	1948	31,784,622	879,029,308	12/31/00

Source: *Foundation Yearbook*, 2002.
*Figures based on a subset of family foundations identified by the Foundation Center using subjective and objective criteria. See Appendix A for details. These funders are included in independent foundation data.
[1]Includes grants, scholarships, and employee matching gifts; excludes set-asides, loans, PRIs, and program expenses.

"New Health" Foundations

- **Giving by private health care conversion foundations totals $362.4 million**

- **California-based funders account for almost seven out of ten grant dollars**

The Foundation Center identified 53 active private grantmaking foundations in 2000 that were created with proceeds from the sale of nonprofit health care entities to for-profit corporations.[1] These independent grantmakers—commonly known as "new health" foundations—held assets totaling nearly $8.1 billion and awarded grants of $362.4 million in the latest year, primarily to improve the health and well-being of residents in their home communities and states.[2]

1. In addition, the Center has identified four private new health foundations that did not award grants in the most recent reporting period and 65 public charities created from the conversion of nonprofit health care entities to for-profit status. (Unlike private foundations, public charities may have a principal purpose other than grantmaking, are not subject to the payout requirements of private foundations, and are required to raise a substantial portion of their revenue each year from the public. Thus, public charities may seek grants from private foundations as one source of revenue.)
2. For an analysis of giving patterns among a subset of these funders, see Lawrence S., and D. Ganguly, *Foundation Giving Trends: Update on Funding Priorities*, New York: Foundation Center, annual.

Led by the California Endowment and the California Wellness Foundation, the nine California-based health care conversion foundations controlled more than three-fifths of the assets (62.5 percent) and almost seven-tenths of the giving (69.5 percent) of private new health foundations. By comparison, the second largest state ranked by new health foundation assets and giving—Kansas—was home to only the Kansas Health Foundation, and this funder accounted for just 5.8 percent of assets and giving. Other states with private new health foundations reporting giving totaling at least $5 million included Colorado, Tennessee, Illinois, New Jersey, Louisiana, and Pennsylvania.

A small number of health care conversion foundations provided the vast majority of support. Table H1 lists the top 25 private health care conversion foundations in 2000 by giving. While these funders accounted for roughly 96 percent of all private new health foundation giving and more than 93 percent of assets, the top five alone controlled over three-fourths of giving and nearly seven-tenths of the assets of these grantmakers.

TABLE H1. 25 Largest Private "New Health" Foundations by Total Giving, 2000*

	Foundation Name	State	Year Created	Total Giving[1]	Assets	Fiscal Date
1.	California Endowment	CA	1996	$189,663,220	$3,490,256,407	2/28/01
2.	California Wellness Foundation	CA	1991	44,715,936	1,029,461,012	12/31/00
3.	Kansas Health Foundation[2]	KS	1978	19,319,277	467,555,588	12/31/00
4.	Colorado Trust	CO	1985	10,400,700	421,238,194	12/31/00
5.	Assisi Foundation of Memphis	TN	1994	9,214,148	214,961,325	2/28/00
6.	Baptist Community Ministries	LA	1995	7,922,359	264,019,557	9/30/00
7.	Healthcare Foundation of New Jersey	NJ	1997	7,875,000	172,223,000	12/31/00
8.	Jewish Healthcare Foundation of Pittsburgh	PA	1990	6,165,478	133,500,000	12/31/00
9.	Archstone Foundation	CA	1985	5,506,946	122,198,875	6/30/01
10.	Alliance Healthcare Foundation	CA	1988	4,798,477	126,823,722	6/30/00
11.	Community Memorial Foundation	IL	1995	4,263,524	96,079,064	12/31/00
12.	Christy-Houston Foundation	TN	1986	4,225,000	87,887,128	12/31/00
13.	Sierra Health Foundation	CA	1984	3,929,321	168,643,990	6/30/00
14.	Michael Reese Health Trust	IL	1995	3,549,908	90,743,537	6/30/01
15.	Alleghany Foundation	VA	1995	3,049,676	51,094,345	5/31/01
16.	Health Foundation of Greater Indianapolis	IN	1985	2,461,642	46,144,706	12/31/00
17.	Cape Fear Memorial Foundation	NC	1996	2,350,155	63,549,139	6/30/00
18.	Presbyterian Health Foundation	OK	1985	2,298,520	215,424,291	9/30/00
19.	VNA Foundation	IL	1995	2,020,150	42,910,871	6/30/01
20.	M Health Foundation	CA	1986	1,872,000	44,586,240	12/31/00
21.	Foundation for Seacoast Health	NH	1984	1,749,610	73,974,141	12/31/00
22.	Hill Crest Foundation[3]	AL	1967	1,636,700	33,277,781	6/30/01
23.	Blowitz-Ridgeway Foundation	IL	1984	1,435,545	26,692,592	9/30/00
24.	Byerly Foundation	SC	1995	1,027,024	28,615,075	9/30/00
25.	Portsmouth General Hospital Foundation	VA	1987	985,834	17,365,029	6/30/01

Source: *Foundation Yearbook*, 2002.

*Overall, the Foundation Center has identified 53 active private grantmaking new health foundations, four private new health foundations that did not award grants in the most recent reporting period, and 65 public charities created from the conversion of nonprofit health care entities to for-profit status.
[1]Includes grants, scholarships, and employee matching gifts; excludes set-asides, loans, PRIs, and program expenses.
[2]The foundation received its principal endowment in 1985 from the sale of the Wesley Medical Center. It became a private foundation in 1992.
[3]The foundation was originally the fundraising arm of Hill Crest Psychiatric Hospital, which converted to a private foundation in 1988 as a result of the sale of the hospital.

Giving and Growth of Independent, Corporate, and Community Foundations

grant dollars (7.9 percent). Overall, more than half (54.8 percent) of corporate foundation giving in the latest year came from foundations sponsored by non-manufacturing enterprises, while the foundations of manufacturing concerns accounted for over two-fifths (44.9 percent). Among manufacturing concerns, the top industries by share of giving included transportation equipment (7.7 percent), industrial and commercial machinery (6.8 percent), and pharmaceuticals (5.4 percent). Interestingly, the paper products sector represented less than 1 percent of corporate foundation giving.

TABLE 31. Analysis of Corporate Foundations by Total Giving Range, 2000*

Total Giving Range	Number of Foundations	%	Total Giving[1]	%
$25 million+	20	1.0	$ 915,462	30.7
$10 million–$25 million	45	2.2	652,442	21.9
$1 million–$10 million	371	18.4	1,115,442	37.4
$100,000–$1 million	761	37.7	271,033	9.1
Under $100,000	821	40.7	30,266	0.9
Total	**2,018**	**100.0**	**$2,984,645**	**100.0**

Source: *Foundation Yearbook*, 2002.
*Dollars in thousands.
[1] Includes grants, scholarships, and employee matching gifts; excludes set-asides, loans, PRIs, and program expenses.

Funding by the Top 50 Corporate Foundations. To qualify for ranking among the top 50 corporate foundations, the minimum spending level was $12.0 million, compared to the maximum of $169.1 million distributed by the Michigan-based Ford Motor Company Fund (Table 33). In addition to the Ford Motor Company Fund, three other funders distributed at least $60 million—the Bank of America (NC), SBC (TX), and Wal-Mart (AR) foundations. An additional nine funders distributed at least $40 million—the J.P. Morgan Chase (NY), Lucent Technologies (NJ), AT&T (NY), General Motors (MI), Citigroup (NY), ExxonMobil (TX), Aventis Pharmaceuticals Health Care (NJ), and Verizon (NY) foundations and the GE Fund (CT). Among the top ten funders, the threshold for giving increased to $42.2 million from last year's $33.9 million.

Top 50 Corporate Foundations with Increased Funding. Giving by the nation's top corporate foundations increased an impressive 23.8 percent in 2000. Forty-two of the top 50 corporate foundations reported increased giving. Among the top ten corporate funders, the Ford Motor Company Fund (noted above) increased grants paid by close to three-quarters in the latest year to $169.1 million. The Citigroup Foundation more than doubled its giving to $43.1 million. Helping to

TABLE 32. Corporate Foundation Giving by Industry, 2000 (Dollars in thousands)*

Industrial Classification	Number of Foundations	%	Total Giving[1]	%	Average Giving
Chemicals	54	2.7	$ 144,585	4.8	$2,678
Computers/Office Equipment	21	1.0	35,368	1.2	1,684
Food and Agriculture	80	4.0	133,038	4.5	1,663
Industrial and Commercial Machinery (Not Computer)	164	8.1	202,647	6.8	1,236
Paper and Like Products	32	1.6	26,074	0.9	815
Petroleum/Gas/Mining	28	1.4	79,786	2.7	2,850
Pharmaceuticals	23	1.1	160,870	5.4	6,994
Primary Metals	49	2.4	58,801	2.0	1,200
Printing/Publishing/Media	71	3.5	76,556	2.6	1,078
Textiles and Apparel	71	3.5	40,159	1.3	566
Transportation Equipment	62	3.1	229,942	7.7	3,709
Other Manufacturing	225	11.1	153,435	5.1	682
Total Manufacturing	**880**	**43.6**	**$1,341,263**	**44.9**	**$1,524**
Banking	189	9.4	470,603	15.8	2,490
Finance	155	7.7	230,545	7.7	1,487
Insurance	99	4.9	204,887	6.9	2,070
Retail and Wholesale Trade	242	12.0	218,065	7.3	901
Telecommunications	31	1.5	236,080	7.9	7,615
Transportation	25	1.2	59,833	2.0	2,393
Utilities	76	3.8	95,739	3.2	1,260
Other Services	266	13.2	120,038	4.0	451
Total Nonmanufacturing	**1,083**	**53.7**	**$1,635,789**	**54.8**	**$1,510**
Unspecified	55	2.7	7,592	0.3	138
Total	**2,018**	**100.0**	**$2,984,645**	**100.0**	**$1,479**

Source: *Foundation Yearbook*, 2002.
*Categories are based on the Conference Board's collapse of corporations using Standard Industrial Codes.
[1] Includes grants, scholarships, and employees matching gifts; excludes set-asides, loans, PRIs, and program expenses.

raise the foundation's giving was a $107.8 million gift from Citigroup in the latest year. In addition, the ExxonMobil Foundation (TX) nearly doubled its giving for education nationwide to $42.2 million. Among the foundation's areas of interest are university-based research related to the petroleum and chemical industries and mathematics education and school reform at the elementary and secondary level. Together, these three foundations were responsible for more than two-fifths (41.0 percent) of the increase in giving by the top 50 funders. If these foundations were excluded from the top 50 in both years, giving by the remaining top corporate foundations would have increased 16.0 percent.

Corporate Foundations New to the Top 50. Eight foundations were new to the top 50 corporate foundations by total giving. The Aventis Pharmaceuticals Health Care Foundation (NJ), ranked eleventh in 2000, increased its giving in the latest year from $3.2 million to $41.6 million. The foundation provides medicine to low-income people. The Intel Foundation (OR), ranked twenty-ninth, raised its funding by seven-tenths to $18.3 million in 2000. Fueling this increase was a $30.5 million gift from its parent company. Other foundations new or returning to the top 50 included the thirty-first-ranked Pfizer Foundation (NY), with giving of $17.2 million; forty-second-ranked Cisco Systems Foundation (CA), with giving of $14.2

TABLE 33. 50 Largest Corporate Foundations by Total Giving, 2000*

	Foundation	State	Total Giving[1]	Qualifying Distributions[2]	Assets	Fiscal Date
1.	Ford Motor Company Fund	MI	$169,100,475	$170,268,431	$247,625,772	12/31/00
2.	Bank of America Foundation	NC	85,755,841	85,755,841	2,212,307	12/31/00
3.	SBC Foundation	TX	68,678,574	68,630,454	328,100,000	12/31/00
4.	Wal-Mart Foundation	AR	62,617,641	62,964,540	359,724	1/31/00
5.	J. P. Morgan Chase Foundation	NY	44,656,806	46,487,686	137,439,675	12/31/00
6.	Lucent Technologies Foundation	NJ	43,932,312	45,009,168	22,970,298	9/30/00
7.	AT&T Foundation	NY	43,539,963	43,000,000	73,252,695	12/31/00
8.	General Motors Foundation	MI	43,280,242	43,317,795	401,916,997	12/31/00
9.	Citigroup Foundation	NY	43,068,029	44,534,882	179,182,168	12/31/00
10.	ExxonMobil Foundation	TX	42,188,567	42,266,873	71,180,930	12/31/00
11.	Aventis Pharmaceuticals Health Care Foundation	NJ	41,558,325	41,558,325	7,039	12/31/00
12.	Verizon Foundation	NY	41,205,556	41,183,299	80,214,080	12/30/00
13.	GE Fund	CT	40,701,047	42,269,513	53,887,325	12/31/00
14.	Prudential Foundation	NJ	36,219,045	39,329,403	156,251,000	12/31/00
15.	Fannie Mae Foundation	DC	34,835,347	108,447,726	272,988,815	12/31/00
16.	UPS Foundation	GA	34,646,311	34,670,693	109,825,286	12/31/00
17.	Avon Products Foundation	NY	31,629,489	31,696,799	38,437,478	12/31/00
18.	Procter & Gamble Fund	OH	30,430,962	30,454,124	11,494,665	6/30/00
19.	DaimlerChrysler Corporation Fund	MI	29,619,272	30,337,489	66,738,102	12/31/00
20.	Merck Company Foundation	NJ	28,795,232	29,203,646	317,420,760	12/31/00
21.	FleetBoston Financial Foundation	MA	24,200,000	24,200,000	99,500,000	12/31/00
22.	First Union Foundation	NC	23,933,599	24,685,171	892,746	12/31/00
23.	Wells Fargo Foundation	CA	21,321,223	21,165,989	279,334,009	12/31/00
24.	Shell Oil Company Foundation	TX	20,877,698	20,877,698	84,687,000	12/31/00
25.	Alcoa Foundation	PA	20,130,756	20,130,756	441,245,083	12/31/00
26.	BP Amoco Foundation	IL	19,154,127	21,397,937	86,644,858	12/31/00
27.	Fidelity Foundation	MA	18,314,415	18,753,964	431,163,790	12/31/00
28.	Emerson Charitable Trust	MO	18,303,933	18,186,587	7,382,376	9/30/00
29.	Intel Foundation	OR	18,303,084	18,303,084	82,175,071	12/31/00
30.	American Express Foundation	NJ	18,271,856	18,255,865	3,708,520	12/31/00
31.	Pfizer Foundation	NY	17,227,882	17,771,643	392,848,769	12/31/00
32.	Eli Lilly and Company Foundation	IN	17,156,681	17,168,881	140,000,000	12/31/00
33.	NCC Charitable Foundation II	OH	17,127,194	17,100,325	44,080,889	6/30/00
34.	Dow Chemical Company Foundation	MI	16,517,636	16,597,451	17,358,915	12/31/00
35.	Bristol-Myers Squibb Foundation	NY	15,836,964	15,862,375	26,867,580	12/31/00
36.	Freddie Mac Foundation	VA	15,719,453	18,932,382	31,820,731	12/31/00
37.	Firstar Foundation	OH	15,215,561	15,215,895	57,295,065	12/31/00
38.	General Mills Foundation	MN	15,009,937	15,010,965	35,034,155	5/31/00
39.	State Farm Companies Foundation	IL	14,957,375	14,980,575	62,511,350	12/31/00
40.	Metropolitan Life Foundation	NY	14,509,741	16,044,292	256,419,866	12/31/00
41.	Merrill Lynch & Co. Foundation	NJ	14,397,241	14,652,581	29,917,334	12/31/00
42.	Cisco Systems Foundation	CA	14,190,789	13,955,869	132,211,438	7/31/00
43.	Levi Strauss Foundation	CA	13,941,796	14,668,625	114,618,305	12/31/00
44.	Monsanto Fund	MO	13,741,661	13,806,258	37,847,443	12/31/00
45.	Cargill Foundation	MN	13,433,801	13,355,525	78,605,924	12/31/00
46.	Key Foundation	OH	13,239,555	13,239,555	47,591,488	12/31/00
47.	Anheuser-Busch Foundation	MO	12,648,330	12,623,148	60,345,116	12/31/00
48.	Coca-Cola Foundation	GA	12,182,611	12,160,368	68,176,408	12/31/00
49.	Medtronic Foundation	MN	12,034,302	12,725,333	15,741,331	4/30/00
50.	Washington Mutual Foundation	WA	12,028,221	12,101,108	3,369,964	12/31/00

Source: *Foundation Yearbook*, 2002.
*Aggregate foundation fiscal information is based on data provided to the Center as of February 2, 2002; fiscal data on individual foundations included in this table may be more current.
[1] Includes grants, scholarships, and employee matching gifts; excludes set-asides, loans, PRIs, and program expenses.
[2] Qualifying distributions is the amount used in calculating the required 5 percent payout; includes total giving, as well as reasonable administrative expenses, set-asides, PRIs, operating program expenses, and amount paid to acquire assets used directly for charitable purposes.

million; forty-fifth-ranked Cargill Foundation (MN), with giving of $13.4 million; forty-sixth-ranked Key Foundation (OH), with giving of $13.2 million; forty-ninth-ranked Medtronic Foundation (MN), with giving of $12.0 million; and fiftieth-ranked Washington Mutual Foundation (WA), with giving of $12.0 million.

Top 50 Corporate Foundations with Reduced Giving. Eight of the top 50 corporate foundations reduced their giving. The largest decline was reported by the BP Amoco Foundation (IL), which decreased paid grants from $36.9 million to $19.2 million in the latest year. As a result, its rank fell from sixth to twenty-sixth. Among other top 50 corporate foundations that reduced their payments in 2000 were the Bank of America (NC), Wal-Mart, Shell Oil Company (TX), General Mills (MN), and Levi Strauss (CA) foundations and the Procter & Gamble (OH) and Monsanto (MO) funds.

New and Large Corporate Foundations. Six corporate funders included in this analysis for the first time reported grants of over $1 million. The largest of these, the St. Paul Companies, Inc. Foundation (MN), was established in 1998 by the St. Paul Companies, Inc., which provides reinsurance and asset management services. The foundation awarded $9.7 million in 2000 primarily for arts and culture, community and neighborhood development, education projects and programs, and advancing the nonprofit, voluntary sector. Among the other newly reporting foundations making at least $1 million in grants were: ADC Foundation (MN), OMNOVA Solutions Foundation (OH), GPU Foundation (NJ), Huntington Foundation (OH), and Pepsi Bottling Group Foundation (NY).

2000 Assets

- **Corporate foundation assets increase by 4.2 percent**
- **Top 50 corporate foundations slightly surpass overall growth**

Growth of Corporate Foundation Assets. Assets of the 2,018 corporate foundations grew a very modest 4.2 percent in 2000, roughly one-quarter of the 16.4 percent gain reported in 1999. Nonetheless, corporate foundation assets have more than doubled since 1994, and these increased resources help them to limit cuts in grantmaking during periods of slumping profits. Overall, assets rose from $15.3 billion to $15.9 billion between 1999 and 2000.

Assets of Large vs. Small Corporate Foundations. Unlike independents, many corporate foundations do not have large endowments but depend instead on their sponsoring companies for continued contributions.

Corporate Profits, Giving, and Foundations

Pre-tax income of U.S. corporations increased nearly 9 percent in 2000, roughly matching the previous year's gain. Estimates from *Giving USA* for 2000 showed total corporate contributions as a percent of income before taxes remained steady at 1.2 percent. In terms of the dollar value of contributions, estimated giving of nearly $10.9 billion represented a 12.1 percent increase between 1999 and 2000.

Corporate giving as a percent of pre-tax income reached a peak of 2.1 percent in 1986 and has gradually dropped off to current levels. Although still less than the ratio in 1986, the current ratio of contributions relative to income remains slightly above the ratios reported in the years 1995 through 1998. Still, estimated corporate income increased 133.2 percent between 1990 and 2000, while estimated charitable contributions grew a smaller 98.9 percent during this period.

Using *Giving USA's* estimate of $10.9 billion in total corporate contributions and the Foundation Center's figure of $3.0 billion in actual corporate foundation giving, 2000 foundation giving represented well under three-tenths of total corporate giving. Still, the $10.9 billion total includes not only cash, but also product, property and equipment, and gifts of securities. Foundation giving—consisting mainly of cash—represents a higher proportion of contributions if only cash gifts are measured.

Looking forward, the Conference Board's latest survey of 207 primarily large companies estimated no growth in overall corporate giving in 2001. By comparison, the Foundation Center estimated 2.6 percent growth in 2001 corporate foundation giving. As a result, giving through foundations is likely to represent an even larger share of overall corporate giving.

Nonetheless, 924 corporate foundations (45.7 percent) held assets of at least $1 million, compared to 906 in 1999 (Table 34). Just over 286 corporate funders (14.1 percent) maintained assets of $10 million or more, yet they provided close to two-thirds (63.2 percent) of corporate foundation giving. In addition, 73 corporate foundations reported assets of at least $50 million, compared to 66 in the previous year and only 21 in 1993.

Finally, the ratio of gifts into foundations from sponsoring companies (pay-in) compared to giving (payout) by foundations differed by foundation size in 2000. For example, although payout exceeded pay-in by 2.8 percent overall, among foundations with at least $10 million in assets, pay-in exceeded payout by roughly 3.8 percent. In contrast, payout exceeded pay-in by about 16.2 percent among corporate funders with assets totaling less than $10 million.

Assets of the Top 50 Corporate Foundations. Reflecting the beginning of a pronounced economic slowdown, assets of the top corporate foundations grew only 4.7 percent in 2000, just slightly exceeding the 4.2 percent overall growth reported. Still, one grantmaker—the Goldman, Sachs Foundation (NY)—realized an asset increase of close to $220 million. If this foundation was excluded, assets of the remaining top funders would have increased 1.8 percent.

The threshold for qualifying among the top 50 corporate funders by asset size grew from $60.7 million in 1999 to $66.5 million in 2000—a more than 7 percent increase. Qualifying asset values ranged from the Mellon Financial Corporation Foundation's (PA) $65.1 million to the Alcoa Foundation's (PA) $441.2 million. Twenty-nine corporate foundations held assets of at least $100 million, up from 28 last year. The new foundations in this asset range included the Goldman, Sachs, HCA (TN), Batchelor (FL), and Cisco Systems (CA) foundations and the Abbott Laboratories Fund (IL).

Top 50 Corporate Foundations with Assets Gains. Only two-fifths (20) of the top 50 corporate foundations showed asset increases in 2000 (Table 35). Still, seven top corporate foundations reported at least a doubling of their endowments. For example, the Goldman, Sachs Foundation's assets grew close to nineteen-fold to $230.7 million following receipt of a $200.0 million gift. Funded by Goldman, Sachs, the New York-based investment firm, the foundation focuses on funding for education. Among other corporate foundations with pronounced percentage gains in asset values were: the Batchelor Foundation, up almost five-fold to $146.9 million; General Motors Foundation (MI), up more than two and one-half-fold to $401.9 million; and Coca-Cola Foundation (GA), up nearly two and one-half-fold to $68.2 million.

Corporate Foundations New to the Top 50. Four foundations were new to the list of top 50 corporate foundations by assets. Leading these funders was the twelfth-ranked Goldman, Sachs Foundation (noted above). Other foundations new or returning to the list included the Batchelor, Verizon (NY), and Coca-Cola foundations.

Top 50 Corporate Foundations with Reduced Assets. Reflecting declining corporate fortunes, 28 of the top 50 business foundations reported decreases in asset values in the latest year. The Fannie Mae Foundation (DC) experienced the sharpest decline in asset value, with its endowment down 33.0 percent to $273.0 million. The foundation paid $34.8 million in grants and received $30.0 million in gifts in the latest year. However, this was not enough to offset large losses in the value of its holdings. In general, decreases in corporate assets result from an imbalance between grants paid out by the foundations relative to gifts received from their sponsoring companies. However, in some cases assets decrease when the value of the company's stock holdings declines.

TABLE 34. Analysis of Corporate Foundations by Asset Range, 2000*

Asset Range	Number of Foundations	%	Assets	%	Total Giving[1]	%
$250 million+	9	0.4	$ 3,040,248	19.1	$ 226,903	7.6
$50 million–$250 million	64	3.1	5,844,318	36.7	901,188	30.2
$10 million–$50 million	213	10.6	4,509,551	28.4	757,463	25.4
$1 million–$10 million	638	31.6	2,228,828	14.0	677,428	22.7
Under $1 million	1,094	54.3	276,148	1.6	421,663	14.2
Total	2,018	100.0	$15,899,090	100.0	$2,984,645	100.0

Source: *Foundation Yearbook*, 2002.
*Dollars in thousands; due to rounding, figures may not add up.
[1]Includes grants, scholarships, and employee matching gifts; excludes set-asides, loans, PRIs, and program expenses.

2000 Gifts Received

- Gifts from companies to their foundations decrease 12.4 percent
- Payout exceeds pay-in by 2.8 percent

Gifts to Corporate Foundations. The aggregate value of gifts from companies to their foundations (pay-in) totaled $2.9 billion in 2000, down from more than $3.3 billion in 1999 (Table 24). This 12.4 percent decrease followed a 24.8 percent gain in 1999 and a record 41.7 percent jump in new gifts in 1998. Moreover, giving (payout) exceeded pay-in by about $82 million, or 2.8 percent, representing a modest drain on the value of corporate foundation assets.

Thirty-one companies gave at least $10 million to their foundations, down from 50 in 1999; additionally, 19 provided gifts of over $25 million, down from 25 in the previous year (Table 36). Nine corporate foundations based in New York received gifts totaling at least

TABLE 35. 50 Largest Corporate Foundations by Asset Size, 2000*

	Foundation	State	Assets	Total Giving[1]	Qualifying Distributions[2]	Fiscal Date
1.	Alcoa Foundation	PA	$441,245,083	$20,130,756	$20,130,756	12/31/00
2.	Fidelity Foundation	MA	431,163,790	18,314,415	18,753,964	12/31/00
3.	General Motors Foundation	MI	401,916,997	286,867,500	43,317,795	12/31/00
4.	Pfizer Foundation	NY	392,848,769	17,227,882	17,771,643	12/31/00
5.	SBC Foundation	TX	328,100,000	68,678,574	68,630,454	12/31/00
6.	Merck Company Foundation	NJ	317,420,760	28,795,232	29,203,646	12/31/00
7.	Wells Fargo Foundation	CA	279,334,009	21,321,223	21,165,989	12/31/00
8.	Fannie Mae Foundation	DC	272,988,815	34,835,347	108,447,726	12/31/00
9.	Metropolitan Life Foundation	NY	256,419,866	14,509,741	16,044,292	12/31/00
10.	Ave Maria Foundation	MI	252,309,239	13,685,047	20,934,131	12/31/00
11.	Ford Motor Company Fund	MI	247,625,772	169,100,475	170,268,431	12/31/00
12.	Goldman, Sachs Foundation	NY	230,721,571	4,932,625	5,010,040	6/30/00
13.	Citigroup Foundation	NY	179,182,168	43,068,029	44,534,882	12/31/00
14.	HCA Foundation	TN	171,207,684	3,286,628	3,444,189	12/31/00
15.	Prudential Foundation	NJ	156,251,000	36,219,045	39,329,403	12/31/00
16.	Alabama Power Foundation	AL	149,170,931	7,937,391	8,721,583	12/31/00
17.	Batchelor Foundation	FL	146,895,493	1,946,675	1,946,675	6/30/01
18.	IBM International Foundation	NY	146,630,946	10,148,618	10,936,076	12/31/00
19.	USAA Foundation, A Charitable Trust	TX	145,237,670	10,837,349	10,774,304	6/30/01
20.	Eli Lilly and Company Foundation	IN	140,000,000	17,156,681	17,168,881	12/31/00
21.	Northwestern Mutual Foundation	WI	137,640,179	11,403,898	11,813,256	6/30/00
22.	J. P. Morgan Chase Foundation	NY	137,439,675	44,656,806	46,487,686	12/31/00
23.	Cisco Systems Foundation	CA	132,211,438	14,190,789	13,955,869	7/31/00
24.	Steelcase Foundation	MI	123,961,148	7,197,364	7,475,593	11/30/00
25.	Abbott Laboratories Fund	IL	117,763,266	11,162,538	12,731,383	12/31/00
26.	Levi Strauss Foundation	CA	114,618,305	13,941,796	14,668,625	12/31/00
27.	Motorola Foundation	IL	110,460,710	9,712,915	9,807,259	12/31/00
28.	UPS Foundation	GA	109,825,286	34,646,311	34,670,693	12/31/00
29.	Georgia Power Foundation	GA	101,998,133	7,764,923	7,774,338	12/31/00
30.	FleetBoston Financial Foundation	MA	99,500,000	24,200,000	24,200,000	12/31/00
31.	First Union Regional Foundation	PA	98,218,561	4,575,000	4,575,000	12/31/00
32.	Bridgestone/Firestone Trust Fund	TN	87,819,753	4,664,329	4,739,529	12/31/00
33.	BP Amoco Foundation	IL	86,644,858	19,154,127	21,397,937	12/31/00
34.	Scripps Howard Foundation	OH	85,838,950	6,676,715	7,714,613	12/31/00
35.	Shell Oil Company Foundation	TX	84,687,000	20,877,698	20,877,698	12/31/00
36.	Intel Foundation	OR	82,175,071	18,303,084	18,303,084	12/31/00
37.	Principal Financial Group Foundation	IA	80,292,635	4,419,654	4,419,654	12/31/00
38.	Verizon Foundation	NY	80,214,080	41,205,556	41,183,299	12/30/00
39.	Cargill Foundation	MN	78,605,924	13,433,801	13,355,525	12/31/00
40.	Transamerica Foundation	CA	74,196,773	2,787,821	2,846,061	12/31/00
41.	Minnesota Mining and Manufacturing Foundation	MN	74,028,370	10,664,904	11,278,743	12/31/00
42.	AT&T Foundation	NY	73,252,695	43,539,963	43,000,000	12/31/00
43.	ExxonMobil Foundation	TX	71,180,930	42,188,567	42,266,873	12/31/00
44.	Baxter Allegiance Foundation	IL	71,038,979	4,997,078	4,997,078	12/31/00
45.	New York Life Foundation	NY	69,783,373	4,570,509	4,516,146	12/31/00
46.	Independence Community Foundation	NY	68,532,842	5,064,524	5,498,112	12/31/00
47.	Coca-Cola Foundation	GA	68,176,408	12,182,611	12,160,368	12/31/00
48.	DaimlerChrysler Corporation Fund	MI	66,738,102	29,619,272	30,337,489	12/31/00
49.	Glaxo Wellcome Foundation	NC	66,455,220	3,410,567	3,917,135	12/31/00
50.	Mellon Financial Corporation Foundation	PA	65,116,758	4,300,349	4,300,349	12/31/00

Source: *Foundation Yearbook*, 2002.
*Aggregate foundation fiscal information is based on data provided to the Center as of February 2, 2002; fiscal data on individual foundations included in this table may be more current.
[1]Includes grants, scholarships, and employee matching gifts; excludes set-asides, loans, PRIs, and program expenses.
[2]Qualifying distributions is the amount used in calculating the required 5 percent payout; includes total giving, as well as reasonable administrative expenses, set-asides, PRIs, operating program expenses, and amount paid to acquire assets used directly for charitable purposes.

$10 million, followed by California, Illinois, and Michigan with three each. None of the remaining states reported more than two corporate foundations with gifts in this range.

TABLE 36. 50 Largest Corporate Foundations by Gifts Received, 2000*

Foundation	State	Gifts Received	Assets	Fiscal Date
1. General Motors Foundation	MI	$286,867,500	$401,916,997	12/31/00
2. Goldman, Sachs Foundation	NY	200,000,000	230,721,571	6/30/00
3. Citigroup Foundation	NY	107,812,500	179,182,168	12/31/00
4. Cisco Systems Foundation	CA	91,024,874	132,211,438	7/31/00
5. Verizon Foundation	NY	70,688,063	80,214,080	12/30/00
6. Ford Motor Company Fund	MI	70,000,000	247,625,772	12/31/00
7. Wells Fargo Foundation	CA	51,337,038	279,334,009	12/31/00
8. Coca-Cola Foundation	GA	51,302,278	68,176,408	12/31/00
9. Avon Products Foundation	NY	50,667,895	38,437,478	12/31/00
10. Monsanto Fund	MO	47,552,201	37,847,443	12/31/00
11. Bristol-Myers Squibb Foundation	NY	39,091,700	26,867,580	12/31/00
12. J. P. Morgan Chase Foundation	NY	37,876,292	137,439,675	12/31/00
13. Lucent Technologies Foundation	NJ	37,518,305	22,970,298	9/30/00
14. Firstar Foundation	OH	35,120,581	57,295,065	12/31/00
15. BP Amoco Foundation	IL	35,073,059	86,644,858	12/31/00
16. Intel Foundation	OR	30,456,908	82,175,071	12/31/00
17. Fannie Mae Foundation	DC	30,000,000	272,988,815	12/31/00
18. AT&T Foundation	NY	27,000,000	73,252,695	12/31/00
19. ExxonMobil Foundation	TX	26,550,000	71,180,930	12/31/00
20. ADC Foundation	MN	22,825,210	21,677,730	10/31/00
21. DaimlerChrysler Corporation Fund	MI	18,940,000	66,738,102	12/31/00
22. GenCorp Foundation	CA	17,939,823	20,019,738	11/30/00
23. GreenPoint Foundation	NY	17,551,000	49,807,395	9/30/00
24. Phoenix Foundation	CT	15,725,734	20,460,675	12/31/00
25. Grand Victoria Foundation	IL	15,246,349	40,167,864	2/28/00
26. Anheuser-Busch Foundation	MO	15,000,000	60,345,116	12/31/00
27. Caterpillar Foundation	IL	12,000,000	54,700,692	12/31/00
28. Corning Incorporated Foundation	NY	11,108,975	26,902,816	12/31/00
29. Nationwide Foundation	OH	10,599,038	53,221,215	12/31/00
30. Batchelor Foundation	FL	10,000,000	146,895,493	6/30/01
31. Nasdaq Stock Market Educational Foundation	MD	10,000,000	36,209,621	12/31/99
32. McKesson Foundation	CA	9,957,893	32,937,949	3/31/00
33. Enterprise Rent-A-Car Foundation	MO	9,698,794	37,654,876	7/31/00
34. PepsiCo Foundation	NY	8,214,000	34,236,614	12/31/99
35. General Mills Foundation	MN	8,000,000	35,034,155	5/31/00
36. Texas Instruments Foundation	TX	7,500,000	29,885,765	12/31/00
37. Federated Department Stores Foundation	OH	7,500,000	21,615,327	1/30/00
38. Vivendi Universal Foundation	NY	7,173,926	20,032,810	6/30/00
39. Pacific Life Foundation	CA	7,022,104	41,876,034	12/31/00
40. New York Stock Exchange Foundation	NY	6,850,289	33,228,852	12/31/99
41. Abbott Laboratories Fund	IL	6,500,000	117,763,266	12/31/00
42. John Deere Foundation	IL	6,214,865	23,555,558	10/31/99
43. T. Rowe Price Associates Foundation	MD	6,045,925	29,925,686	12/31/00
44. Micron Technology Foundation	ID	5,805,000	19,381,131	12/31/00
45. Morgan Stanley Dean Witter Foundation	NY	5,545,313	32,329,164	12/31/99
46. HCA Foundation	TN	5,442,753	171,207,684	12/31/00
47. Steelcase Foundation	MI	5,000,000	123,961,148	11/30/00
48. GE Fund	CT	5,000,000	53,887,325	12/31/00
49. PacifiCorp Foundation for Learning	OR	5,000,000	43,720,955	3/31/00
50. Whirlpool Foundation	MI	5,000,000	21,557,173	3/31/00

Source: *Foundation Yearbook*, 2002.
*Aggregate foundation fiscal information is based on data provided to the Center as of February 2, 2002; fiscal data on individual foundations included in this table may be more current.

Largest Gifts Received. The largest gift amount reported was $286.9 million to the Michigan-based Ford Motor Company Fund from its parent company. Other recipients of especially large gifts included the New York-based Goldman, Sachs Foundation ($200.0 million), and the New York-based Citigroup Foundation ($107.8 million).

Trends of Corporate Foundations, 1987 to Present

The growth pattern of corporate foundations contrasts sharply with independent foundations. Although corporate foundations have been operating since the post-war period, growth in corporate philanthropy was most pronounced in the 1970s and mid-1980s. Corporate foundations fared much better than independent foundations in the inflationary economy of the 1970s; by the late 1980s, however, many long-established corporate giants fell prey to reduced profits, slumping oil prices, the decline of the manufacturing sector, business downsizing and restructuring, and the turmoil of mergers and acquisitions. On the brighter side, several industries that prospered in the 1980s—e.g., telecommunications, utilities, and financial services—were active in forming corporate foundations and bringing new resources to the field.

The development of a global economy has also affected corporate foundation grantmaking. As companies realize a greater share of their profits from overseas operations, many are increasing their giving outside the U.S. This global grantmaking is largely funded through companies' overseas affiliates and not through their foundations. Thus, overall growth in company giving may be underrepresented in foundation data.

To measure the growth of corporate foundations over time, the Foundation Center has compiled data on all corporate foundations since 1987.[4] An analysis of these foundations reveals the following trends in giving and assets.

Growth of Corporate Foundations. Overall, the number of corporate foundations has increased from 1,295 in 1987 to 2,018 in 2000, a 55.8 percent gain (Table 37). Still, most of this growth in number occurred through 1993. Since then, corporate mergers and buyouts, leading to foundation mergers and terminations, have cut down the rate of establishment of new corporate foundations. As a result, the net gain in number of active corporate foundations since 1993 totals only 62, a 3.2 percent rise.

4. Prior to the 2001 edition of *Foundation Yearbook*, this report presented biennial data on changes in the number of foundations, total giving, and total assets of larger corporate foundations, beginning with 1975.

Giving by Corporate Foundations. Support from corporate foundations grew almost two and two-thirds times (164.9 percent) since 1987 to nearly $3.0 billion in 2000. Adjusted for inflation, the thirteen-year increase was almost 75 percent. Growth in corporate foundation giving began to slip in the late 1980s, and annual increases averaged between 1 and 5 percent from the beginning of the 1990s through mid-decade. In 1996, spurred by the strong economy, corporate foundation giving began to rebound and reached a high of 15.0 percent growth in 1999. In 2000, the stock market fall and economic slowdown ended three straight years of double-digit growth in corporate foundation giving.

Assets of Corporate Foundations. Corporate foundation assets totaled $15.9 billion in 2000, up more than three-fold from $4.9 billion in 1987. In constant dollars, assets rose almost 115 percent. (In contrast, independent foundations' inflation-adjusted asset values increased by 173.5 percent over the same thirteen-year time period.) With the exception of 1989, corporate foundations realized only modest growth in the value of their assets through 1994. In 1995, the strengthening economy led corporations to begin replenishing their foundations' assets. The bull stock market of the late 1990s also added tremendous value to company stock. As a result, despite the current year's slowdown in asset growth, corporate foundations realized a more than four-fifths jump in their asset values since mid-decade.

Community Foundations

Community foundations represent a relatively small but extremely vital and influential component of the foundation universe. Not only were community foundations one of the fastest growing segments of philanthropy in the 1980s, but their leadership role in many communities increased along with stepped-up demands for private initiatives to solve local problems, such as crime, drugs, AIDS, homelessness, and the failure of many public school systems. In the 1990s, the role of community foundations was further heightened by the impact of economic restructuring and government downsizing on local economies. With government support of many nonprofits sharply reduced, community foundations have sought to expand resources by forging partnerships between public and private funding sources.

2000 Giving

- **Giving by community foundations grows 17 percent**
- **Giving by the largest community foundations increases faster**
- **Community funds account for nearly one-in-twelve grant dollars**

Growth in Number of Community Foundations. 560 community foundations reported grant activity in 2000, up almost 8 percent from the previous year. Overall, the number of community foundations in the

TABLE 37. Growth of Corporate Foundation Giving and Assets, 1987 to 2000*

			Total Giving (in millions)[1]				Assets (in millions)			
			Current Dollars		Constant Dollars[2]		Current Dollars		Constant Dollars[2]	
Year	Number of Foundations	% Change	Amount	% Change	Amount	% Change	Amount	% Change	Amount	% Change
1987	1,295		$1,127		$1,127		$4,884		$4,884	
1988	1,449	11.9	1,267	12.4	1,217	7.9	5,101	4.4	4,898	0.3
1989	1,587	9.5	1,366	7.8	1,252	2.9	5,727	12.3	5,247	7.1
1990	1,718	8.3	1,444	5.7	1,255	0.2	5,876	2.6	5,107	(2.7)
1991	1,775	3.3	1,490	3.2	1,243	(1.0)	6,038	2.8	5,036	(1.4)
1992	1,897	6.9	1,565	5.0	1,267	2.0	6,598	9.3	5,343	6.1
1993	1,956	3.1	1,585	1.3	1,246	(1.7)	6,885	4.3	5,412	1.3
1994	1,951	(0.3)	1,626	2.6	1,246	0.0	7,256	5.4	5,562	2.8
1995	1,946	(0.3)	1,699	4.5	1,266	1.6	8,687	19.7	6,476	16.4
1996	1,969	1.2	1,836	8.1	1,336	5.5	9,459	8.9	6,884	6.3
1997	2,029	3.0	2,066	12.6	1,466	9.7	10,887	15.1	7,725	12.2
1998	2,022	(0.3)	2,446	18.4	1,705	16.3	13,109	20.4	9,136	18.3
1999	2,019	(0.1)	2,814	15.0	1,918	12.5	15,258	16.4	10,404	13.9
2000	2,018	(0.0)	2,985	6.1	1,969	2.6	15,899	4.2	10,489	0.8

Source: *Foundation Yearbook*, 2002.
*The Foundation Center began tracking separate information on all corporate foundations in 1987.
[1] Includes grants, scholarships, and employee matching gifts; excludes set-asides, loans, PRIs, and program expenses.
[2] Constant 1987 dollars based on annual average Consumer Price Index, all urban consumers, U.S. Department of Labor, Bureau of Labor Statistics, as of March 2002.

Foundation Center's census has more than doubled since 1988.[5]

Community Foundations as a Share of All Giving. Community foundations accounted for 1 percent of the total number of active grantmaking foundations (Figure 27) but were responsible for 7.9 percent of giving (Figure 28) and 13.9 percent of gifts received (Figure 30). As the growth of corporate foundation giving diminished after 1987, community foundations' share of all philanthropic giving steadily increased.

Giving by Large vs. Small Community Funds. Of the 560 community foundations identified in the latest year, 217 made grants totaling $1 million or more—up 18.6 percent from the 183 reported in 1999 (Table 38). Together these foundations paid out close to $2.1 billion in grants or 95.5 percent of community foundation giving. The remaining 343 funders collectively gave away about $98.6 million.

Growth in funding among the category of largest community foundations was responsible for the biggest gains in grantmaking in 2000. For example, support in the highest category of funders (those making grants of $10 million or more) increased by 21.9 percent. By comparison, overall community foundation giving was up by 17.1 percent, while support in the range of large to mid-size funders (those making grants totaling between $1 million and $10 million) increased by 8.2 percent; and among those funders making grants totaling less than $1 million by 4.2 percent.

Established vs. New Community Foundations' Support. Established funders accounted for most of the increase in giving in 2000. The 34 newly reporting community funds provided only $16.9 million or approximately 5 percent of the $316.9 million in increased giving reported by community foundations. Excluding the grants of newly reporting community foundations, giving by established funders grew 16.2 percent.

Funding by the Top 25 Community Foundations. Giving by the nation's top 25 community foundations increased 14.1 percent in 2000, falling below the 17.1 percent gain reported for all community foundations. Four foundations—the San Francisco Foundation (CA), Peninsula Community Foundation (CA), Seattle Foundation (WA), and Oklahoma City Community Foundation (OK)—were responsible for two-thirds of this increase. If these foundations were excluded from the top 50 in both years, giving by the remaining top community funds would have increased a very modest 5.5 percent (Table 39).

To qualify for ranking among the top 25 community foundations, the minimum spending level was $22.3 million, distributed by the Rhode Island Foundation (RI), compared to the maximum of $144.0 million, awarded by the New York Community Trust (NY). In addition to the Trust, four other funders distributed at least $60 million: the San Francisco Foundation, Greater Kansas City Community Foundation and Affiliated Trusts (MO), California Community Foundation (CA), and Peninsula Community Foundation. An additional nineteen funders distributed at least $25 million. Among the top five funders, the threshold for giving remained unchanged at $64.0 million.

Top 25 Community Foundations with Increased Funding. Eighteen of the top 25 community foundations by giving increased funding in 2000. Among the top five funders, the Peninsula Community Foundation increased giving by nearly seven-tenths to $64.2 million after receiving gifts totaling $230.3 million in the latest year. Primary areas of foundation interest include homelessness and housing, children and youth, adult services, social services, and education.

Among other top 25 community foundations, the Oklahoma City Community Foundation more than tripled its giving to $30.9 million in 2000. The foundation received gifts of $62.4 million in the latest year. In addition, the Seattle Foundation raised its giving more than two and two-thirds times to $48.8 million.

Top 25 Community Foundations with Reduced Giving. Although many of the top 25 community funds increased their giving in 2000, seven reported decreases. Among those reporting declines in grant payments of at least 10 percent, the California Community Foundation's giving dropped by three-tenths; the

---

5. The Foundation Center's count of community foundations falls short of the number identified by other national sources, explained in part by different methods of tracking supporting organizations. The Center reports as one fiscal unit a community foundation and the supporting funds that it administers, if those funds are jointly reported in the foundation's IRS tax form 990. The Center's data on active grantmakers also excludes startup community foundations that have not yet awarded grants.

TABLE 38. Analysis of Community Foundations by Total Giving Range, 2000*

Total Giving Range	Number of Foundations	%	Total Giving[1]	%
$100 million+	1	0.2	$ 143,951	6.6
$25 million–$100 million	21	3.8	1,008,311	46.5
$10 million–$25 million	22	3.9	349,225	16.1
$1 million–$10 million	173	30.9	566,257	26.2
$100,000–$1 million	216	38.6	93,356	4.3
Under $100,000	127	22.7	5,243	0.2
Total	**560**	**100.0**	**$2,166,343**	**100.0**

Source: *Foundation Yearbook*, 2002.
*Dollars in thousands.
[1]Includes grants, scholarships, and employee matching gifts; excludes set-asides, loans, PRIs, and program expenses.

TABLE 39. 25 Largest Community Foundations by Total Giving, 2000*

	Foundation	State	Total Giving[1]	Assets	Fiscal Date
1.	New York Community Trust	NY	$143,950,743	$1,930,370,263	12/31/00
2.	San Francisco Foundation	CA	86,000,000	741,000,000	6/30/01
3.	Greater Kansas City Community Foundation and Affiliated Trusts	MO	85,426,000	719,476,000	12/31/00
4.	California Community Foundation	CA	78,300,000	547,793,000	6/30/01
5.	Peninsula Community Foundation	CA	64,243,451	449,062,871	12/31/00
6.	Columbus Foundation and Affiliated Organizations	OH	57,605,631	677,889,306	12/31/00
7.	Cleveland Foundation	OH	57,030,931	1,600,206,255	12/31/00
8.	Community Foundation Silicon Valley[2]	CA	52,145,296	583,088,268	6/30/01
9.	Marin Community Foundation	CA	50,524,713	1,150,556,205	6/30/01
10.	Boston Foundation	MA	48,952,445	656,806,419	6/30/01
11.	Seattle Foundation	WA	48,833,167	305,644,179	12/30/00
12.	Communities Foundation of Texas	TX	42,798,517	657,906,999	6/30/00
13.	Chicago Community Trust and Affiliates	IL	41,243,732	1,302,626,633	9/30/00
14.	Omaha Community Foundation	NE	40,927,643	378,324,615	12/31/00
15.	San Diego Foundation	CA	38,000,000	401,000,000	6/30/01
16.	Oregon Community Foundation	OR	36,406,143	471,989,656	12/31/00
17.	Community Foundation of Greater Memphis	TN	33,099,247	207,867,607	4/30/01
18.	Oklahoma City Community Foundation	OK	30,855,478	400,661,819	6/30/01
19.	Minneapolis Foundation	MN	28,961,477	542,651,730	3/31/01
20.	Community Foundation for Greater Atlanta	GA	28,892,461	396,512,792	6/30/01
21.	Saint Paul Foundation	MN	27,547,750	449,062,871	12/31/00
22.	Community Foundation for the National Capital Region	DC	26,729,312	153,896,592	3/31/01
23.	Foundation For The Carolinas	NC	26,405,093	250,975,459	12/31/00
24.	Hartford Foundation for Public Giving	CT	25,897,228	647,516,680	9/30/00
25.	Rhode Island Foundation	RI	22,329,586	391,199,463	12/31/00

Source: *Foundation Yearbook*, 2002.
*Aggregate foundation fiscal information is based on data provided to the Center as of February 2, 2002; fiscal data on individual foundations included in this table may be more current.
[1] Includes grants, scholarships, and employee matching gifts; excludes set-asides, loans, PRIs, and program expenses.
[2] Figures based on unaudited financial information.

Community Foundation for the National Capitol Region (DC) reduced distributions by 16.1 percent; the Foundation For The Carolinas (NC) decreased funding by 13.6 percent; and the Cleveland Foundation's giving declined by 11.0 percent.

2000 Assets

- Community foundations' assets grow 10.2 percent
- Assets reach $30.5 billion, nearly doubling since 1996

Growth of Community Foundation Assets. Assets of community foundations grew 10.2 percent in 2000 (Table 24), amounting to just half of the prior year's 20.4 percent increase. Assets totaled $30.5 billion, up from $27.6 billion in 1999 and close to double the $15.9 billion reported in 1996.

Assets of Large vs. Small Community Foundations. 266 community foundations held assets of $10 million or over in 2000, up 10.4 percent from the 241 tracked last year (Table 40). These foundations held 96.9 percent of all community fund assets. A total of 205 funders reported assets ranging from $1 million to $10 million, while 89 had not yet reached the $1 million mark in asset accumulation. In all, 58 community foundations now hold assets of $100 million or more, up from 55 last year, and more than four times the 14 reported in 1990.

Not surprising given dramatic market gains and new gifts to all foundations, many community foundations have increased the value of their endowments, and the biggest gains in total assets have been reported in the highest asset ranges. For example, the total value of endowments of at least $50 million grew by 10.5 percent, while endowments in the less than $10 million range experienced a 4.4 percent gain.

Assets of Top 25 Community Foundations. Qualifying asset values among the 25 largest community funds ranged from the Arizona Community Foundation's

TABLE 40. Analysis of Community Foundations by Asset Range, 2000*

Asset Range	Number of Foundations	%	Assets	%	Total Giving[1]	%
$1 billion+	4	0.7	$ 5,983,759	19.6	$ 292,750	13.5
$250 million–$1 billion	26	4.6	11,930,594	39.2	991,045	45.7
$50 million–$250 million	78	13.9	8,046,397	26.4	547,795	25.3
$10 million–$50 million	158	28.2	3,553,282	11.7	252,925	11.7
$1 million–$10 million	205	36.6	910,298	3.0	73,992	3.4
Under $1 million	89	15.9	39,343	0.1	7,835	0.3
Total	560	100.0	$30,463,674	100.0	$2,166,343	100.0

Source: *Foundation Yearbook*, 2002.
*Dollars in thousands; due to rounding, figures may not add up.
[1] Includes grants, scholarships, and employee matching gifts; excludes set-asides, loans, PRIs, and program expenses.

$320.0 million to the $1.9 billion held by the New York Community Trust (Table 41). Overall, assets of these leading grantmakers grew by 8.1 percent, falling below the 10.2 percent growth reported for all community foundations.

Top 25 Community Foundations with Asset Gains. In 2000, 19 of the leading community foundations realized asset increases. Three reported gains of at least 40 percent, and six additional funders showed increases of at least 20 percent. Interestingly, most of the fastest growing funds were located west of the Mississippi.

TABLE 41. 25 Largest Community Foundations by Asset Size, 2000*

	Foundation	State	Assets	Total Giving[1]	Fiscal Date
1.	New York Community Trust	NY	$1,930,370,263	$143,950,743	12/31/00
2.	Cleveland Foundation	OH	1,600,206,255	57,030,931	12/31/00
3.	Chicago Community Trust and Affiliates	IL	1,302,626,633	41,243,732	9/30/00
4.	Marin Community Foundation	CA	1,150,556,205	50,524,713	6/30/01
5.	San Francisco Foundation	CA	741,000,000	86,000,000	6/30/01
6.	Greater Kansas City Community Foundation and Affiliated Trusts	MO	719,476,000	85,426,000	12/31/00
7.	Columbus Foundation and Affiliated Organizations	OH	677,889,306	57,605,631	12/31/00
8.	Communities Foundation of Texas	TX	657,906,999	42,798,517	6/30/00
9.	Boston Foundation	MA	656,806,419	48,952,445	6/30/01
10.	Hartford Foundation for Public Giving	CT	647,516,680	25,897,228	9/30/00
11.	Saint Paul Foundation	MN	588,426,310	27,547,750	12/31/00
12.	Community Foundation Silicon Valley[2]	CA	583,088,268	52,145,296	6/30/01
13.	Pittsburgh Foundation	PA	548,374,723	22,090,867	12/31/00
14.	California Community Foundation	CA	547,793,000	78,300,000	6/30/01
15.	Minneapolis Foundation	MN	542,651,730	28,961,477	3/31/01
16.	Oregon Community Foundation	OR	471,989,656	36,406,143	12/31/00
17.	Peninsula Community Foundation	CA	449,062,871	64,243,451	12/31/00
18.	San Diego Foundation	CA	401,000,000	38,000,000	6/30/01
19.	Oklahoma City Community Foundation	OK	400,661,819	30,855,478	6/30/01
20.	Greater Cincinnati Foundation	OH	400,057,095	21,211,019	12/31/00
21.	Rhode Island Foundation	RI	391,199,463	22,329,586	12/31/00
22.	Community Foundation Serving Richmond & Central Virginia	VA	379,000,000	21,300,000	12/31/00
23.	Omaha Community Foundation	NE	378,324,615	40,927,643	12/31/00
24.	Greater Milwaukee Foundation	WI	324,905,682	13,443,138	12/31/00
25.	Arizona Community Foundation	AZ	319,959,000	17,522,000	12/31/00

Source: *Foundation Yearbook*, 2002.
*Aggregate foundation fiscal information is based on data provided to the Center as of February 2, 2002; fiscal data on individual foundations included in this table may be more current.
[1] Includes grants, scholarships, and employee matching gifts; excludes set-asides, loans, PRIs, and program expenses.
[2] Figures based on unaudited financial information.

For example, the Peninsula Community Foundation (CA) experienced the strongest growth, increasing its assets by close to half in 2000. Gifts to the foundation more than doubled in the latest year to $230.3 million. Other funders posting strong growth included: the Greater Kansas City Community Foundation, with assets up by two-fifths to $719.5 million; and the San Diego Foundation, with assets increasing by two-fifths to $401.0 million.

Community Foundations New to the Top 25. All of the top 25 community foundations ranked by assets in 1999 continued to rank among the top 25 in 2000, although ranks did change for many funders. For example, the Chicago Community Trust (IL) moved up from fourth to third and the Greater Kansas City Community Foundation climbed from twelfth to sixth, while the Boston Foundation (MA) slipped from sixth to ninth and the Pittsburgh Foundation (PA) moved down from ninth to thirteenth.

Top 25 Community Foundations with Reduced Assets. Despite the gains noted above, six of the top 25 community foundations reported decreases in asset values in the latest year. The Omaha Community Foundation (NE) reported the largest decrease in giving between 1999 and 2000, with assets down 15.1 percent to $378.3 million. For the remaining community foundations, asset decreases ranged from 0.7 percent to 7.8 percent.

2000 Gifts Received

- **Gifts to community foundations grow over 16 percent**
- **71 community funds receive gifts totaling at least $10 million**

Gifts and Bequests to Community Foundations. Unlike independent foundations, which rely primarily on investment performance to increase assets, community foundations seek to raise their asset base both through the growth of their existing pooled funds and through the cultivation of new donors. Gifts to endowments and "pass-through" funds increased from $3.3 billion to $3.8 billion—up 16.2 percent—following a 27.6 percent increase in 1999. Moreover, new gifts to community foundations exceeded grants paid out by nearly $1.7 billion, contributing to an increase in asset values.

The number of community foundations receiving gifts totaling at least $80 million increased from eight to nine in the latest year, while those with gifts of $10 million or more totaled 71, up from 64 in 1999. Ten foundations based in California received gifts totaling at least $10 million, followed by Ohio (5), and North Carolina (4). None of the remaining states reported more than three foundations with gifts in this range.

Largest Gifts Received. Community Foundation Silicon Valley received the largest amount of gifts into a community foundation in 2000—$243.1 million (Table 42). The foundation provides support to organizations located primarily in Santa Clara County for education, health and social services, performing arts, community development and urban affairs, and the environment. The nearby Peninsula Community Foundation ranked second in the latest year with gifts totaling $230.3 million (noted earlier).

Other Notable Gifts. Other community foundations reporting gifts totaling at least $100 million in 2000 included: the Communities Foundation of Texas (TX), New York Community Trust, Greater Kansas City Community Foundation, California Community Foundation, and San Francisco Foundation. An additional 11 foundations reported gifts totaling at least $50 million.

Trends of Community Foundations, 1987 to Present

- **Community foundation giving more than doubles since 1996**

Formation and growth patterns of community foundations have differed substantially from independent and corporate foundations. While the 1950s and early 1960s were peak

TABLE 42. 50 Largest Community Foundations by Gifts Received, 2000*

	Foundation	State	Gifts Received	Assets	Fiscal Date
1.	Community Foundation Silicon Valley[1]	CA	$243,128,235	$ 583,088,268	6/30/01
2.	Peninsula Community Foundation	CA	230,268,777	449,062,871	12/31/00
3.	Communities Foundation of Texas	TX	148,932,294	657,906,999	6/30/00
4.	New York Community Trust	NY	126,156,270	1,930,370,263	12/31/00
5.	Greater Kansas City Community Foundation and Affiliated Trusts	MO	119,047,000	719,476,000	12/31/00
6.	California Community Foundation	CA	103,996,063	547,793,000	6/30/01
7.	San Francisco Foundation	CA	103,000,000	741,000,000	6/30/01
8.	Oregon Community Foundation	OR	81,322,109	471,989,656	12/31/00
9.	Community Foundation for the National Capital Region	DC	80,994,401	153,896,592	3/31/01
10.	Baton Rouge Area Foundation	LA	79,713,000	229,406,000	12/31/00
11.	Community Foundation for Southeastern Michigan	MI	71,834,623	309,173,270	12/31/00
12.	Columbus Foundation and Affiliated Organizations	OH	70,417,959	677,889,306	12/31/00
13.	Hartford Foundation for Public Giving	CT	65,883,751	647,516,680	9/30/00
14.	Oklahoma City Community Foundation	OK	62,423,801	400,661,819	6/30/01
15.	Community Foundation of Middle Tennessee	TN	60,588,238	125,518,170	12/31/00
16.	Seattle Foundation	WA	58,138,462	305,644,179	12/30/00
17.	Community Foundation Serving Richmond & Central Virginia	VA	57,700,000	379,000,000	12/31/00
18.	Delaware Community Foundation	DE	57,618,328	111,647,400	6/30/99
19.	San Diego Foundation	CA	49,263,000	401,000,000	6/30/01
20.	Central Indiana Community Foundation	IN	46,979,817	170,665,591	12/31/00
21.	Chicago Community Trust and Affiliates	IL	45,296,495	1,302,626,633	9/30/00
22.	Cleveland Foundation	OH	44,112,658	1,600,206,255	12/31/00
23.	Boston Foundation	MA	43,925,289	656,806,419	6/30/01
24.	Minneapolis Foundation	MN	43,394,237	542,651,730	3/31/01
25.	Arizona Community Foundation	AZ	41,072,000	319,959,000	12/31/00
26.	Greater Cincinnati Foundation	OH	36,705,255	400,057,095	12/31/00
27.	Foundation For The Carolinas	NC	36,441,020	250,975,459	12/31/00
28.	Community Foundation of Greater Memphis	TN	35,919,582	207,867,607	4/30/01
29.	Orange County Community Foundation	CA	34,370,424	72,451,652	6/30/00
30.	New Hampshire Charitable Foundation	NH	31,069,263	237,664,323	12/31/00
31.	Omaha Community Foundation	NE	30,542,480	378,324,615	12/31/00
32.	Tulsa Community Foundation	OK	29,468,654	30,732,623	6/30/00
33.	Greater New Orleans Foundation	LA	28,982,182	93,408,483	12/31/00
34.	Winston-Salem Foundation	NC	28,758,342	192,885,819	12/31/00
35.	Dayton Foundation	OH	26,757,806	237,115,343	6/30/00
36.	Marin Community Foundation	CA	26,377,249	1,150,556,205	6/30/01
37.	Maine Community Foundation	ME	25,561,777	95,872,327	12/31/00
38.	Community Foundation for Fox Valley Region	WI	24,446,851	83,232,564	6/30/00
39.	Greater Milwaukee Foundation	WI	24,337,684	324,905,682	12/31/00
40.	East Bay Community Foundation	CA	24,185,999	99,825,401	6/30/00
41.	Saint Paul Foundation	MN	22,489,345	588,426,310	12/31/00
42.	Community Foundation of Tampa Bay	FL	20,655,175	108,947,323	6/30/00
43.	Austin Community Foundation for the Capital Area	TX	20,092,028	53,417,453	12/31/00
44.	Greater Houston Community Foundation	TX	19,563,240	52,262,075	12/31/00
45.	Community Foundation of Louisville	KY	16,933,254	175,783,559	6/30/00
46.	Idaho Community Foundation	ID	16,851,412	47,823,330	12/31/00
47.	Pittsburgh Foundation	PA	16,573,729	548,374,723	12/31/00
48.	Community Foundation of Western North Carolina	NC	16,092,000	93,218,729	6/30/01
49.	Toledo Community Foundation	OH	16,000,000	96,000,000	12/31/00
50.	Greater Kanawha Valley Foundation	WV	15,673,709	101,331,230	12/31/00

Source: *Foundation Yearbook,* 2002.
*Aggregate foundation fiscal information is based on data provided to the Center as of February 2, 2002; fiscal data on individual foundations included in this table may be more current.
[1]Figures based on unaudited financial information.

years for private foundation development, followed by a sharp decline in the 1970s, community foundations expanded rapidly in the 1970s and continued to grow throughout the 1980s and 1990s. (For more details, see the next chapter on "Foundation Development".)

To measure the growth of community foundations, the Foundation Center has compiled data on all community foundations for roughly two decades.[6] An analysis of these foundations reveals the following trends in giving and assets.

Growth of Community Foundations. From 1981 to 2000, the number of community foundations rose more than two and two-thirds times, from 208 to 560 (Table 43), and this growth can be expected to continue. Since 1979, the development of community foundations has been actively promoted by special projects of the Council on Foundations and of regional associations of grantmakers, and by special gift matching programs of several large foundations, including C.S. Mott, Ford, Kellogg, Lilly, Kresge, Hewlett, and others.

---

6. Prior to the 2001 edition of *Foundation Yearbook*, this report presented biennial data on changes in the number of foundations, total giving, and total assets of larger community foundations, beginning with 1975.

Giving by Community Foundations. Among community foundations, grants have increased almost twelve-fold, from $183 million in 1981 to $2.2 billion in 2000 (Table 43). After adjusting for inflation, contributions have increased more than six-fold (525.1 percent). Community foundations have realized positive growth in giving in all but one year (1994) since the start of the 1980s. Nonetheless, the consecutive double-digit annual increases in giving after 1994 represent the strongest period of growth on record.

Assets of Community Foundations. Between 1981 and 2000, assets of community foundations increased fourteen-fold, from close to $2.2 billion to more than $30.5 billion. In constant dollars, their value grew more than seven-fold. Community foundation assets rose more rapidly than those of independent foundations in part because they did not suffer the same declines that characterized independent foundation assets at the start of the 1980s (resulting from the high payout rates required for private foundations); and in part due to the extraordinary success of many community foundations in attracting new endowed funds. As a result, compared to independent and corporate foundations since 1995, community foundations have sustained a longer consistent run of double-digit annual asset growth.

TABLE 43. Growth of Community Foundation Giving and Assets, 1981 to 2000*

Year	Number of Foundations	% Change	Total Giving[1] (in millions) Current Dollars Amount	% Change	Constant Dollars[2] Amount	% Change	Assets (in millions) Current Dollars Amount	% Change	Constant Dollars[2] Amount	% Change
1981	208		$183		$183		$2,174		$2,174	
1982	225	8.2	233	27.4	219	20.0	2,668	22.7	2,513	15.6
1983	236	4.9	242	4.1	221	0.8	2,792	4.7	2,548	1.4
1984	243	3.0	278	15.0	244	10.2	3,134	12.3	2,742	7.6
1985	250	2.9	290	4.1	245	0.5	4,049	29.2	3,421	24.8
1986	—	—	—	—	—	—	—	—	—	—
1987	232	(7.2)	313	8.1	251	2.4	4,596	13.5	3,678	7.5
1988	256	10.3	405	29.4	312	24.3	4,938	7.4	3,794	3.2
1989	282	10.2	427	5.4	313	0.5	6,002	21.5	4,400	16.0
1990	328	16.3	496	16.1	345	10.1	6,622	10.3	4,606	4.7
1991	335	2.1	545	9.8	364	5.4	8,046	21.5	5,370	16.6
1992	353	5.4	638	17.1	413	13.7	8,726	8.5	5,654	5.3
1993	374	5.9	718	12.6	452	9.3	9,691	11.1	6,096	7.8
1994	403	7.8	653	(9.1)	400	(11.4)	10,071	3.9	6,177	1.3
1995	413	2.5	806	23.5	481	20.1	12,383	23.0	7,386	19.6
1996	411	(0.5)	951	18.1	554	15.3	15,858	28.1	9,235	25.0
1997	403	(1.9)	1,192	25.3	677	22.2	19,700	24.2	11,185	21.1
1998	437	8.4	1,458	22.3	813	20.1	22,955	16.5	12,801	14.4
1999	519	18.8	1,849	26.9	1,009	24.1	27,649	20.4	15,086	17.8
2000	560	7.9	2,166	17.1	1,144	13.3	30,464	10.2	16,081	6.6

Source: *Foundation Yearbook*, 2002.
*The Foundation Center began tracking separate fiscal information on all community foundations in 1981.
[1]Includes grants, scholarships, and employee matching gifts; excludes set-asides, loans, PRIs, and program expenses.
[2]Constant 1981 dollars based on annual average Consumer Price Index, all urban consumers, U.S. Department of Labor, Bureau of Labor Statistics, as of March 2002.
— = not available

Grantmaking Operating Foundations

Operating foundations primarily conduct their own programs or provide a direct service. Nevertheless, three-fifths (60.1 percent) of the 5,780 operating foundations in the U.S. report some level of grant activity. Most of these grantmaking operating foundations make only a tiny number of grants related to their primary purpose. However, a few have established distinct grants programs. For various reasons, grantmaking operating foundations experienced very strong growth in the mid-1990s, prompting the Center to include them in this analysis of trends by foundation type. Since operating foundations are not required to make grants, however, recent trends are not necessarily predictors of future giving.

The dynamic growth of operating foundations in recent years suggests that more donors are choosing to develop and administer their own programs instead of serving as funding resources for other groups. It also suggests that the lines between operating and independent foundations may be blurring, since operating foundations in some cases are becoming large grantmakers.

2000 Giving

- Operating foundations provide grants totaling nearly $1.1 billion

- Operating foundation grants represent 3.9 percent of all foundation giving

- Number of grantmaking operating foundations rises by more than one-fifth

Growth in Number of Operating Foundations. In 2000, 3,472 operating foundations reported grant activity, up 22.3 percent from last year and more than three and one-third times the 1,040 grantmakers reported for 1987 (see Table 47 in Chapter 5). In the 1980s and early 1990s, the number of operating foundations grew faster than all other types of foundations. From 1993 to 1999, operating foundations maintained a roughly consistent 5.5 percent share of the overall number of grantmaking foundations. In the latest year, however, operating foundations climbed to 6.1 percent of the total number of grantmaking foundations (Figure 27).

Operating Foundations as a Share of All Giving. Consistent with the growth in their share of number of grantmaking foundations, operating foundations provided 3.9 percent of grant dollars in 2000, up from 2.9 percent in 1999 (Figure 28). Moreover, this share amounts to three times the 1.3 percent of total giving they accounted for in 1993.

Giving by operating foundations grew by nearly three-fifths (59.2 percent) in 2000, from $669.1 million to nearly $1.1 billion. In addition, operating foundation support in the latest year was more than nine times greater than the $114 million reported in 1990. A small number of recently established foundations—such as the Searle Patients in Need Foundation (NJ), Bristol-Myers Squibb Patient Assistance Foundation (NJ), and Lilly Care Foundation (IN)—were largely responsible for the increased giving in the latest year.

Top Ten Operating Foundations with Increased Funding. The ten largest operating foundations by giving accounted for $601.1 million or 56.4 percent of all grants paid by grantmaking operating foundations. The three largest by giving—Open Society Institute (NY), Searle Patients in Need Foundation (IL), and Bristol-Myers Squibb Patient Assistance Foundation—were alone responsible for $307.1 million or close to three-tenths (28.8 percent) of dollars distributed (Table 44).

While the Open Society Institute continued to hold the top position among grantmaking operating foundations, the Searle Patients in Need Foundation moved into second place after increasing giving in the latest year from $22.4 million to nearly $96 million.

TABLE 44. Ten Largest Grantmaking Operating Foundations by Total Giving, 2000*

	Foundation	State	Total Giving[1]	Qualifying Distributions[2]	Fiscal Date
1.	Open Society Institute	NY	**$116,342,544**	$160,496,757	12/31/00
2.	Searle Patients in Need Foundation	NJ	**95,975,582**	96,311,112	12/31/00
3.	Bristol-Myers Squibb Patient Assistance Foundation	NJ	**94,805,585**	98,269,671	12/31/00
4.	Lilly Cares Foundation	IN	**86,650,335**	87,695,970	12/31/00
5.	Janssen Ortho Patient Assistance Foundation	NJ	**81,294,984**	81,294,984	12/31/00
6.	Freedom Forum	VA	**36,320,040**	N/A	12/31/00
7.	Karfunkel Family Foundation	NY	**34,203,777**	34,204,277	6/30/00
8.	Packard Humanities Institute	CA	**20,655,346**	35,022,214	12/31/00
9.	Samuel Roberts Noble Foundation	OK	**17,554,773**	41,290,165	10/31/00
10.	J. Paul Getty Trust	CA	**17,344,634**	279,747,018	6/30/00

Source: *Foundation Yearbook*, 2002.

*Aggregate foundation fiscal information is based on data provided to the Center as of February 2, 2002; fiscal data on individual foundations included in this table may be more current.

[1]For some operating foundations, total giving includes grants and program expenses; for others, total giving includes only grants. Most operating foundations' qualifying distributions are paid out for administration of operating programs and not for grants.

[2]Qualifying distributions is the amount used in calculating the required payout; includes total giving, as well as reasonable administrative expenses, set-asides, PRIs, operating program expenses, and amount paid to acquire assets used directly for charitable purposes.

Established in 1990, the foundation provides prescription drugs to indigent people.

Operating Foundations New to the Top Ten. Five funders were new to the list of top ten grantmaking operating foundations in 2000, including the Bristol-Myers Squibb Patient Assistance Foundation, Lilly Cares Foundation (IN), Karfunkel Family Foundation (NY), Packard Humanities Institute (CA), and Samuel Roberts Noble Foundation (OK).

2000 Assets

- Operating foundation assets grow more than 27 percent

Growth of Operating Foundation Assets. Asset values of the 3,472 grantmaking operating foundations rose by 27.3 percent in 2000, far surpassing independent, community, and corporate foundations (Table 23). Contributing to this faster growth in assets was the J. Paul Getty Trust (CA), which reported a one-quarter increase in the value of its assets, from $8.7 billion in 1999 to $10.9 billion in the latest year.

Assets of Large vs. Small Operating Foundations. Of the 3,472 active grantmaking operating foundations, roughly one-fourth held assets of at least $1 million. Yet together these funders controlled 98.2 percent of operating foundations' assets (Table 45). By far the largest operating foundation by asset size was the J. Paul Getty Trust, with assets of $10.9 billion (Table 46). Established in 1953 and fully endowed in 1982, Getty ranks fourth by assets among foundations overall. In the latest year, it gave out $17.3 million in grants for arts conservation and scholarships in the history of art, up from $14.6 million in 1999.

2000 Gifts Received

- Grantmaking operating foundations receive $1.7 billion in gifts

Gifts and Bequests to Operating Foundations. Grantmaking operating foundations received gifts and bequests totaling $1.7 billion in 2000, a 26.0 percent increase over the $1.4 billion reported last year. Four foundations received gifts from their donors of $90 million or more—Open Society Institute, Searle Patients in Need Foundation, Bristol-Myers Squibb Patient Assistance Foundation, and Janssen Ortho Patient Assistance Foundation—compared to one in 1999.

TABLE 45. Analysis of Grantmaking Operating Foundations by Asset Range, 2000*

Asset Range	Number of Foundations	%	Assets	%	Total Giving[1]	%	Programs	%
$1 billion+	4	0.1	$16,166,552	52.2	$ 73,157	6.9	$ 433,026	36.8
$250 million–$1 billion	11	0.3	5,743,396	18.5	187,380	17.6	97,679	8.3
$50 million–$250 million	38	1.1	3,933,332	12.7	45,100	4.2	120,600	10.3
$10 million–$50 million	118	3.4	2,426,753	7.8	224,491	21.1	203,089	17.3
$1 million–$10 million	690	19.9	2,167,362	7.0	321,956	30.2	283,652	24.1
Under $1 million	2,611	75.2	535,761	1.7	213,862	20.1	39,265	3.3
Total	**3,472**	**100.0**	**$30,973,156**	**100.0**	**$1,065,947**	**100.0**	**$1,177,311**	**100.0**

Source: *Foundation Yearbook,* 2002.
*Dollars in thousands; due to rounding, figures may not add up.
[1]For some operating foundations, total giving amount includes grants and program expenses; for others, total giving amount includes only grants. Most operating foundations' qualifying distributions are paid out for administration of operating programs and not for grants.

TABLE 46. Ten Largest Grantmaking Operating Foundations by Asset Size, 2000*

	Foundation	State	Assets	Total Giving[1]	Qualifying Distributions[2]	Gifts Received	Fiscal Date
1.	J. Paul Getty Trust	CA	$10,929,809,811	$17,344,634	$279,747,018	$1,573,357	6/30/00
2.	Casey Family Programs	WA	2,811,000,726	1,824,177	136,683,045	5,133,194	12/31/00
3.	Packard Humanities Institute	CA	1,302,804,659	20,655,346	35,022,214	0	12/31/00
4.	Freedom Forum	VA	1,037,110,607	36,320,040	N/A	N/A	12/31/00
5.	Samuel Roberts Noble Foundation	OK	971,672,378	17,554,773	41,290,165	25,000	10/31/00
6.	Kimbell Art Foundation	TX	912,000,000	775,000	21,000,000	285,000	12/31/00
7.	John E. Fetzer Institute	MI	372,922,306	1,287,320	15,378,625	637,102	7/31/00
8.	Gerry Foundation	NY	185,542,521	1,977,770	4,598,057	6,665,625	10/31/00
9.	Christensen Fund	CA	158,572,533	8,903,454	8,677,411	2,720,107	11/30/00
10.	Research Corporation	AZ	158,566,094	6,067,278	6,067,278	198,053	12/31/00

Source: *Foundation Yearbook,* 2002.
*Aggregate foundation fiscal information is based on data provided to the Center as of February 2, 2002; fiscal data on individual foundations included in this table may be more current.
[1]For some operating foundations, total giving includes grants and program expenses; for others, total giving includes only grants. Most operating foundations' qualifying distributions are paid out for administration of operating programs and not for grants.
[2]Qualifying distributions is the amount used in calculating the required payout; includes total giving, as well as reasonable administrative expenses, set-asides, PRIs, operating program expenses, and amount paid to acquire assets used directly for charitable purposes.

CHAPTER 5

Foundation Development

Overview through 2000

- Foundation community grows a record 12.7 percent in latest year
- Number of grantmaking foundations grows by nearly 6,400
- Close to 56,600 active grantmaking foundations reported

According to the Foundation Center's latest census, there are now nearly 56,600 grantmaking foundations in the U.S.[1] This figure comprises more than 50,500 independent foundations (including family foundations), more than 2,000 corporate foundations, 560 community foundations, and close to 3,500 grantmaking operating foundations.

Between 1999 and 2000, the foundation community grew from 50,201 to 56,582, up by 6,381 funders or 12.7 percent—the largest annual increase reported by the Foundation Center since tracking of all U.S. foundations began in 1975 (Figure 31 and Table 47). This gain surpassed a 7 percent rise in 1999 and represented more than double the roughly 6 percent increases reported in 1998 and 1997. Moreover, the current annual growth rate of foundations represents more than triple the growth rate seen in the years 1994 through 1996. In addition, 2000's net gain of close to 6,400 foundations that made grants is the largest on record in absolute terms. The vast majority of these foundations were formed in 1999 and 1998 and started grantmaking in 2000.

Foundation Creation Before 1970

- Modern foundations date to early 1900s
- Foundations established in 1940s and 50s hold disproportionately large share of assets

To put recent formation in context, we must look back over a century of development. The concept of private foundations as they exist today dates back to the beginning of the 1900s when the first general purpose or "modern" foundations were created by wealthy individuals, including the Russell Sage Foundation (1907), Carnegie Corporation of New York (1911), and Rockefeller Foundation (1913).

The first community fund, the Cleveland Foundation, was established in 1914, and by 1930 another 36 trusts still active today had been formed. Although corporations were not allowed federal tax deductions for charitable contributions until 1936, a few corporate foundations, such as the Dayton Hudson Foundation[2] (1918) and the Belk Foundation (1928), were formed in these early years as well.

More than one-in-six (15.5 percent) of the giant foundations of today—those with assets of $100 million or over—were established before 1940 (Table 48). Still, the overall number of foundations was quite small. It was only after World War II that the foundation movement experienced explosive growth, attributed to societal needs that surfaced in the wake of the war, the emergence of corporate foundations, a new emphasis on family foundations with living donors, and the very high income tax rates then in effect.

The rate of foundation creation nearly tripled in the 1940s and grew slightly faster in the 1950s (Table 49), the highest growth rates of any period. These decades

---

1. For detailed information on the Foundation Center's methodology for identifying and counting grantmaking foundations, see Appendix A. The Center's criteria exclude entities in the IRS private foundation file that are failed public charities, that have been inactive for more than three years, or have not yet filed a 990-PF or reported any grant activity.

2. The Dayton Hudson Foundation (MN) has since been renamed the Target Foundation (MN).

FIGURE 31. Number of Grantmaking Foundations, 1975 to 2000*

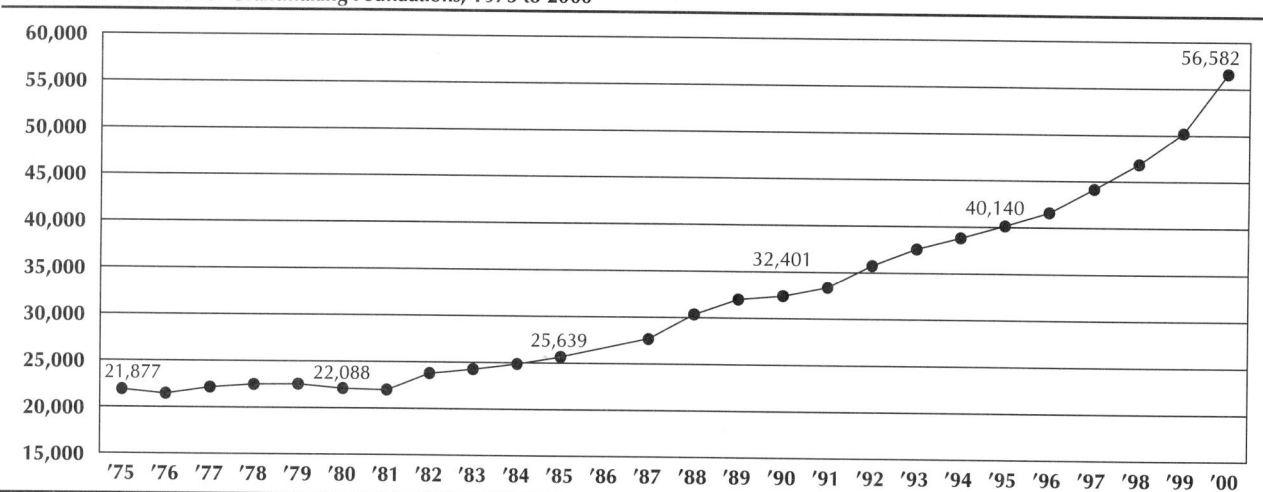

Source: *Foundation Yearbook,* 2002.

*The close to 35,000 grantmaking foundations added between 1975 and 2000 represent an increase in newly created foundations (approx. 34,000), the addition of nonexempt charitable trusts to the IRS file of "private" foundations, and an increase in the number of grantmaking operating foundations.

TABLE 47. Number of Active Grantmaking Foundations, 1975 to 2000*

	All Types		Private Foundations							Community Foundations[1]	
Year	Number	% Change	Number	IN	% Change	CS	% Change	OP	% Change	Number	% Change
1975	21,887		21,877	—		—		—		—	
1976	21,447	(2.0)	21,447	—		—		—		—	
1977	22,152	3.3	21,982	—		—		—		170	
1978	22,484	1.5	22,325	—		—		—		159	(6.5)
1979	22,535	0.2	22,348	—		—		—		187	17.6
1980	22,088	(2.0)	21,906	—		—		—		182	(2.7)
1981	21,967	(0.5)	21,759	—		—		496		208	14.3
1982[2]	23,770	8.2	23,545	—		—		817	64.7	225	8.2
1983	24,261	2.1	24,025	—		—		676	(17.3)	236	4.9
1984	24,859	2.5	24,616	—		—		907	34.2	243	3.0
1985	25,639	3.1	25,389	—		—		677	(25.4)	250	2.9
1986	26,650		—	—		—		—		—	
1987[3]	27,661		27,429	25,094		1,295		1,040		232	
1988	30,338	9.7	30,082	27,411	9.2	1,449	11.9	1,222	17.5	256	10.3
1989	31,990	5.4	31,708	28,669	4.6	1,587	9.5	1,452	18.8	282	10.2
1990	32,401	1.3	32,073	28,743	0.3	1,718	8.3	1,612	11.0	328	16.3
1991	33,356	2.9	33,021	29,476	2.6	1,775	3.3	1,770	9.8	335	2.1
1992	35,765	7.2	35,412	31,604	7.2	1,897	6.9	1,911	8.0	353	5.4
1993	37,571	5.0	37,197	33,224	5.1	1,956	3.1	2,017	5.5	375	6.2
1994	38,807	3.3	38,404	34,319	3.3	1,951	(0.3)	2,134	5.8	403	7.5
1995	40,140	3.4	39,727	35,602	3.7	1,946	(0.3)	2,179	2.1	413	2.5
1996	41,588	3.6	41,177	36,885	3.6	1,969	1.2	2,323	6.6	411	(0.5)
1997	44,146	6.2	43,743	39,248	6.4	2,029	3.0	2,466	6.2	403	(1.9)
1998	46,832	6.1	46,395	41,751	6.4	2,022	(0.3)	2,622	6.3	437	8.4
1999	50,201	7.2	49,682	44,824	7.4	2,019	(0.1)	2,839	8.3	519	18.8
2000	56,582	12.7	56,022	50,532	12.7	2,018	(0.0)	3,472	22.3	560	7.9

Source: *The Foundation Center,* 2002.

— = not available; IN = Independent; CS = Corporate; OP = Operating

[1]Collection of data on community foundations began with the fiscal year 1977. Data solicited annually by questionnaire; community foundations are not required to file Form 990-PF.

[2]Increase largely due to improved, computerized data collection techniques scanning multiple year IRS transaction tapes to identify eligible grantmaking foundations.

[3]Primary source of data changed from IRS transaction tape to direct entry by Foundation Center staff from Form 990-PF, facilitating manual coding of independent and corporate foundations.

also produced a disproportionate share of the very largest endowed foundations. Of the roughly 21,000 larger foundations still active today, roughly one-seventh (2,885) were created in the 1940s and 1950s, yet these foundations hold close to three-tenths ($131.8 billion) of the combined assets of larger foundations. Moreover, of the 562 active foundations with assets in excess of $100 million, more than one-third (34.5 percent) were created in the 1940s and 1950s.

In the 1960s, the rate of establishment dropped to less than 59 percent. Still, more than 2,000 foundations still active today were formed, or 9.7 percent of larger foundations. Proportionally, fewer of the foundations with assets of $100 million or more were formed during this decade.

Formation may also be measured in absolute numbers, by averaging the number of births per year. From that perspective, creation climbed from 82 a year in the 1940s to 206 in the 1950s, but decreased slightly to 203 a year in the 1960s (Table 50).

Foundation Creation in the 1970s

• **Establishment rate falls after 1969 Tax Act**

Foundation creation plummeted in the 1970s. Although 1,238 new larger foundations were formed, the increase in the birth rate dropped to less than 23 percent (Table 49). In terms of absolute numbers, creation declined to just 124 a year, a two-fifths drop from the 1950s (Table 50).

The sharp fall in the birth rate followed the passage of the 1969 Tax Act. As reported in Chapter 2, the new legislation introduced stringent regulations on private foundations that some in the field considered excessively burdensome, accorded less favorable tax treatment to donors to private foundations, and imposed annual pay-out requirements and a 4 percent excise tax. Regulation, and the generally hostile climate that surrounded it, resulted in a chilling effect on new formation, especially of independent and family foundations. Questions about the favorability of corporate direct giving programs over company foundations and a weak economy also contributed to the overall downturn.

TABLE 49. Growth of Number of Larger Foundations by Decade

Decade Created	Total Population*	Net Increase	% Increase
Before 1900	99		
1900–1909	125	26	26.3
1910–1919	204	79	63.2
1920–1929	367	163	79.9
1930–1939	576	209	56.9
1940–1949	1,399	823	142.9
1950–1959	3,461	2,062	147.4
1960–1969	5,492	2,031	58.7
1970–1979	6,730	1,238	22.5
1980–1989	11,266	4,536	67.4
1990–1999[1]	19,830	8,564	76.0

Source: *Foundation Yearbook*, 2002. Based on Foundation Center survey of grantmaking foundations with at least $1 million in assets or making grants of $100,000 or more in 1999–2000.
*Excludes 1,099 foundations missing establishment data.
[1]Data incomplete for the period 1998 to 1999.
Note: Not represented are 35 active foundations established in 2000.

TABLE 48. Period of Establishment for Larger Foundations by Asset Categories*

Decade Created	Total Foundations No.	%	$100 million or more No.	%	$25 million–under $100 million No.	%	$10 million–under $25 million No.	%	$5 million–under $10 million No.	%	$1 million–under $5 million No.	%	Under $1 million No.	%
Before 1900	99	0.5	0	0.0	6	0.4	12	0.5	19	0.6	61	0.6	1	0.0
1900–1909	26	0.1	2	0.4	4	0.3	4	0.2	4	0.1	11	0.1	1	0.0
1910–1919	79	0.4	23	4.1	12	0.8	7	0.3	13	0.4	24	0.2	0	0.0
1920–1929	163	0.8	25	4.4	36	2.5	23	1.0	25	0.8	51	0.5	3	0.1
1930–1939	209	1.0	37	6.6	39	2.7	37	1.6	35	1.2	56	0.5	5	0.2
1940–1949	823	3.9	83	14.8	124	8.4	137	6.0	136	4.6	311	2.9	32	1.1
1950–1959	2,062	9.8	111	19.8	264	18.0	333	14.5	325	10.9	867	8.0	162	5.7
1960–1969	2,031	9.7	73	13.0	195	13.3	288	12.5	341	11.5	955	8.8	179	6.3
1970–1979	1,238	5.9	54	9.6	127	8.7	179	7.8	205	6.9	556	5.1	117	4.1
1980–1989	4,536	21.6	81	14.4	347	23.6	511	22.3	665	22.4	2,267	21.0	665	23.2
1990–1999[1]	8,564	40.9	68	12.1	304	20.7	728	31.7	1098	37.0	4,860	45.0	1,506	52.6
Data not available	1,099	5.2	3	0.5	9	0.6	34	1.5	99	3.3	767	7.1	187	6.5
Total[2]	20,964	100.0	562	100.0	1,468	100.0	2,296	100.0	2,970	100.0	10,804	100.0	2,864	100.0

Source: *Foundation Yearbook*, 2002. Based on Foundation Center survey of grantmaking foundations with at least $1 million in assets or making grants of $100,000 or more in 1999–2000.
*Due to rounding, figures may not add up.
[1]Data incomplete for the period 1998 to 1999.
[2]Total includes 35 active foundations established in 2000.

Foundation Creation in the 1980s and 1990s

- **Number of grantmaking foundations more than doubles since 1980**

At the start of the 1980s, the foundation population totaled 22,000 and was shrinking (Figure 31). Foundation decline was of paramount concern to the philanthropic community, which responded with efforts to improve the regulatory environment, attract new philanthropists, and expand organized philanthropy. By the mid-1980s, a period favored by vibrant economic growth and new wealth creation, the Foundation Center was able to report substantial evidence of renewed foundation growth and vitality.

In terms of overall numbers, the foundation population increased more than two and one-half times between 1980 and 2000, from 22,088 to 56,582 (Table 47). Growth began slowly and then accelerated in the mid-1980s. Between 1980 and 1989, 9,900 foundations were added to the Center's database, most of them independent foundations. Since 1987 (when comprehensive coding of all private foundations according to type was initiated by the Foundation Center) the number of independent foundations jumped by nearly 25,438 (up 101.4 percent) and the number of corporate foundations increased by 723 (up 55.8 percent).

Comprehensive tracking of community foundations and grantmaking operating foundations started earlier, in 1977 and 1981, respectively. Since 1977, the number of community foundations has grown more than three times, from 170 to 560.[3] Since 1981, the

[3]. The Foundation Center's count of community foundations falls short of the number identified by other national sources, explained in part by different methods of tracking supporting organizations. The Center reports as one fiscal unit a community foundation and the supporting funds that it administers, if those funds are jointly reported in the foundation's IRS tax form 990. The Center's data on active grantmakers also excludes startup community foundations that have not yet awarded grants.

number of grantmaking operating foundations has grown close to sevenfold, from fewer than 500 to nearly 3,500.

Overall growth in foundation numbers has resulted primarily from the creation of new foundations. Other factors include:

- Fewer terminations since 1984, with the termination rate hovering around 1 percent. In the most recent year, 649 foundations (1.1 percent) ceased operation or merged into other foundations. However, an additional 283 were presumed inactive or in the process of ceasing operations.

- An increase to nearly 3,500 operating foundations (both new and established) actively awarding grants, as noted above.

- More accurate data gathering on smaller foundations by the Foundation Center, achieved by examining the IRS Form 990-PF of every reporting foundation.

- The addition on a one-time basis of more than 2,100 non-exempt charitable trusts (NECTs) into the IRS file due to a filing requirement that took effect in the mid-1980s. (Most private foundation NECTs fall into the category of the smallest foundations with assets of less than $1 million or awarding grants totaling less than $100,000.)

While precise birth year data are not known for all 56,582 active grantmaking foundations, intensive research by Center staff in the past decade has identified over 34,000 foundations—large and small—created after 1979. In the latest year, close to 6,400 recently established foundations were added to the 2002 edition of the *Guide to U.S. Foundations*.

TABLE 50. Growth of Number of Larger Foundations by Decade and by Foundation Type*

Decade Created	All Foundations[1] Total Population	All Foundations[1] Net Increase	All Foundations[1] Average No. per Year	Independent Net Increase	Independent Average No. per Year	Corporate Net Increase	Corporate Average No. per Year	Community Net Increase	Community Average No. per Year
1920–1929	367	163	16	134	13	4	0	19	2
1930–1939	576	209	21	193	19	8	1	3	0
1940–1949	1,399	823	82	720	72	60	6	21	2
1950–1959	3,461	2,062	206	1,714	171	292	29	32	3
1960–1969	5,492	2,031	203	1,797	180	152	15	48	5
1970–1979	6,730	1,238	124	1,036	104	98	10	75	8
1980–1989	11,266	4,536	454	3,982	398	315	32	115	12
1990–1999[2]	19,830	8,564	856	7,769	777	336	34	123	12

Source: *Foundation Yearbook*, 2002. Based on Foundation Center survey of grantmaking foundations with at least $1 million in assets or making grants of $100,000 or more in 1999–2000.
*Excludes 1,099 foundations missing establishment data.
[1]All foundations figure includes operating foundations.
[2]Data incomplete for the period 1998 to 1999.
Note: Not represented are 35 active foundations established in 2000.

Larger Foundation Creation

• **Over two-fifths of larger foundations formed in 1990s**

As a result of ongoing research since the 1960s for *The Foundation Directory*, we can precisely identify and compare formation periods of the larger foundations—those nearly 21,000 funders reporting assets of $1 million or over or giving of at least $100,000 in 2000. Figure 32 shows that of these larger foundations, 4,536 (21.6 percent) were created in the 1980s, more than three and one-half times the number formed in the 1970s. An even greater 8,564 foundations—more than two-fifths of larger foundations (40.9 percent)—have been formed since 1990. Taken together, the number of larger-size 1980s and 90s foundations now comprises the majority—nearly 63 percent—of all larger active foundations. Furthermore, the 1990's share of the foundation world has grown rapidly and can be expected to exceed 10,000 new larger grantmakers, far surpassing the record-setting 1980s.

This dramatic resurgence in foundation growth is based on absolute numbers of larger new foundations. From the perspective of rate of new creation, the news is less striking. Foundation births grew by 67.3 percent in the 1980s, three times faster than in the 1970s, but still far below the record rates of increase in the 1950s and 1940s. Still, the formation rate for the 1990s (through 1998) has now exceeded the rate for the 1980s. With data not yet complete for the 1990s, the rate for the latest decade can be expected to climb further.

Larger Foundation Formation from 1970 through 1999

Figure 33 and Table 51 map from year-to-year the decline and recovery in foundation formation that took place after 1969. Only 94 foundations active today with assets of at least $1 million or paying out $100,000 in grants were created in 1970. Annual creation numbers had nearly doubled by 1979, tripled by 1981, increased more than four times by 1984, and were about nine times greater in 1986, when a then record 872 mid-size and larger foundations were created. In just two years—1985 and 1986—roughly 1,400 larger new foundations were formed, more than the number created throughout the 1970s.

After peaking in 1986, new creation dropped sharply in the next two years. Yet, by the end of the 1980s, the number of new foundations created annually had surpassed pre-1986 levels. For most of the 1990s, formation was steady or increased. In 1997, in anticipation of the sun-setting of a federal tax law provision, formation soared to 1,602, the largest number created in any year. (Numbers for 1998 and 1999 are incomplete since newly-formed foundations may delay the start of grantmaking for a few years.)

What explains fluctuations in growth trends in the 1980s and 1990s? Possible explanations include changes in income tax policy, economic conditions,

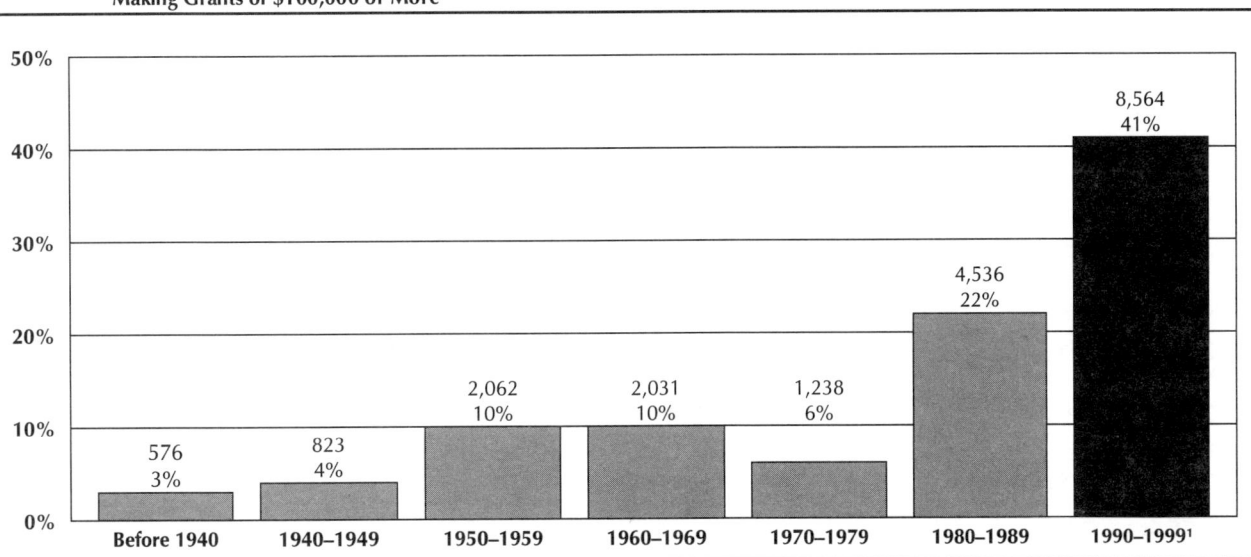

FIGURE 32. Decade of Establishment of Active Grantmaking Foundations with Assets of at Least $1 Million or Making Grants of $100,000 or More

Period	Number	Percent
Before 1940	576	3%
1940–1949	823	4%
1950–1959	2,062	10%
1960–1969	2,031	10%
1970–1979	1,238	6%
1980–1989	4,536	22%
1990–1999[1]	8,564	41%

Source: *Foundation Yearbook*, 2002.
Note: Based on Foundation Center survey of 20,964 grantmaking foundations of at least $1 million or making grants of $100,000 or more in 1999–2000. Establishment data was not available for 1,099 foundations. The number above each bar indicates the number of foundations formed in that period and still active in 1999–2000. Not represented are 35 active foundations established in 2000.
[1] Data incomplete for the period 1998 to 1999.

and wealth accumulation (cited earlier). Contributions to foundations peaked in 1986 as wealthy individuals responded to greater incentives for giving. Lower personal income tax rates enacted by the Tax Reform Act of 1986 led to a decline in the growth of overall charitable contributions and created a disincentive for establishing foundations. One year later, the stock market tumbled, ending an era of unprecedented accumulation of wealth and ushering in a period of instability in the financial markets. Finally, the economy faltered and then moved into a painful recession, which for many areas of the country lingered into 1992. After a period of uncertainty, the mid-1990s restored the blessings of a robust economy, extremely low inflation, and a roaring stock market. These conditions continued unabated throughout the late 1990s.

FIGURE 33. Establishment of Larger Foundations by Year, 1970 to 1998*

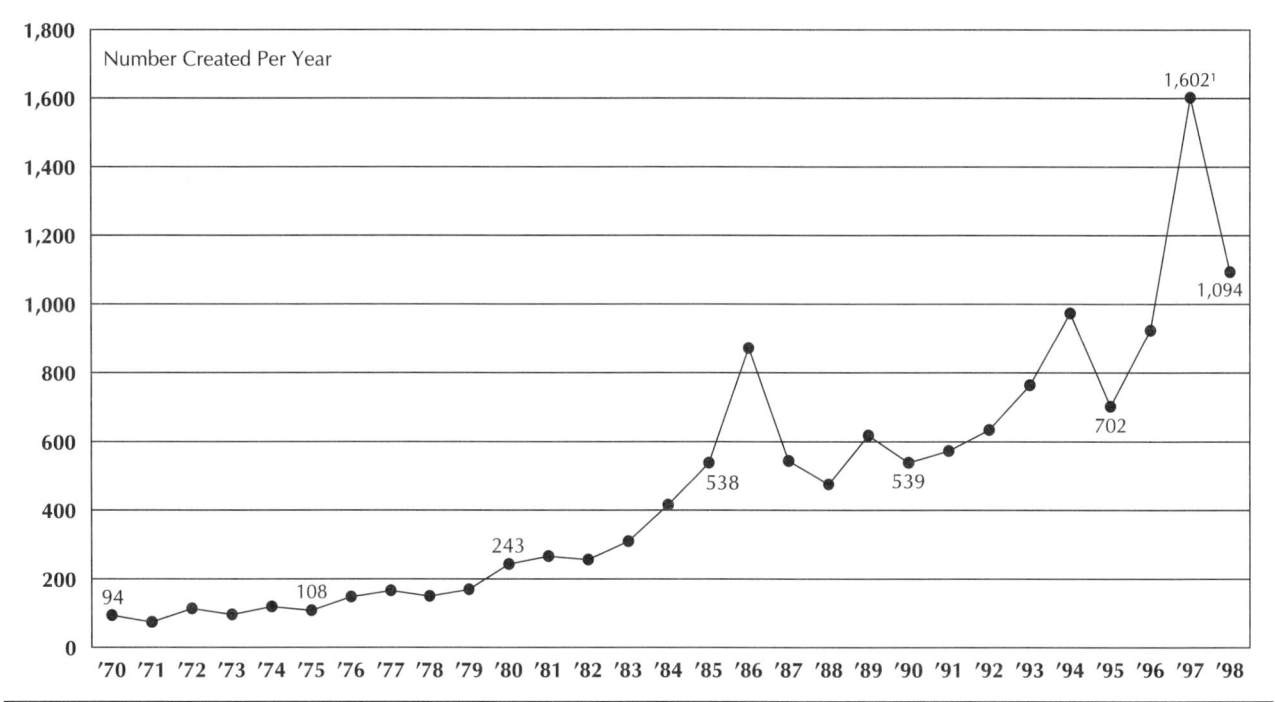

Source: *Foundation Yearbook,* 2002.
* Based on Foundation Center survey of grantmaking foundations with at least $1 million in assets or making grants of $100,000 or more in 1999–2000.
[1] Data incomplete after 1997.

TABLE 51. Number and Assets of Larger Foundations Created Per Year After 1969*

1970s			1980s			1990s[1]		
Year	No.	Assets	Year	No.	Assets	Year	No.	Assets
1970	94	$ 5,498,932	1980	243	$ 2,279,518	1990	539	$ 4,412,288
1971	74	794,496	1981	266	4,363,937	1991	573	7,023,796
1972	114	2,542,937	1982	256	4,064,136	1992	634	5,722,428
1973	96	2,184,805	1983	309	3,460,865	1993	764	5,796,670
1974	119	2,093,576	1984	415	6,001,531	1994	974	27,879,532
1975	108	3,681,270	1985	538	5,734,209	1995	702	4,725,217
1976	148	2,960,070	1986	872	9,719,464	1996	924	10,562,432
1977	166	3,116,977	1987	544	7,513,892	1997	1,602	7,714,781
1978	150	5,902,992	1988	475	4,227,395	1998	1,094	5,420,463
1979	169	3,071,513	1989	618	9,688,189	1999[2]	758	4,106,732
Total	1,238	$31,847,568	Total	4,536	$57,053,138	Total	8,564	$83,364,340

Source: *Foundation Yearbook,* 2002. Based on Foundation Center survey of grantmaking foundations with at least $1 million in assets or making grants of $100,000 or more in 1999–2000.
*Dollars in thousands.
[1] Data incomplete for the period 1998 to 1999.
[2] Most foundations established in 1999 did not yet report fiscal 2000 giving activity to the IRS.
Note: Not represented are 35 active foundations established in 2000.

Birth Rates Per Year for Larger Foundations by Type

Measuring larger foundation births per year (Table 50), the mean number created annually between 1980 and 1989 was 454, more than double the 206 created annually in the high growth period of the 1950s. For independent foundations, the number created per year in the 1980s (398) is more than double the number of births per year in the 1950s and close to four times greater than the number of births per year in the 1970s. An analysis of recent data (although incomplete) suggests that independent foundations were being formed at an even higher rate in the 1990s—about 780 a year.

Corporations were also active in the 1980s and formed foundations at the rate of 32 per year that decade, roughly equal to the number formed in the 1950s and triple the number created in the 1970s. The increase in births, however, was overshadowed by terminations caused by company mergers and buy-outs and by a downturn for many of the corporate giants. Despite sweeping changes in corporate America in the 1990s, recent data show that companies are continuing to form foundations. Through 1998-99, 34 corporate foundations were formed a year, up slightly from the 1980s.

The development of community foundations, free from the more punitive tax and regulatory burdens imposed on private foundations, has differed dramatically from that of private foundations over the last few decades. While many of the very largest community foundations were established early in the century, the formation rate did not accelerate appreciably until the 1970s, when 75 community trusts, currently holding assets of $1 million or more or making grants of at least $100,000, were established. Development continued at a rapid rate in the 1980s, with support from the Council on Foundations, regional associations of grantmakers, and from several of the largest private foundations. In all, 115 larger community foundations were formed in the 1980s—or close to 12 per year. This record volume of establishment was surpassed in the 1990s, with 123 larger community foundations established. When information for the decade is complete, the rate of community foundation formation will total roughly 13 foundations per year.

Total Assets of Larger 1980s and 90s Foundations

While more than three-fifths of all larger foundations were formed in the 1980s and 1990s, these newer foundations held $140.4 billion in assets or three-tenths (30.4 percent) of the total wealth of larger foundations (Table 52). The lower asset share, however, seems consistent with established patterns of foundation development. A study has shown that the largest independent foundations received their primary endowments about 18 years after creation, following the death of the principal founder and his/her spouse.[4] In fact, the assets of these newer foundations are increasing rapidly and are important to growth: between 1999 and 2000, asset values of the 1980s and 90s foundations grew $18.5 billion (15.2 percent) and represented close to three-fifths (56.9 percent) of all larger foundation asset growth.

Larger 1980s and 90s Foundations by Assets and Giving

Of the more than 13,000 larger foundations formed since 1980, a substantial majority are quite small—just over seven out of ten (71.0 percent) have assets under

---

4. See Nelson, R., "An Economic History of Large Foundations," *America's Wealthy and the Future of Philanthropy*, Ed. By T. Odendahl, New York: Foundation Center, 1987.

New Foundation Philanthropists

The priorities of new foundations reflect the strong personal interests of their founders. Since the mid-1980s, a new generation of younger philanthropists has emerged, many of whom built their fortunes over the past twenty years. Among the many thousands of individuals or families who have created foundations, either during their lifetimes or in the form of a bequest, we can identify a number of wealthy celebrities, from entrepreneurs to artists to media moguls, among them: Paul Allen, Edward Albee, Tom Brokaw, Warren Buffet, Johnny Carson, Tracy Chapman, Liz Claiborne, Bill Cosby, Kirk Douglas, Doris Duke, Gloria Estefan, Bill Gates, David Geffen, Hugh Hefner, Kirk Kerkorian, George Lucas, Michael Milken, Gordon Moore, George Soros, Stephen Spielberg, Barbra Streisand, Ted Turner, and Tiger Woods. This trend toward creating foundations by a new generation of Americans attests to the rise of vast new personal fortunes combined with a strongly positive view of the role of foundations in society.

$5 million (Table 48). Yet, in a relatively few years, the 1980s and the 1990s have produced a number of very large foundations: 800 have assets over $25 million, and of those, 149 reported assets of $100 million or more, up from 128 in 1999. These 149 foundations represented more than one-quarter (26.5 percent) of the 562 foundations in that top size range.

Table 53 presents the assets, giving, and gifts received of 56 foundations with assets of $125 million or more formed since 1990. Six are corporate, three are operating, and two are community foundations, while the vast majority are independent (including family and new health foundations). Thirteen are found in California, including three of the top ten newer foundations by assets. Seven are found in New York, including the third-ranked Doris Duke Charitable Foundation. By comparison, only two Washington State foundations were included in the list, but these included the top-ranked Bill & Melinda Gates Foundation.

Finally, Table 54 ranks the 49 foundations created since 1990 that made grants of $10 million or more in 2000 (or 1999 for one). First in rank by giving was the Bill and Melinda Gates Foundation ($994.9 million), a family foundation. A total of seven operating foundations appeared in this list, while ten corporate foundations were included. The list contained only one community foundation. The balance of foundations were independents, which include family foundations.

Many of these newer large foundations limit their giving to highly specialized interests:

- The Lumina Foundation for Education (IN)—created from the conversion of USA Group, a nonprofit student loan guarantor and administrator—seeks to encourage Americans to obtain a post-secondary education. The foundation funds nationally in the areas of financial access, retention and attainment, and non-traditional learners and learning.

- The California Endowment (CA), California Wellness Foundation (CA), and Healthcare Foundation of New Jersey, with assets derived from the sale of nonprofit health care providers to profit-making companies, concentrate largely on health promotion. For example, the California Wellness Foundation has developed a violence prevention initiative and is active in statewide health policy initiatives, while the Healthcare Foundation of New Jersey addresses the healthcare needs of families and individuals in Newark, Essex County, and the State of New Jersey.

- The Turner Foundation (GA) has a principal interest in environmental causes, including conservation of natural resources, protection of wildlife, and promotion of sound population policies.

Future Prospects for Foundation Creation

Among the factors responsible for recent growth in foundation number, by far the most compelling one has been the choice of individuals, families, businesses, and communities to create new foundations. The revitalization of organized philanthropy in the

TABLE 52. Period of Establishment for Larger Foundations by Foundation Type with Aggregate Assets*

Decade Created	All Foundations No.	All Foundations Assets	Independent Foundations No.	Independent Foundations Assets	Corporate Foundations No.	Corporate Foundations Assets	Community Foundations No.	Community Foundations Assets	Operating Foundations No.	Operating Foundations Assets
Before 1900	99	$ 748,231	84	$ 636,346	0	$ 0	0	$ 0	15	$ 111,885
1900–1909	26	561,027	23	374,661	0	0	0	0	3	186,367
1910–1919	79	15,031,657	57	8,152,649	1	25,000	17	6,678,489	4	175,519
1920–1929	163	17,740,098	134	13,104,596	4	82,751	19	4,427,559	6	125,191
1930–1939	209	64,770,475	193	64,454,572	8	55,082	3	133,918	5	126,904
1949–1949	823	53,141,695	720	47,004,706	60	816,498	21	3,361,996	22	1,958,496
1950–1959	2,062	78,695,626	1,714	59,352,604	292	4,421,682	32	2,888,187	24	12,033,152
1960–1969	2,031	52,449,428	1,797	44,155,969	152	1,898,680	48	3,122,479	34	3,272,299
1970–1979	1,238	31,847,568	1,036	25,816,481	98	1,797,804	75	4,016,865	29	216,419
1980–1989	4,536	57,053,138	3,982	46,659,650	315	3,603,457	115	4,203,765	124	2,586,266
1990–1999[1]	8,564	83,364,340	7,769	75,792,398	336	2,990,453	123	1,502,496	336	3,078,993
Data not available	1,099	4,242,099	973	2,880,640	25	56,774	26	77,426	75	1,227,260
Total[2]	20,964	$461,230,903	18,513	$389,941,300	1,291	$15,748,181	479	$30,413,180	681	$25,128,242

Source: *Foundation Yearbook*, 2002. Based on Foundation Center survey of grantmaking foundations with at least $1 million in assets or making grants of $100,000 or more in 1999–2000.
*Dollars in thousands. Due to rounding, figures may not add up.
[1]Data incomplete for the period 1998 to 1999.
[2]Total includes 35 active foundations established in 2000.

TABLE 53. Foundations Created Since 1990 with Assets of $125 Million or More*

	Foundation Name	State	Year Created	Type[1]	Assets	Gifts Received	Total Giving[2]	Qualifying Distributions[3]	Fiscal Date
1.	Bill & Melinda Gates Foundation	WA	1994	IN	$21,149,100,000	$5,068,000,000	$994,900,000	$994,900,000	12/31/00
2.	California Endowment	CA	1996	IN	3,490,256,407	262,680,840	189,663,220	211,000,000	2/28/01
3.	Doris Duke Charitable Foundation	NY	1996	IN	1,574,746,419	10,186,116	86,310,650	84,676,886	12/31/00
4.	Freedom Forum[4]	VA	1991	OP	1,037,110,607	N/A	36,320,040	N/A	12/31/00
5.	California Wellness Foundation	CA	1991	IN	1,029,461,012	0	44,715,936	49,793,244	12/31/00
6.	Lumina Foundation for Education	IN	2000	IN	928,954,681	0	212,848	1,978,617	12/31/00
7.	Goizueta Foundation	GA	1992	IN	686,026,134	603,900	33,802,380	34,794,152	12/31/00
8.	Wallace H. Coulter Foundation	FL	2000	IN	508,683,997	454,354,473	5,569,869	5,489,330	9/30/00
9.	H. N. & Frances C. Berger Foundation	CA	1993	IN	403,833,632	0	10,378,667	15,616,121	12/31/00
10.	Nina Mason Pulliam Charitable Trust	IN	1997	IN	398,000,103	0	16,730,932	18,811,099	12/31/00
11.	Albert & Bessie Mae Kronkosky Charitable Foundation	TX	1991	IN	366,257,167	0	15,492,858	17,090,154	12/31/00
12.	Charles and Helen Schwab Foundation	CA	1993	IN	344,542,135	0	7,854,900	8,654,031	6/30/00
13.	F. B. Heron Foundation	NY	1992	IN	282,484,643	0	10,864,669	15,380,710	12/31/00
14.	Baptist Community Ministries	LA	1995	IN	264,019,557	0	7,922,359	9,771,641	9/30/00
15.	Lemelson Foundation	NV	1994	IN	262,702,507	0	6,525,638	6,751,534	12/31/00
16.	Summit Charitable Foundation	DC	1991	IN	242,190,489	17,993,391	11,935,902	13,333,076	12/31/00
17.	Michael and Susan Dell Foundation	TX	1999	IN	224,270,856	0	5,475,861	5,475,861	12/31/00
18.	Broad Foundation	CA	1998	IN	222,308,387	194,414,188	3,283,100	2,104,891	12/31/00
19.	Assisi Foundation of Memphis	TN	1994	IN	214,961,325	0	9,214,148	9,883,265	2/28/00
20.	Albert and Margaret Alkek Foundation	TX	1996	IN	211,208,729	27,034	8,935,625	8,959,558	12/31/00
21.	Turner Foundation	GA	1990	IN	209,515,569	4,861	44,441,523	47,802,254	12/31/00
22.	Waitt Family Foundation	CA	1993	IN	207,252,015	111,190,015	14,632,347	15,632,874	12/31/00
23.	Oberkotter Foundation	PA	1992	IN	195,278,685	31,505,476	21,334,724	25,097,298	11/30/00
24.	Gerry Foundation[4]	NY	1997	OP	185,542,521	6,665,625	1,977,770	4,598,057	10/31/00
25.	Highland Street Connection	MA	1994	IN	183,397,594	1,408,949	8,813,613	9,208,488	12/31/00
26.	Dr. Ralph and Marian Falk Medical Research Trust	IL	1991	IN	181,845,264	0	8,595,814	8,875,426	11/30/00
27.	Citigroup Foundation	NY	1994	CS	179,182,168	107,812,500	43,068,029	44,534,882	12/31/00
28.	Gill Foundation	CO	1994	IN	177,613,525	55,056,399	4,105,215	5,945,598	12/31/00
29.	Noyce Foundation	CA	1990	IN	173,718,164	0	10,069,446	10,069,446	12/31/00
30.	Healthcare Foundation of New Jersey	NJ	1997	IN	172,223,000	0	7,875,000	8,588,000	12/31/00
31.	HCA Foundation	TN	1992	CS	171,207,684	5,442,753	3,286,628	3,444,189	12/31/00
32.	Central Indiana Community Foundation	IN	1997	CM	170,665,591	46,979,817	4,200,451	4,200,451	12/31/00
33.	Daniels Fund	CO	1998	IN	170,097,179	204,327,857	1,220,708	1,220,708	12/31/00
34.	Janaki Foundation	NY	1997	IN	165,483,740	0	6,551,670	6,543,379	12/31/00
35.	Colburn Foundation	CA	1999	IN	163,704,657	0	3,970,000	4,521,332	12/31/00
36.	Iowa West Foundation	IA	1994	IN	161,216,643	12,515,000	21,192,574	21,376,958	12/31/00
37.	Flora Family Foundation	CA	1998	IN	148,348,802	108,260,903	7,812,301	8,129,267	12/31/00
38.	Batchelor Foundation	FL	1990	CS	146,895,493	10,000,000	1,946,675	1,946,675	6/30/01
39.	William G. McGowan Charitable Fund	DC	1992	IN	146,532,189	0	6,841,036	6,841,036	6/30/01
40.	USAA Foundation, A Charitable Trust	TX	1994	CS	145,237,670	0	10,837,349	10,774,304	6/30/01
41.	Drs. Bruce and Lee Foundation	SC	1995	IN	144,950,899	350	974,277	1,364,963	12/31/00
42.	McCune Charitable Foundation	NM	1992	IN	142,111,891	0	6,087,100	10,217,097	12/31/00
43.	Eisner Foundation	CA	1996	IN	140,784,990	0	6,820,946	7,002,957	12/31/00
44.	V. Kann Rasmussen Foundation	MA	1991	IN	140,492,408	0	7,476,910	8,172,640	6/30/00
45.	Northwestern Mutual Foundation	WI	1992	CS	137,640,179	0	11,483,498	11,813,256	6/30/00
46.	Wallace Global Fund	DC	1995	IN	135,544,196	1,000,000	6,113,512	7,563,097	12/31/00
47.	Open Society Institute[4]	NY	1993	OP	135,447,900	363,639,131	116,342,544	160,496,757	12/31/00
48.	Russell Family Foundation	WA	1994	IN	134,382,352	0	4,182,400	5,201,860	12/31/00
49.	Soros Charitable Foundation	NY	1992	IN	134,116,994	0	37,000,000	37,033,871	11/30/00
50.	Jewish Healthcare Foundation of Pittsburgh	PA	1990	IN	133,500,000	1,868,964	6,165,478	7,100,000	12/31/00
51.	William K. Bowes, Jr. Foundation	CA	1991	IN	133,110,273	22,009,485	5,061,780	5,485,397	12/31/00
52.	Thomas and Stacey Siebel Foundation	CA	1996	IN	132,876,402	0	2,070,000	1,547,322	12/31/99
53.	Cisco Systems Foundation	CA	1997	CS	132,211,438	91,024,874	14,190,789	13,955,869	7/31/00
54.	Carlos and Marguerite Mason Fund	GA	1991	IN	129,053,398	0	5,554,775	6,163,811	12/31/00
55.	Kemper and Ethel Marley Foundation	AZ	1990	IN	126,341,178	22,877,937	3,804,046	3,896,808	2/28/00
56.	Community Foundation of Middle Tennessee	TN	1991	CM	125,518,170	60,588,238	12,910,100	13,095,864	12/31/00

Source: *Foundation Yearbook*, 2002.

*Aggregate foundation fiscal information is based on data provided to the Center as of February 2, 2002; fiscal data on individual foundations included in this table may be more current.

[1] Foundation type: IN=Independent; CS=Corporate; CM=Community; and OP=Operating.

[2] Includes grants, scholarship, employee matching gifts; excludes set-asides, loans, PRIs, and program expenses.

[3] Qualifying distributions is the amount used in calculating the required 5 percent payout; includes total giving, as well as reasonable administrative expenses, set-asides, PRIs, operating program expenses, and amount paid to acquire assets used directly for charitable purposes.

[4] For some operating foundations, total giving amount includes grants and program expenses; for others, total giving amount includes only grants. Most operating foundations' qualifying distributions are paid out for administration of operating programs and not for grants.

1980s and 1990s—its unparalleled growth in giving and assets—owes much to new donors and the creation of new wealth, as well as to market performance and a strong economy. With the precipitous decline in the stock market, beginning in mid-2000, and the start of a recession in 2001, there will be weaker incentives for donors to create foundations.

Despite the economic slowdown, future new foundation growth will continue to benefit from a positive change in federal tax policy enacted in the late 1990s. At issue was a temporary provision in the tax law permitting living donors to deduct the full market value of gifts of appreciated stock to private foundations. The provision expired in 1994, possibly spurring high formation in that year. It was reinstated twice after 1995 for brief periods (hailed as windows of opportunity for gifts from living donors to new and existing foundations). It expired again in mid-1998. After strong lobbying by foundation associations and nonprofit leaders, the provision was made a permanent part of the tax code at the end of that year. To the extent possible, we will monitor the results of these policy changes on new formation as data become available.

TABLE 54. Foundations Created Since 1990 with Total Giving of $10 Million or More*

	Foundation Name	State	Year Created	Type[1]	Total Giving[2]	Qualifying Distributions[3]	Gifts Received	Assets	Fiscal Date
1.	Bill & Melinda Gates Foundation	WA	1994	IN	$994,900,000	$994,900,000	$5,068,000,000	$21,149,100,000	12/31/00
2.	California Endowment	CA	1996	IN	189,663,220	211,000,000	262,680,840	3,490,256,407	2/28/01
3.	Open Society Institute[4]	NY	1993	OP	116,342,544	160,496,757	363,639,131	135,447,900	12/31/00
4.	Searle Patients in Need Foundation[4]	NJ	1990	OP	95,975,582	96,311,112	110,123,451	10,163,451	12/31/00
5.	Bristol-Myers Squibb Patient Assistance Foundation[4]	NJ	1999	OP	94,805,585	98,269,671	99,161,807	1,675,064	12/31/00
6.	Lilly Cares Foundation[4]	IN	1996	OP	86,650,335	87,695,970	69,747,680	2,861,597	12/31/00
7.	Doris Duke Charitable Foundation	NY	1996	IN	86,310,650	N/A	N/A	1,574,746,419	12/31/00
8.	Janssen Ortho Patient Assistance Foundation[4]	NJ	1998	OP	81,294,984	81,294,984	90,687,633	895,057	12/31/00
9.	California Wellness Foundation	CA	1991	IN	44,715,936	49,793,244	0	1,029,461,012	12/31/00
10.	Turner Foundation	GA	1990	IN	44,441,523	47,802,254	4,861	209,515,569	12/31/00
11.	Lucent Technologies Foundation	NJ	1996	CS	43,932,312	45,009,168	37,518,305	22,970,298	9/30/00
12.	Citigroup Foundation	NY	1994	CS	43,068,029	44,534,882	107,812,500	179,182,168	12/31/00
13.	Aventis Pharmaceuticals Health Care Foundation	NJ	1992	CS	41,558,325	41,558,325	41,558,325	7,039	12/31/00
14.	Freedom Forum[4]	VA	1991	OP	36,320,040	N/A	N/A	1,037,110,607	12/31/00
15.	Karfunkel Family Foundation[4]	NY	1991	OP	34,203,777	34,204,277	6,736,292	18,588,413	6/30/00
16.	Goizueta Foundation	GA	1992	IN	33,802,380	34,794,152	603,900	686,026,134	12/31/00
17.	James H. Clark Charitable Foundation	NV	1999	IN	30,000,000	29,968,171	96,487	96,023,990	3/31/01
18.	Michael R. Bloomberg Family Foundation Trust	NY	1998	IN	22,500,000	22,495,939	0	3,445,077	12/31/00
19.	Oberkotter Foundation	PA	1992	IN	21,334,724	25,097,298	31,505,476	195,278,685	11/30/00
20.	Iowa West Foundation	IA	1994	IN	21,192,574	21,376,958	12,515,000	161,216,643	12/31/00
21.	Chartwell Charitable Foundation	CA	1998	IN	17,524,700	17,365,585	0	10,667,435	12/31/00
22.	John W. Kluge Foundation	MD	1990	IN	17,191,770	17,199,910	13,075,000	71,109,123	9/30/00
23.	NCC Charitable Foundation II	OH	1993	CS	17,127,194	17,100,325	0	44,080,889	6/30/00
24.	Nina Mason Pulliam Charitable Trust	IN	1997	IN	16,730,932	18,811,099	0	398,000,103	12/31/00
25.	Sierra Foundation	NJ	1994	IN	16,387,952	16,373,754	18,335,952	16,258,212	10/31/00
26.	Freddie Mac Foundation	VA	1990	CS	15,719,453	18,932,382	2,903,365	31,820,731	12/31/00
27.	Albert & Bessie Mae Kronkosky Charitable Foundation	TX	1991	IN	15,492,858	17,090,154	0	366,257,167	12/31/00
28.	McKnight Brain Research Foundation	FL	1998	IN	14,863,622	14,835,165	61,336,287	52,851,612	6/30/00
29.	Waitt Family Foundation	CA	1993	IN	14,632,347	15,632,874	111,190,015	207,252,015	12/31/00
30.	Energy Foundation	CA	1991	IN	14,360,105	14,360,105	25,798,798	48,884,433	12/31/00
31.	Cisco Systems Foundation	CA	1997	CS	14,190,789	13,955,869	91,024,874	132,211,438	7/31/00
32.	Huberfeld-Bodner Family Foundation	NY	1994	IN	13,185,300	2,106,237	7,667,437	23,824,929	12/31/99
33.	Community Foundation of Middle Tennessee	TN	1991	CM	12,910,100	13,095,864	60,588,238	125,518,170	12/31/00
34.	Helen Bader Foundation	WI	1991	IN	12,385,092	13,843,681	14,800,000	3,278,008	8/31/00
35.	Summit Charitable Foundation	DC	1991	IN	11,935,902	13,333,076	17,993,391	242,190,489	12/31/00
36.	Garmar Foundation	MN	1998	IN	11,894,351	11,884,501	11,500	22,607,432	6/30/00
37.	Craig and Susan McCaw Foundation	WA	1998	IN	11,817,686	11,816,204	10,244,000	22,525,138	12/31/00
38.	Jean C. Tempel Charitable Foundation	MA	1996	IN	11,548,500	11,419,811	14,578,126	2,620,834	12/31/00
39.	Federated Department Stores Foundation	OH	1995	CS	11,513,341	11,637,357	7,500,000	21,615,327	1/30/00
40.	Northwestern Mutual Foundation	WI	1992	CS	11,403,898	11,813,256	0	137,640,179	6/30/00
41.	Chicago Annenberg Challenge Foundation	IL	1995	IN	11,331,874	12,796,300	50,250	74,633,836	12/31/00
42.	USAA Foundation, A Charitable Trust	TX	1994	CS	11,292,579	11,039,433	4,048	171,33,825	6/30/00
43.	Capital Group Companies Charitable Foundation	CA	1997	IN	11,076,765	11,088,631	1,102,070	44,637,056	6/30/00
44.	F. B. Heron Foundation	NY	1992	IN	10,864,669	15,380,710	0	282,484,643	12/31/00
45.	Tenet Healthcare Foundation	CA	1998	CS	10,852,268	10,794,585	0	67,827,267	5/31/00
46.	Florik Charitable Trust	IL	1995	IN	10,299,474	10,339,288	0	61,900,878	4/30/00
47.	Meijer Foundation	MI	1990	IN	10,238,836	10,238,836	7,000,000	33,473,313	9/30/00
48.	Gerald J. & Dorothy R. Friedman New York Foundation For Medical Research	NY	1999	IN	10,200,096	10,348,123	0	3,964,409	2/28/01
49.	Noyce Foundation	CA	1990	IN	10,069,446	10,069,446	0	173,718,164	12/31/00

Source: *Foundation Yearbook*, 2002.

*Aggregate foundation fiscal information is based on data provided to the Center as of February 2, 2002; fiscal data on individual foundations included in this table may be more current.

[1] Foundation type: IN=Independent; CS=Corporate; CM=Community; and OP=Operating.
[2] Includes grants, scholarship, employee matching gifts; excludes set-asides, loans, PRIs, and program expenses.
[3] Qualifying distributions is the amount used in calculating the required 5 percent payout; includes total giving, as well as reasonable administrative expenses, set-asides, PRIs, operating program expenses, and amount paid to acquire assets used directly for charitable purposes.
[4] For some operating foundations, total giving amount includes grants and program expenses; for others, total giving amount includes only grants. Most operating foundations' qualifying distributions are paid out for administration of operating programs and not for grants.

APPENDIX A

Methodology

Foundation Yearbook analyzes and interprets in one volume the entire body of data collected by the Foundation Center on active grantmaking foundations. Its purpose is fourfold: (1) to measure the dimensions of U.S. grantmaking foundations by number, assets, giving, and gifts received as a means of documenting their capacity for supporting the nonprofit sector; (2) to examine differences in the growth and distribution of foundations and their resources by foundation location and type; (3) for the largest foundations, to track growth over time by foundation type; and (4) to monitor new foundation formation.

Foundation Yearbook draws from a range of current and historical data sources. It adheres to underlying foundation definitions and criteria used throughout the Foundation Center's publications. The following methodology discussion examines the universe of philanthropic foundations covered by *Foundation Yearbook*, the sources of data for smaller and larger foundations, and the timeliness of fiscal information.

Counting Foundations: How We Differ from the IRS

The Internal Revenue code defines the category of "private foundation" only by the exclusion of other nonprofit organizations. Under IRS regulations, organizations such as libraries, museums, and homes for the aged may be counted as foundations if they "happen to be endowed by an individual or single family, or if they were established as public charities and lose that status by failing to prove they have received ongoing financial support from the general public."[1]

The Foundation Center supports a narrower private foundation definition: a nongovernmental, nonprofit organization with its own funds (usually from a single source, either an individual, a family, or a corporation) and program managed by its own trustees and directors, established to maintain or aid educational, social, charitable, religious, or other activities serving the common welfare, primarily by making grants to other nonprofit organizations. Included among these foundations are operating foundations (which conduct their own research or direct service programs) that also make grants.

In addition, the Foundation Center tracks community foundations. Like private foundations, these funders make grants, but they receive their funding from the public, generally through contributions received from many donors. (For definitions of foundations by type, see Figure 24 in Chapter 4.)

In counting "active grantmaking foundations," the Foundation Center excludes organizations deemed terminated or inactive and those not intended to fulfill the philanthropic functions the Center ascribes to private foundations. In general, those falling into the latter category are failed public charities.

In early 2002, staff research documented 56,582 active grantmaking foundations. All of these foundations had made grants of at least one dollar in their most current fiscal year on record—which ranged from 1998 to 2001—and had not terminated operations.

Among those foundations filing 990-PF tax returns in the most recent year, but not included in this total, were 3,609 foundations that did not award any grants (including many newly established funders); 2,308 operating foundations that did not make grants to outside organizations; and 932 foundations that had either terminated operations, merged into another foundation or corporate giving program, changed status to a public charity, or become inactive.

---
1. Freeman, D. and the Council on Foundations. *The Handbook of Private Foundations*. Washington, DC: Council on Foundations, 1997.

Sources of Historical Data

To establish time-line data going back to 1975, *Foundation Yearbook* consolidates summary information published by the Foundation Center in the statistical introductions to its major reference publications. Fiscal data summaries were drawn from the *National Data Book of Foundations* (editions 2-16), and the Foundation Center database.

Sources of Current Data

The Foundation Center's sources of data on active grantmaking foundations include:

- the yearly transaction tape produced by the Internal Revenue Service from the annual information returns (Form 990-PF) filed by private foundations during the given period

- CD-ROMs of Form 990-PF that the Center receives monthly from the IRS

- financial and program information provided by foundations in annual reports, other foundation publications, Web sites, or in questionnaires mailed out annually by the Foundation Center to more than 24,000 larger foundations (including those in *The Foundation Directory* and *The Foundation Directory, Part 2*). These questionnaires are the primary source of detailed information on foundation establishment, staffing, and reporting, and of detailed financial reporting on loans and other program-related investments, and grants and scholarships to individuals

Gathering Data on Active Community Foundations

Most community foundations are not included on the IRS tape or in the shipments of 990-PF tax returns since they are classified as public charities and file different information returns (IRS Form 990). Thus, the Center, after working with the Council on Foundations to identify existing community foundations, has gathered information on these foundations primarily through annual surveys. In 2001, the Center received responses from 560 community foundations, and this information was added to the foundation database file by our staff. Most of the community foundations appearing in either of the *Directory* publications also publish an annual report or program statement.

The 2000 Report Year: How Consistent Is the Information?

Because the Foundation Center depends on a range of fiscal reporting sources—some far more timely than others—a single snapshot of the 56,582 active foundations typically contains fiscal data spanning three to four years. By updating foundation listings directly from questionnaires, annual reports, and Form 990-PF, the Center has been able to improve the timeliness of data by at least 50 percent over that reported on the IRS transaction tape. For this analysis, 70 percent of the 56,582 foundation listings contained 2000 or early 2001 fiscal data, 24 percent contained 1999 data, and the balance contained 1998 data.

Those 39,488 foundations reporting 2000 or early 2001 fiscal information accounted for 81 percent of the total assets and 78 percent of the total giving reported in this edition. An additional nearly 18 percent of assets and 21 percent of grant dollars reflected 1999 fiscal data. Finally, less than 2 percent of asset and grants information reflected 1998 fiscal data.

Analyses of Larger Foundations

Throughout this report, expanded analyses have been conducted on foundations holding assets of at least $1 million or making grants totaling $100,000 or more. A total of nearly 21,000 private and community foundations met this standard for report year 2000.

The special reports on these foundations include foundation formation by decade. Historical data were taken from *The Foundation Directory* (editions 6–14), while more recent fiscal data came directly from the Center's database.

Tracking New Foundations

Reporting on new foundation formation is an important and unique feature of *Foundation Yearbook*. The Center has researched and maintained comprehensive records on foundation establishment for the larger foundations since the 1970s, allowing us to chart the growth of foundations across decades. Since 1987, when the Center began to process data directly from the 990-PF tax return, our staff has researched formation year data for small foundations. As a result, in early 2002, we were able to identify 33,300 active foundations established since 1980.

These new foundations represent almost 97 percent of the nearly 34,500 foundation records added to the

Center's database since 1980. Others are not new foundations but rather "private foundation" non-exempt charitable trusts (NECTs). Starting around 1982, the IRS required that these trusts file Form 990-PF.

Family Foundations

Measuring the activities of so called "family foundations"—i.e., independent foundations in which individual donors and/or family members are directly involved in guiding operations—poses unique difficulties for researchers on philanthropy. Since there is no legal definition of a family foundation, there is not yet and may never be a precise way to identify these grantmakers. Nonetheless, in an effort to begin collecting information on this set of funders, the Foundation Center has developed several subjective and objective means to identify family foundations.

Beginning in the mid-1990s, the Center added a question to its annual survey of top foundations asking them to self-identify as family foundations. Although this "subjective" method captures only a fraction of the total number of foundations that are believed to be operated by individual donors and/or families, it provides a starting point for identifying these funders.

In addition to this subjective measure, the Center has added three "objective" criteria for identifying family foundations. First, family foundation data include any independent foundation that has identified itself as a family foundation through the use of the term "Family" or "Families" in its name. Thus, grantmakers such as the Nelson D. Abell Family Foundation (LA) and the Marion and Robert Rosenthal Family Foundation (VA) are captured in family foundation statistics. Second, family foundation data include any grantmaker with a living donor whose surname matches the foundation name, based on the assumption that living donors will take an active role in the governance of a foundation that carries their name. Third, data on family foundations include any independent foundation with at least two trustees whose surnames match a living or deceased donor's name, based on the assumption that a foundation with at least two family members on its board shows meaningful family involvement in its governance.

These subjective and objective criteria are imperfect and by no means identify all foundations operated with significant donor and/or family involvement. Anecdotal information suggests that the majority of independent foundations, most of which are quite small, are to some degree donor and/or family operated. Nonetheless, these measures are effective in identifying most of the "newer" family foundations, as data received by the Center for these funders often includes information on living donors, who are presumed to play an important role in governance. Over the next several years, the Center will endeavor to enhance its capacity for tracking family foundations.

APPENDIX B

Regulation of Private Foundations

Nonprofit organizations that are defined as private foundations by the IRS must be organized and operated under specific regulations, which are primarily derived from the Tax Reform Act of 1969, with some significant modifications as a result of the 1976 Tax Reform Act, the Economic Recovery Tax Act of 1981 (ERTA), and tax legislation enacted in 1984, 1986, 1987, and 1988. The Tax Reform Act of 1969 established the criteria for distinguishing private foundations from public charities and set up a separate category of private foundations with a more favorable tax status for operating foundations.

Provisions of the 1969 Tax Reform Act. The Act set forth special rules that, among other things, prohibit certain transactions between foundations and "disqualified persons," including their donors and managers, as "self-dealing;" restrict foundation ownership and control of private business; limit the percentage of an individual's annual income that can be donated to a private foundation as a tax-deductible contribution; and regulate foundation giving to individuals, other foundations, non-exempt organizations, and activities that influence legislation or political campaigns.

To offset costs incurred by the IRS in regulating tax-exempt organizations, the 1969 Act imposed an excise tax on foundations at the rate of 4 percent of net investment income. Because this excise tax generated revenues that greatly exceeded the annual budget of the exempt organizations branch of the IRS, the Revenue Act of 1978 reduced the tax to 2 percent. With tax revenues still many times greater than regulatory costs, the Deficit Reduction Act of 1984 reduced the tax from 2 to 1 percent for any foundation that, in a given tax year, makes sufficient qualifying distributions to meet certain requirements.

Payout Requirements. The 1969 Act also required a private foundation to distribute for charitable purposes, either of all its "adjusted net income" or a percentage, to be set each year, of the market value of that year's investment assets, whichever was higher. This "payout requirement" was later set at 5 percent of the average market value of that year's investment assets, to be paid out in the following year. Tax legislation in 1984 limited to .65 percent of net investment assets the amount of administrative expenses incurred in making grants that could be counted as part of the 5 percent payout requirement. The intention was to assure that private foundations could not meet the payout requirement by paying excessive trustee fees or similar non-charitable distributions. The ".65 percent rule" was allowed to lapse at the end of 1990, following a study by the Treasury Department that concluded that it was complex and burdensome and that there was no evidence of excessive administrative expenses on the part of the vast majority of foundations.

Reporting Requirements. The 1969 legislation called for foundations to file two annual information returns with the IRS (Form 990-AR and 990-PF), to make the forms available for inspection by the public, and to file two copies of the forms with state authorities in the state where the foundation is incorporated and maintains its principal offices. Beginning in 1982, foundations have been required to file only one form, a revised version of the Form 990-PF that incorporates all information previously required on the separate forms, and calls for additional information on the foundation's grantmaking policies.

Legislation passed in 1998 and regulations finalized in early 2000 now require private foundations to provide "take home" copies of their current Form 990-PF to any individual who makes a request in person or in writing. These regulations apply to all returns filed after March 13, 2000. Foundations are required to make each annual return filed after this date available for three years. If a foundation's Form

990-PF is widely available through the Internet in a manner that complies with the regulations, it will have satisfied its disclosure requirements and need not provide take home copies.

Other Provisions. The Tax Reform Act of 1969 further prohibits or circumscribes a number of activities on the part of private foundations, including attempts to influence legislation, intervention in political campaigns, and making grants to individuals or to other private foundations or non-501(c)(3) organizations. Making grants in these areas entails a certain amount of planning and paperwork for foundations. For instance, a foundation must have an IRS-approved individual grants program in order to make grants to individuals for study or travel purposes, and must follow up such grants with special reports. A foundation may make a grant for a charitable purpose to an organization that does not qualify as a public charity so long as it exercises "expenditure responsibility," which entails a pre-grant inquiry, a grant contract and follow-up reports to the IRS as part of the 990-PF. Foundations may even support groups that include lobbying or voter education and registration in their activities, provided that they and their grantee follow the regulations governing these areas. More recent directives from the Treasury outline procedures that foundations may follow in connection with grant-making to foreign organizations.

State Regulation. The IRS is responsible for enforcing the federal regulations on foundations, and it accomplishes this primarily through review of the 990-PF reports and through audits of individual foundations. At the state level, regulation is typically the concern of the state attorney general, who enforces the state's not-for-profit corporation law and any statutory or common laws governing charitable trustees. The federal regulatory system was designed to encourage more active state regulation of foundations. The 990-PFs must, for instance, be filed with the appropriate state authorities as well as with the IRS. Thus, in many states, the office of the attorney general serves as another resource for those interested in researching a foundation located in that state.

APPENDIX C

Foundation Center Cooperating Collections
Free Funding Information Centers

The Foundation Center is an independent national service organization established by foundations to provide an authoritative source of information on foundation and corporate giving. The New York, Washington D.C., Atlanta, Cleveland, and San Francisco reference collections operated by the Foundation Center offer a wide variety of services and comprehensive resources on foundations and grants. Cooperating Collections are libraries, community foundations, and other nonprofit agencies that make accessible a collection of Foundation Center print and electronic publications, as well as a variety of supplementary materials and education programs in areas useful to grantseekers. The collection includes:

FC SEARCH: THE FOUNDATION CENTER'S DATABASE ON CD-ROM
THE FOUNDATION DIRECTORY 1 AND 2, AND SUPPLEMENT
FOUNDATION FUNDAMENTALS
THE FOUNDATION 1000

FOUNDATIONS TODAY SERIES
FOUNDATION GRANTS TO INDIVIDUALS
THE FOUNDATION CENTER'S GUIDE TO GRANTSEEKING ON THE WEB
THE FOUNDATION CENTER'S GUIDE TO PROPOSAL WRITING

GUIDE TO U.S. FOUNDATIONS, THEIR TRUSTEES, OFFICERS, AND DONORS
NATIONAL DIRECTORY OF CORPORATE GIVING
NATIONAL GUIDE TO FUNDING IN.... (SERIES)
SECURING YOUR ORGANIZATION'S FUTURE

All five Foundation Center libraries and most Cooperating Collections have *FC: Search: The Foundation Center's Database on CD-ROM* available for public use and all provide Internet access. Increasingly, those seeking information on fundraising and nonprofit management are referring to our Web site (http://www.fdncenter.org) for a wealth of data and advice on grantseeking, including links to foundation IRS information returns (990-PFs). Because the Cooperating Collections vary in their hours, it is recommended that you call the collection in advance of a visit. To check on new locations or current holdings, call toll-free 1-800-424-9836, or visit our site at http://fdncenter.org/collections/index.html.

REFERENCE COLLECTIONS OPERATED BY THE FOUNDATION CENTER

THE FOUNDATION CENTER
2nd Floor
79 Fifth Ave.
New York, NY 10003
(212) 620-4230

THE FOUNDATION CENTER
312 Sutter St., Suite 606
San Francisco, CA 94108
(415) 397-0902

THE FOUNDATION CENTER
1627 K St., NW, 3rd floor
Washington, DC 20006
(202) 331-1400

THE FOUNDATION CENTER
Kent H. Smith Library
1422 Euclid Ave., Suite 1600
Cleveland, OH 44115
(216) 861-1933

THE FOUNDATION CENTER
Suite 150, Grand Lobby
Hurt Bldg., 50 Hurt Plaza
Atlanta, GA 30303
(404) 880-0094

ALABAMA

BIRMINGHAM PUBLIC LIBRARY
Government Documents
2100 Park Place
Birmingham 35203
(205) 226-3620

HUNTSVILLE PUBLIC LIBRARY
915 Monroe St.
Huntsville 35801
(256) 532-5940

AUBURN UNIVERSITY AT MONTGOMERY LIBRARY
74-40 East Dr.
Montgomery 36117-3596
(334) 244-3200

ALASKA

CONSORTIUM LIBRARY
3211 Providence Dr.
Anchorage 99508
(907) 786-1848

JUNEAU PUBLIC LIBRARY
292 Marine Way
Juneau 99801
(907) 586-5267

ARIZONA

FLAGSTAFF CITY-COCONINO COUNTY PUBLIC LIBRARY
300 W. Aspen Ave.
Flagstaff 86001
(928) 779-7670

PHOENIX PUBLIC LIBRARY
Information Services Department
1221 N. Central Ave.
Phoenix 85004
(602) 262-4636

TUCSON PIMA PUBLIC LIBRARY
101 N. Stone Ave.
Tucson 87501
(520) 791-4393

ARKANSAS

WESTARK COLLEGE—BOREHAM LIBRARY
5210 Grand Ave.
Ft. Smith 72913
(479) 788-7204

CENTRAL ARKANSAS LIBRARY SYSTEM
100 Rock St.
Little Rock 72201
(501) 918-3000

CALIFORNIA

KERN COUNTY LIBRARY
Beale Memorial Library
701 Truxtun Ave.
Bakersfield 93301
(661) 868-0700

HUMBOLDT AREA FOUNDATION
Rooney Resource Center
373 Indianola
Bayside 95524
(707) 442-2993

VENTURA COUNTY COMMUNITY FOUNDATION
Resource Center for Nonprofit Organizations
1317 Del Norte Rd., Suite 150
Camarillo 93010-8504
(805) 988-0196

FRESNO REGIONAL FOUNDATION
Nonprofit Advancement Center
3425 N. First St., Suite 101
Fresno 93726
(559) 226-0216

CENTER FOR NONPROFIT MANAGEMENT IN SOUTHERN CALIFORNIA
Nonprofit Resource Library
606 South Olive St. #2450
Los Angeles 90014
(213) 623-7080

LOS ANGELES PUBLIC LIBRARY
Mid-Valley Regional Branch Library
16244 Nordhoff St.
North Hills 91343
(818) 895-3654

PHILANTHROPY RESOURCE CENTER
Flintridge Foundation
1040 Lincoln Ave, Suite 100
Pasadena 91103
(626) 449-0839

GRANT & RESOURCE CENTER OF NORTHERN CALIFORNIA
Bldg. C, Suite A
2280 Benton Dr.
Redding 96003
(530) 244-1219

RICHMOND PUBLIC LIBRARY
325 Civic Center Plaza
Richmond 94804
(510) 620-6561

RIVERSIDE CITY PUBLIC LIBRARY
3581 Mission Inn Ave.
Riverside 92501
(909) 826-5201

SACRAMENTO PUBLIC LIBRARY
328 I St., 2nd Floor
Sacramento 95814
(916) 264-2772

APPENDIX C

SAN DIEGO FOUNDATION
Funding Information Center
1420 Kettner Blvd., Suite 500
San Diego 92101
(619) 235-2300

COMPASSPOINT NONPROFIT
SERVICES
Nonprofit Development Library
1922 The Alameda, Suite 212
San Jose 95126
(408) 248-9505

PENINSULA COMMUNITY
FOUNDATION
Peninsula Nonprofit Center
1700 S. El Camino Real, #R201
San Mateo 94402-3049
(650) 358-9392

LOS ANGELES PUBLIC LIBRARY
San Pedro Regional Branch
931 S. Gaffey St.
San Pedro 90731
(310) 548-7779

VOLUNTEER CENTER OF GREATER
ORANGE COUNTY
Nonprofit Resource Center
1901 E. 4th St., Suite 100
Santa Ana 92705
(714) 953-5757

SANTA BARBARA PUBLIC LIBRARY
40 E. Anapamu St.
Santa Barbara 93101-1019
(805) 962-7653

SANTA MONICA PUBLIC LIBRARY
1343 6th St.
Santa Monica 90401-1603
(310) 458-8600

SONOMA COUNTY LIBRARY
3rd & E Sts.
Santa Rosa 95404
(707) 545-0831

SEASIDE BRANCH LIBRARY
550 Harcourt Ave.
Seaside 93955
(831) 899-8131

SIERRA NONPROFIT SUPPORT
CENTER
20100 Cedar Rd., N.
Sonora 95370
(209) 533-2596

COLORADO

PENROSE LIBRARY
20 N. Cascade Ave.
Colorado Springs 80903
(719) 531-6333

DENVER PUBLIC LIBRARY
10 W. 14th Ave. Pkwy.
Denver 80204
(720) 865-1363

CONNECTICUT

DANBURY PUBLIC LIBRARY
170 Main St.
Danbury 06810
(203) 797-4527

GREENWICH LIBRARY
101 W. Putnam Ave.
Greenwich 06830
(203) 622-7900

HARTFORD PUBLIC LIBRARY
500 Main St.
Hartford 06103
(860) 543-8656

NEW HAVEN FREE PUBLIC LIBRARY
133 Elm St.
New Haven 06510-2057
(203) 946-7091

DELAWARE

UNIVERSITY OF DELAWARE
Hugh Morris Library
Newark 19717-5267
(302) 831-2432

FLORIDA

VOLUSIA COUNTY LIBRARY CENTER
City Island
105 E. Magnolia Ave.
Daytona Beach 32114-4484
(386) 257-6036

NOVA SOUTHEASTERN UNIVERSITY
Einstein Library
3301 College Ave.
Fort Lauderdale 33314
(954) 262-4513

INDIAN RIVER COMMUNITY
COLLEGE
Learning Resources Center
3209 Virginia Ave.
Fort Pierce 34981-5596
(561) 462-4757

JACKSONVILLE PUBLIC LIBRARIES
Grants Resource Center
122 N. Ocean St.
Jacksonville 32202
(904) 630-2665

MIAMI-DADE PUBLIC LIBRARY
Humanities/Social Science
101 W. Flagler St.
Miami 33130
(305) 375-5575

ORANGE COUNTY LIBRARY SYSTEM
Social Sciences Department
101 E. Central Blvd.
Orlando 32801
(407) 425-4694

SELBY PUBLIC LIBRARY
Reference
1331 1st St.
Sarasota 34236
(941) 316-1181

HILLSBOROUGH COUNTY PUBLIC
LIBRARY COOPERATIVE
900 N. Ashley Dr.
Tampa 33602
(813) 273-3652

COMMUNITY FOUNDATION OF
PALM BEACH & MARTIN COUNTIES
324 Datura St., Suite 340
West Palm Beach 33401
(561) 659-6800

GEORGIA

ATLANTA-FULTON PUBLIC LIBRARY
Foundation Collection—Ivan Allen
Department
1 Margaret Mitchell Square
Atlanta 30303-1089
(404) 730-1909

HALL COUNTY LIBRARY SYSTEM
127 Main Street NW
Gainesville 30501
(770) 532-3311

UNITED WAY OF CENTRAL GEORGIA
Community Resource Center
277 Martin Luther King Jr. Blvd.,
Suite 301
Macon 31201
(478) 745-4732

SAVANNAH STATE UNIVERSITY
Asa Gordon Library
Thompkins Rd.
Savannah 31404
(912) 356-2185

THOMAS COUNTY PUBLIC LIBRARY
201 N. Madison St.
Thomasville 31792
(912) 225-5252

HAWAII

UNIVERSITY OF HAWAII
Hamilton Library
2550 The Mall
Honolulu 96822
(808) 956-7214

HAWAII COMMUNITY
FOUNDATION
Funding Resource Library
900 Fort St., Suite 1300
Honolulu 96813
(808) 537-6333

IDAHO

BOISE PUBLIC LIBRARY
Funding Information Center
715 S. Capitol Blvd.
Boise 83702
(208) 384-4024

CALDWELL PUBLIC LIBRARY
1010 Dearborn St.
Caldwell 83605
(208) 459-3242

ILLINOIS

DONORS FORUM OF CHICAGO
208 S. LaSalle, Suite 735
Chicago 60604
(312) 578-0175

EVANSTON PUBLIC LIBRARY
1703 Orrington Ave.
Evanston 60201
(847) 866-0300

ROCK ISLAND PUBLIC LIBRARY
401 19th St.
Rock Island 61201-8143
(309) 732-7323

UNIVERSITY OF ILLINOIS
AT SPRINGFIELD, LIB 23
Brookens Library
Springfield 62794-9243
(217) 206-6633

INDIANA

EVANSVILLE–VANDERBURGH
PUBLIC LIBRARY
22 SE 5th St.
Evansville 47708
(812) 428-8200

ALLEN COUNTY PUBLIC LIBRARY
900 Webster St.
Ft. Wayne 46802
(260) 421-1200

INDIANAPOLIS–MARION COUNTY
PUBLIC LIBRARY
Social Sciences
40 E. St. Clair
Indianapolis 46206
(317) 269-1733

VIGO COUNTY PUBLIC LIBRARY
1 Library Square
Terre Haute 47807
(812) 232-1113

IOWA

CEDAR RAPIDS PUBLIC LIBRARY
500 1st St., SE
Cedar Rapids 52401
(319) 398-5123

SOUTHWESTERN COMMUNITY
COLLEGE
Learning Resource Center
1501 W. Townline Rd.
Creston 50801
(515) 782-7081

PUBLIC LIBRARY OF DES MOINES
100 Locust
Des Moines 50309-1791
(515) 283-4152

SIOUX CITY PUBLIC LIBRARY
Siouxland Funding Research Center
529 Pierce St.
Sioux City 51101-1203
(712) 255-2933

KANSAS

PIONEER MEMORIAL LIBRARY
375 West 4th St.
Colby 67701
(785) 462-4470

DODGE CITY PUBLIC LIBRARY
1001 2nd Ave.
Dodge City 67801
(316) 225-0248

KEARNY COUNTY LIBRARY
101 East Prairie
Lakin 67860
(620) 355-6674

TOPEKA AND SHAWNEE COUNTY
PUBLIC LIBRARY
1515 SW 10th Ave.
Topeka 66604
(785) 580-4400

WICHITA PUBLIC LIBRARY
223 S. Main St.
Wichita 67202
(316) 261-8500

KENTUCKY

WESTERN KENTUCKY UNIVERSITY
Helm-Cravens Library
110 Helm Library
Bowling Green 42101-3576
(270) 745-6163

LEXINGTON PUBLIC LIBRARY
140 E. Main St.
Lexington 40507-1376
(859) 231-5520

LOUISVILLE FREE PUBLIC LIBRARY
301 York St.
Louisville 40203
(502) 574-1617

LOUISIANA

EAST BATON ROUGE PARISH
LIBRARY
Centroplex Branch Grants Collection
120 St. Louis St.
Baton Rouge 70802
(225) 389-4967

BEAUREGARD PARISH LIBRARY
205 S. Washington Ave.
De Ridder 70634
(337) 463-6217

OUACHITA PARISH PUBLIC LIBRARY
1800 Stubbs Ave.
Monroe 71201
(318) 327-1490

NEW ORLEANS PUBLIC LIBRARY
Business & Science Division
219 Loyola Ave.
New Orleans 70112
(504) 596-2580

SHREVE MEMORIAL LIBRARY
424 Texas St.
Shreveport 71120-1523
(318) 226-5894

MAINE

UNIVERSITY OF SOUTHERN
MAINE LIBRARY
Maine Philanthropy Center
314 Forrest Ave.
Portland 04104-9301
(207) 780-5029

Foundation Center Cooperating Collections

MARYLAND

ENOCH PRATT FREE LIBRARY
Social Science & History Dept.
400 Cathedral St.
Baltimore 21201
(410) 396-5430

MASSACHUSETTS

ASSOCIATED GRANT MAKERS OF
MASSACHUSETTS
55 Court St.
Room 520
Boston 02108
(617) 426-2606

BOSTON PUBLIC LIBRARY
Soc. Sci. Reference
700 Boylston St.
Boston 02116
(617) 536-5400

WESTERN MASSACHUSETTS
FUNDING RESOURCE CENTER
65 Elliot St.
Springfield 01101-1730
(413) 452-0697

WORCESTER PUBLIC LIBRARY
Grants Resource Center
2 Salem Sq.
Worcester 01608
(508) 799-1654

MICHIGAN

ALPENA COUNTY LIBRARY
211 N. 1st St.
Alpena 49707
(989) 356-6188

UNIVERSITY OF
MICHIGAN–ANN ARBOR
Graduate Library
Reference & Research Services
  Department
Ann Arbor 48109-1205
(734) 763-1539

WILLARD PUBLIC LIBRARY
Nonprofit & Funding Resource
  Collections
7 W. Van Buren St.
Battle Creek 49017
(616) 968-8166

HENRY FORD CENTENNIAL LIBRARY
16301 Michigan Ave.
Dearborn 48124
(313) 943-2330

WAYNE STATE UNIVERSITY
134 Purdy/Kresge Library
Detroit 48202
(313) 577-6424

MICHIGAN STATE UNIVERSITY
LIBRARIES
Main Library
Funding Center
100 Library
East Lansing 48824-1049
(517) 353-8700

FARMINGTON COMMUNITY
LIBRARY
32737 W. 12 Mile Rd.
Farmington Hills 48334
(248) 553-0300

UNIVERSITY OF MICHIGAN—FLINT
Frances Willson Thompson Library
Flint 48502-1950
(810) 762-3413

GRAND RAPIDS PUBLIC LIBRARY
1100 Hynes Ave.
Grand Rapids 49507
(616) 988-5400

MICHIGAN TECHNOLOGICAL
UNIVERSITY
Van Pelt Library
1400 Townsend Dr.
Houghton 49931
(906) 487-2507

NORTHWESTERN MICHIGAN
COLLEGE
Mark & Helen Osterlin Library
1701 E. Front St.
Traverse City 49686
(231) 995-1060

MINNESOTA

DULUTH PUBLIC LIBRARY
520 W. Superior St.
Duluth 55802
(218) 723-3802

SOUTHWEST STATE UNIVERSITY
University Library
N. Hwy. 23
Marshall 56253
(507) 537-6108

MINNEAPOLIS PUBLIC LIBRARY
Sociology Department
300 Nicollet Mall
Minneapolis 55401
(612) 630-6300

ROCHESTER PUBLIC LIBRARY
101 2nd St. SE
Rochester 55904-3777
(507) 285-8002

ST. PAUL PUBLIC LIBRARY
90 W. 4th St.
St. Paul 55102
(651) 266-7000

MISSISSIPPI

LIBRARY OF HATTIESBURG, PETAL
AND FORREST COUNTY
329 Hardy Street
Hattiesburg 39401-3824
(601) 582-4461'

JACKSON/HINDS LIBRARY SYSTEM
300 N. State St.
Jackson 39201
(601) 968-5803

MISSOURI

COUNCIL ON PHILANTHROPY
University of Missouri—Kansas City
Center for Business Innovation
4747 Troost
Kansas City 64113-0680
(816) 235-1176

KANSAS CITY PUBLIC LIBRARY
311 E. 12th St.
Kansas City 64106
(816) 701-3541

METROPOLITAN ASSOCIATION FOR
PHILANTHROPY, INC.
211 N. Broadway, Suite 1200
St. Louis 63102
(314) 621-6220

SPRINGFIELD-GREENE
COUNTY LIBRARY
The Library Center
4653 S. Campbell
Springfield 65810
(417) 874-8110

MONTANA

MONTANA STATE UNIVERSITY—
BILLINGS
Library—Special Collections
1500 N. 30th St.
Billings 59101-0245
(406) 657-1687

BOZEMAN PUBLIC LIBRARY
220 E. Lamme
Bozeman 59715
(406) 582-2402

MONTANA STATE LIBRARY
Library Services
1515 E. 6th Ave.
Helena 59620-1800
(406) 444-3115

UNIVERSITY OF MONTANA
Mansfield Library
32 Campus Dr. #9936
Missoula 59812-9936
(406) 243-6800

NEBRASKA

UNIVERSITY OF NEBRASKA—
LINCOLN
Love Library
14th & R Sts.
Lincoln 68588-2848
(402) 472-2848

OMAHA PUBLIC LIBRARY
W. Dale Clark Library
Social Sciences Dept.
215 S. 15th St.
Omaha 68102
(402) 444-4826

NEVADA

CLARK COUNTY LIBRARY
1401 E. Flamingo
Las Vegas 89119
(702) 733-3642

WASHOE COUNTY LIBRARY
301 S. Center St.
Reno 89501
(775) 327-8300

NEW HAMPSHIRE

CONCORD PUBLIC LIBRARY
45 Green St.
Concord 03301
(603) 225-8670

PLYMOUTH STATE COLLEGE
Herbert H. Lamson Library
Plymouth 03264
(603) 535-2258

NEW JERSEY

CUMBERLAND COUNTY LIBRARY
800 E. Commerce St.
Bridgeton 08302
(856) 453-2210

FREE PUBLIC LIBRARY OF ELIZABETH
11 S. Broad St.
Elizabeth 07202
(908) 354-6060

NEWARK ENTERPRISE COMMUNITY
RESOURCE DEVELOPMENT CENTER
303-309 Washington St.
Newark 07102
(973) 624-8300

COUNTY COLLEGE OF MORRIS
Learning Resource Center
214 Center Grove Rd.
Randolph 07869
(973) 328-5296

NEW JERSEY STATE LIBRARY
185 W. State St.
Trenton 08625-0520
(609) 292-6220

NEW MEXICO

JEMEZ PUEBLO COMMUNITY
LIBRARY
020 Mission Road
Jemez Pueblo 87024
(505) 834-9171

NEW MEXICO STATE LIBRARY
Information Services
1209 Camino Carlos Rey
Santa Fe 87505-9860
(505) 476-9702

NEW YORK

NEW YORK STATE LIBRARY
Humanities Reference
Cultural Education Center, 6th Fl.
Empire State Plaza
Albany 12230
(518) 474-5355

SUFFOLK COOPERATIVE
LIBRARY SYSTEM
627 N. Sunrise Service Rd.
Bellport 11713
(631) 286-1600

BROOKLYN PUBLIC LIBRARY
Society, Science and Technology
  Division
Grand Army Plaza
Brooklyn 11238
(718) 230-2122

BUFFALO & ERIE COUNTY
PUBLIC LIBRARY
Business, Science & Technology Dept.
1 Lafayette Square
Buffalo 14203-1887
(716) 858-7097

HUNTINGTON PUBLIC LIBRARY
338 Main St.
Huntington 11743
(631) 427-5165

QUEENS BOROUGH PUBLIC
LIBRARY
Social Sciences Division
89-11 Merrick Blvd.
Jamaica 11432
(718) 990-0700

LEVITTOWN PUBLIC LIBRARY
1 Bluegrass Ln.
Levittown 11756
(516) 731-5728

ADRIANCE MEMORIAL LIBRARY
Special Services Department
93 Market St.
Poughkeepsie 12601
(914) 485-3445

ROCHESTER PUBLIC LIBRARY
Social Sciences
115 South Ave.
Rochester 14604
(716) 428-8120

ONONDAGA COUNTY PUBLIC
LIBRARY
447 S. Salina St.
Syracuse 13202-2494
(315) 435-1900

UTICA PUBLIC LIBRARY
303 Genesee St.
Utica 13501
(315) 735-2279

WHITE PLAINS PUBLIC LIBRARY
100 Martine Ave.
White Plains 10601
(914) 422-1480

YONKERS PUBLIC LIBRARY
Reference Department, Getty
  Square Branch
7 Main St.
Yonkers 10701
(914) 476-1255

Appendix C

NORTH CAROLINA

PACK MEMORIAL LIBRARY
Community Foundation of Western
North Carolina
67 Haywood St.
Asheville 28801
(828) 254-4960

THE DUKE ENDOWMENT
100 N. Tryon St., Suite 3500
Charlotte 28202-4012
(704) 376-0291

DURHAM COUNTY PUBLIC LIBRARY
300 N. Roxboro St.
Durham 27702
(919) 560-0100

FORSYTH COUNTY PUBLIC LIBRARY
660 W. 5th St.
Winston-Salem 27408
(336) 727-2264

NORTH DAKOTA

BISMARCK PUBLIC LIBRARY
515 N. 5th St.
Bismarck 58501-4081
(701) 222-6410

FARGO PUBLIC LIBRARY
102 N. 3rd St.
Fargo 58102
(701) 241-1491

MINOT PUBLIC LIBRARY
516 Second Avenue SW
Minot 58701-3792
(701) 852-1045

OHIO

STARK COUNTY DISTRICT LIBRARY
715 Market Ave. N.
Canton 44702
(330) 452-0665

PUBLIC LIBRARY OF CINCINNATI &
HAMILTON COUNTY
Grants Resource Center
800 Vine St.—Library Square
Cincinnati 45202-2071
(513) 369-6000

COLUMBUS METROPOLITAN
LIBRARY
Business and Technology
96 S. Grant Ave.
Columbus 43215
(614) 645-2590

DAYTON & MONTGOMERY
COUNTY PUBLIC LIBRARY
Grants Information Center
215 E. Third St.
Dayton 45402
(937) 227-9500

MANSFIELD/RICHLAND COUNTY
PUBLIC LIBRARY
42 W. 3rd St.
Mansfield 44902
(419) 521-3100

PORTSMOUTH PUBLIC LIBRARY
1220 Gallia St.
Portsmouth 45662
(740) 354-5688

TOLEDO–LUCAS COUNTY
PUBLIC LIBRARY
325 Michigan St.
Toledo 43612
(419) 259-5209

PUBLIC LIBRARY OF
YOUNGSTOWN & MAHONING
COUNTY
305 Wick Ave.
Youngstown 44503
(330) 744-8636

OKLAHOMA

OKLAHOMA CITY UNIVERSITY
Dulaney Browne Library
2501 N. Blackwelder
Oklahoma City 73106
(405) 521-5822

TULSA CITY–COUNTY LIBRARY
400 Civic Center
Tulsa 74103
(918) 596-7977

OREGON

OREGON INSTITUTE OF
TECHNOLOGY
Library
3201 Campus Dr.
Klamath Falls 97601-8801
(541) 885-1770

PACIFIC NON-PROFIT NETWORK
Southern Oregon University
1600 N. Riverside #1094
Medford 97501
(541) 779-6044

MULTNOMAH COUNTY LIBRARY
801 SW 10th Ave.
Portland 97205
(503) 988-5123

OREGON STATE LIBRARY
State Library Bldg.
250 Winter St. NE
Salem 97301-3950
(503) 378-4277

PENNSYLVANIA

NORTHAMPTON COMMUNITY
COLLEGE
Learning Resource Center
3835 Green Pond Rd.
Bethlehem 18017
(610) 861-5360

ERIE COUNTY LIBRARY SYSTEM
160 E. Front St.
Erie 16507
(814) 451-6927

DAUPHIN COUNTY LIBRARY
SYSTEM
East Shore Area Library
4501 Ethel St.
Harrisburg 17109
(717) 652-9380

LANCASTER COUNTY LIBRARY
125 N. Duke St.
Lancaster 17602
(717) 394-2651

FREE LIBRARY OF PHILADELPHIA
Regional Foundation Center
1901 Vine St.
Philadelphia 19103-1189
(215) 686-5423

CARNEGIE LIBRARY OF PITTSBURGH
Foundation Collection
4400 Forbes Ave.
Pittsburgh 15213-4080
(412) 622-1917

POCONO NORTHEAST
DEVELOPMENT FUND
James Pettinger Memorial Library
1151 Oak St.
Pittston 18643
(570) 655-5581

READING PUBLIC LIBRARY
100 S. 5th St.
Reading 19602
(610) 655-6355

JAMES V. BROWN LIBRARY
19 East Fourth Street
Williamsport 17701
(570) 326-0536

MARTIN LIBRARY
159 E. Market St.
York 17401
(717) 846-5300

RHODE ISLAND

PROVIDENCE PUBLIC
LIBRARY
225 Washington St.
Providence 02906
(401) 455-8088

SOUTH CAROLINA

ANDERSON COUNTY LIBRARY
300 N. McDuffie St.
Anderson 29622
(864) 260-4500

CHARLESTON COUNTY LIBRARY
68 Calhoun St.
Charleston 29401
(843) 805-6930

SOUTH CAROLINA STATE LIBRARY
1500 Senate St.
Columbia 29211-1469
(803) 734-8666

COMMUNITY FOUNDATION OF
GREATER GREENVILLE
27 Cleveland St., Suite 101
Greenville 29601
(864) 233-5925

SOUTH DAKOTA

SINTE GLESKA UNIVERSITY LIBRARY
Rosebud Sioux Reservation
Mission 57555-0107
(605) 856-2355

SOUTH DAKOTA STATE LIBRARY
800 Governors Dr.
Pierre 57501-2294
(605) 773-3131
(800) 592-1841 (SD residents)

DAKOTA STATE LIBRARY
Nonprofit Grants Assistance
2505 Career Ave.
Sioux Falls 57108
(605) 367-5380

SIOUXLAND LIBRARIES
201 N. Main Ave.
Sioux Falls 57104
(605) 367-8720

TENNESSEE

UNITED WAY OF GREATER
CHATTANOOGA
Center for Nonprofits
406 Frazier Ave.
Chattanooga 37405
(423) 265-0514

KNOX COUNTY PUBLIC LIBRARY
500 W. Church Ave.
Knoxville 37902
(865) 215-8751

MEMPHIS & SHELBY COUNTY
PUBLIC LIBRARY
3030 Poplar Ave.
Memphis 38111
(901) 415-2734

NASHVILLE PUBLIC LIBRARY
615 Church St.
Nashville 37219
(615) 862-5800

TEXAS

NONPROFIT RESOURCE CENTER
Funding Information Library
500 S. Chestnut, Suite 1634
Abilene 79604
(915) 677-8166

AMARILLO AREA FOUNDATION
Grants Center
801 S. Filmore, Suite 700
Amarillo 79101
(806) 376-4521

HOGG FOUNDATION FOR
MENTAL HEALTH
Regional Foundation Library
3001 Lake Austin Blvd., Suite 400
Austin 78703
(512) 471-5041

BEAUMONT PUBLIC LIBRARY
801 Pearl St.
Beaumont 77704-3827
(409) 838-6606

CORPUS CHRISTI PUBLIC LIBRARY
Funding Information Center
805 Comanche St.
Reference Dept.
Corpus Christi 78401
(361) 880-7000

DALLAS PUBLIC LIBRARY
Urban Information
1515 Young St.
Dallas 75201
(214) 670-1487

SOUTHWEST BORDER NONPROFIT
RESOURCE CENTER
1201 W. University Dr.
Edinburgh 78539
(956) 384-5920

UNIVERSITY OF TEXAS AT EL PASO
Institute for Community-Based
Teaching and Learning Community
Non-profit Grant Library
500 W. University, Benedict Hall, Rm. 103
El Paso 79968-0547
(915) 747-7969

FUNDING INFORMATION CENTER
OF FORT WORTH
329 S. Henderson St.
Ft. Worth 76104
(817) 334-0228

HOUSTON PUBLIC LIBRARY
Bibliographic Information Center
500 McKinney
Houston 77002
(832) 236-1313

NONPROFIT MANAGEMENT AND
VOLUNTEER CENTER
Laredo Public Library
1120 E. Calton Rd.
Laredo 78041
(956) 795-2400

LONGVIEW PUBLIC LIBRARY
222 W. Cotton St.
Longview 75601
(903) 237-1350

LUBBOCK AREA FOUNDATION, INC.
1655 Main St., Suite 209
Lubbock 79401
(806) 762-8061

NONPROFIT RESOURCE CENTER
OF TEXAS
7404 Hwy. 90 W.
San Antonio 78212-8270
(210) 227-4333

WACO-MCLENNAN COUNTY
LIBRARY
1717 Austin Ave.
Waco 76701
(254) 750-5941

NONPROFIT MANAGEMENT
CENTER OF WICHITA FALLS
2301 Kell Blvd., Suite 218
Wichita Falls 76308
(940) 322-4961

Foundation Center Cooperating Collections

UTAH

SALT LAKE CITY PUBLIC LIBRARY
209 E. 500 S.
Salt Lake City 84111
(801) 524-8200

VERMONT

VERMONT DEPT. OF LIBRARIES
Reference & Law Info. Services
109 State St.
Montpelier 05609
(802) 828-3261

VIRGINIA

WASHINGTON COUNTY
PUBLIC LIBRARY
205 Oak Hill St.
Abingdon 24210
(540) 676-6222

HAMPTON PUBLIC LIBRARY
4207 Victoria Blvd.
Hampton 23669
(757) 727-1312

RICHMOND PUBLIC LIBRARY
Business, Science & Technology Dept.
101 E. Franklin St.
Richmond 23219
(804) 646-7223

ROANOKE CITY PUBLIC
LIBRARY SYSTEM
Main Library
706 S. Jefferson
Roanoke 24016
(540) 853-2471

WASHINGTON

MID-COLUMBIA LIBRARY
1620 South Union St.
Kennewick 99338
(509) 783-7878

KING COUNTY LIBRARY SYSTEM
Redmond Regional Library
15990 NE 85th
Redmond 98052
(425) 885-1861

SEATTLE PUBLIC LIBRARY
Fundraising Resource Center
800 Pike St.
Seattle 98101
(206) 386-4645

SPOKANE PUBLIC LIBRARY
Funding Information Center
906 W. Main Ave.
Spokane 99201
(509) 444-5300

UNIVERSITY OF WASHINGTON
TACOMA LIBRARY
1900 Commerce St.
Tacoma 98402-3100
(253) 692-4440

GREATER WENATCHEE
COMMUNITY FOUNDATION AT
THE WENATCHEE PUBLIC LIBRARY
310 Douglas St.
Wenatchee 98807
(509) 662-5021

WEST VIRGINIA

KANAWHA COUNTY PUBLIC
LIBRARY
123 Capitol St.
Charleston 25301
(304) 343-4646

WISCONSIN

UNIVERSITY OF
WISCONSIN–MADISON
Memorial Library, Grants Information
   Center
728 State St.
Madison 53706
(608) 262-3242

MARQUETTE UNIVERSITY
MEMORIAL LIBRARY
Funding Information Center
1415 W. Wisconsin Ave.
Milwaukee 53201-3141
(414) 288-1515

UNIVERSITY OF WISCONSIN—
STEVENS POINT
Library—Foundation Collection
900 Reserve St.
Stevens Point 54481-3897
(715) 346-2540

WYOMING

CASPER COLLEGE
Goodstein Foundation Library
125 College Dr.
Casper 82601
(307) 268-2269

LARAMIE COUNTY COMMUNITY
COLLEGE
Instructional Resource Center
1400 E. College Dr.
Cheyenne 82007-3299
(307) 778-1206

CAMPBELL COUNTY
PUBLIC LIBRARY
2101 4-J Rd.
Gillette 82718
(307) 687-0115

TETON COUNTY LIBRARY
125 Virginian Ln.
Jackson 83001
(307) 733-2164

ROCK SPRINGS LIBRARY
Grantwriting Collection
400 C St.
Rock Springs 82901
(307) 352-6667

PUERTO RICO

UNIVERSIDAD DEL SAGRADO
CORAZON
M.M.T. Guevara Library
Santurce 00914
(787) 728-1515

Participants in the Foundation Center's Cooperating Collections network are libraries or nonprofit information centers that provide fundraising information and other funding-related technical assistance in their communities. Cooperating Collections agree to provide free public access to a basic collection of Foundation Center publications during a regular schedule of hours, offering free funding research guidance to all visitors. Many also provide a variety of services for local nonprofit organizations, using staff or volunteers to prepare special materials, organize workshops, or conduct orientations.

A key initiative of the Foundation Center is to reach under-resourced and underserved populations throughout the United States, who are in need of useful information and training to become successful grantseekers. One of the ways we intend to accomplish this goal is by designating new Cooperating Collection libraries in regions that have the ability to serve the nonprofit communities most in need of Foundation Center resources. We are seeking proposals from qualified institutions (i.e. public, academic or special libraries) that can help us carry out this important initiative. If you are interested in establishing a funding information library in your area, or would like to learn more about the program, please contact the Coordinator of Cooperating Collections: Erika Wittlieb, The Foundation Center, 79 Fifth Avenue, New York, NY 10003 (E-mail: eaw@fdncenter.org).

APPENDIX D

Resources/Bibliography

AAFRC Trust for Philanthropy. *Giving USA.* Ed. by M. Brown. New York: AAFRC Trust for Philanthropy (annual).

Cambridge Associates. *Sustainable Payout for Foundations: A Study Commisioned by the Council of Michigan Foundations.* Grand Haven, MI: Council of Michigan Foundations, 2000.

Council on Foundations. *Foundation Management Report.* Washington, D.C.: Council on Foundations (biennial).

DeMarche Associates, Inc. *Spending Policies and Investment Planning for Foundations: A Structure for Determining a Foundation's Asset Mix.* Washington, D.C.: Council on Foundations, 1999.

Edie, J. *First Steps in Starting a Foundation.* Washington, D.C.: Council on Foundations, 1997.

Foundation Center. *Corporate Foundation Profiles.* New York: Foundation Center (biennial).

Foundation Center. *Directory of Missouri Grantmakers.* New York: Foundation Center, 2001.

Foundation Center. *The Foundation Directory.* New York: Foundation Center (annual).

Foundation Center. *The Foundation Directory, Part 2.* New York: Foundation Center (annual).

Foundation Center. *Foundation Fundamentals.* Ed. by P.J. Johnson and M. Morth. New York: Foundation Center, 1999.

Foundation Center. *Foundation Grants to Individuals.* New York: Foundation Center (biennial).

Foundation Center. *The Foundation 1000.* New York: Foundation Center (annual).

Foundation Center. *Grant Guides.* New York: Foundation Center (annual).

Foundation Center. *Guide to Greater Washington D.C. Grantmakers on CD-ROM.* New York: Foundation Center, 2002.

Foundation Center. *Guide to Ohio Grantmakers.* New York: Foundation Center, 2001.

Foundation Center. *Guide to U.S. Foundations, Their Trustees, Officers, and Donors.* New York: Foundation Center (annual).

Foundation Center. *National Directory of Corporate Giving.* New York: Foundation Center (biennial).

Foundation Center. *New York State Foundations: A Comprehensive Directory.* New York: Foundation Center, 2001.

Foundation Center. *The PRI Directory: Charitable Loans and Other Program-Related Investments by Foundations.* New York, NY: Foundation Center, 2001.

Freeman, D. and the Council on Foundations. *The Handbook of Private Foundations.* Washington, D.C.: Council on Foundations, 1997.

Gluck, R., and D. Ganguly. *Foundation Reporting: Update on Public Reporting Trends of Private and Community Foundations.* New York: Foundation Center (annual).

Gluck, R., and D. Ganguly. *Foundation Staffing: Update on Staffing Trends of Private and Community Foundations.* New York: Foundation Center (annual).

Kao, A. *Corporate Contributions.* New York: Conference Board (annual).

Lawrence, S. *Family Foundations: A Profile of Funders and Trends.* New York: Foundation Center 2000.

Lawrence, S. *Health Funding Update.* New York: Foundation Center, 2001.

Lawrence, S. and D. Ganguly *Foundation Giving Trends: Update on Funding Priorities.* New York: Foundation Center (annual).

Lawrence, S. and D. Ganguly. *Foundation Yearbook: Facts and Figures on Private and Community Foundations.* New York: Foundation Center (annual).

Lawrence, S., R. Gluck, and D. Ganguly. *California Foundations: A Profile of the State's Grantmaking Community.* New York: Foundation Center, 2001.

Renz, L. *Arts Funding Update.* New York: Foundation Center, 2002.

Renz, L. *Foundations Today: Current Facts and Figures on Private and Community Foundations.* New York: Foundation Center, 1988–1990.

Renz, L. *Giving in the Aftermath of 9/11: Foundations and Corporations Respond.* New York: Foundation Center, 2002.

Renz, L. and J. Samson–Atienza. *International Grantmaking II: An Update on U.S. Foundation Trends.* New York: Foundation Center, 2000.

Renz, L., C. Atlas, and J. Kendzior. *Arts Funding 2000: Funder Perspectives on Current and Future Trends.* New York: Foundation Center, 1999.

Renz, L., and S. Lawrence. "Encouraging a Caring Society Through the Promotion of Volunteerism and Philanthropy: The Role of Grantmaking Foundations." Paper presented at INDEPENDENT SECTOR Research Forum, San Antonio, March 1993.

Renz, L. and S. Lawrence. *Foundation Growth and Giving Estimates.* New York: Foundation Center (annual).

Renz, L., and S. Lawrence. *Health Policy Grantmaking: A Report on Foundation Trends.* New York: Foundation Center, 1998.

Renz, L., and S. Lawrence. "A Primer on Foundation Science Support." *Science,* 257, Sept. 18, 1992.

Renz, L., S. Lawrence, C. Camposeco, and J. Kendzior. *Southeastern Foundations II: A Profile of the Region's Grantmaking Community.* New York: Foundation Center, 1999.

Renz, L., et al. *Foundation Giving: Yearbook of Facts and Figures on Private, Corporate and Community Foundations.* New York: Foundation Center, 1991–1999.

Salamon, L. *America's Nonprofit Sector: A Primer.* New York: Foundation Center, 1999.

Weitzman, M., et al. *The New Nonprofit Almanac and Desk Reference: The Essential Facts and Figures for Managers, Researchers, and Volunteers.* New York: Josey-Bass, 2002.